BENGAL RENAISSANCE AND CULTURAL AWAKENING IN NORTH BENGAL

Bengal Renaissance and Cultural Awakening in North Bengal

SUPAM BISWAS

MANOHAR
2026

Cover illustration: India, West Bengal, Murshidabad, late 19th century Sculpture Ivory. By Image: http://collections.lacma.org/sites/default/files/remote_images/piction/ma-31967667-O3.jpgGallery: http://collections.lacma.org/node/243991 archive copy at the Wayback Machine, Public Domain, https://commons.wikimedia.org/w/index.php?curid=27292375

First published 2026
First eBook edition 2026

ISBN 978-93-6080-528-9 (hardbound)
ISBN 978-93-6080-788-7 (eBook)

Published by

Ajay Kumar Jain *for*
Manohar Publishers & Distributors
4753/23 Ansari Road, Daryaganj
New Delhi 110 002

Cover design by Manoj Kumar

Typeset by Kohli Print, Delhi 110 051

Printed and bound in India

Dedicated to my Parents

Contents

Preface 9

Introduction: Cultural Awakening in North Bengal 11

1. History of Brahmo Samaj in North Bengal 27

2. Press, Periodicals and Libraries 48

3. The Zamindars and their Cultural Contribution 75

4. Changes in Educational Scenario 94

5. Growth and Development of Sabha-Samitis 112

6. Performing Art, Music and Culture 127

7. Influence of the Renaissance on Muslim Community 141

Conclusion 159

Bibliography 169

Index 181

Preface

The idea of writing the book emerged when one found that there is indeed an acute dearth of research publications on the impact of Renaissance in North Bengal. Some of the chapters in the book were initially written over the past few years while others have been prepared in recent times. It's the belief of this author that this book is the first of its kind to open a new chapter in studying the cultural history of undivided North Bengal.

I owe a deep debt of gratitude to my teacher Professor Ananda Gopal Ghosh (Professor Emeritus, University of North Bengal) who inspired me to bring out the book at the earliest and has greatly helped me to understand the historical significance of the theme within a short space. I am grateful to Dr Shyamal Guha Roy (former Associate Professor, Siliguri College), with whom I discussed various aspects of my work at length. I express my sincere thanks to Professor Ratna Roy Sanyal, Professor Anita Bagchi, Professor Nirban Basu, Professor Anil Kumar Sarkar, Professor Rup Kuamr Barman, Professor Pronob Kumar Bhattacharya, Professor Madhab Chandra Adhikary, Dr Sailen Debnath, Dr Sudash Lama, Dr Dahlia Bhattacharya, Dr Kartik Ch. Sutradhar, Dr Debajit Dutta. I also thank my scholars Dr Arun Ghosh and Subrata Barai who helped me a lot with the book. I am also thankful to Dr Rajarshi Biswas, Dr Kartik Saha, Dr Papiya Dutta, Dr Gouri Dey, Pranay Rajak, Soumendra Prasad Saha, Sushmita Pandit, Krishna Barman, Kalidas Roy, Sanat Adhikary, Suman Roy, Manojit Das, Sujay Debnath, Bappa Mahanta. I have a long list of well-wishers who inspired me in preparing this volume. For lack of space, I could not mention their names here. I think it is the right place to express my thanks to the staff of National Library Kolkata, West Bengal State Archives Kolkata, and Central Library University of North Bengal.

Once more I have to thank my parents, wife Dipa and daughter Moubani for their continued and warm support of my scholarly endeavours. I hope that this work will encourage others to make a deep study in this area. I take the opportunity to thank Manohar Publishers & Distributors, New Delhi for bringing this book into light. For any mistakes I take the responsibility.

Siliguri SUPAM BISWAS
March 2024

Introduction
Cultural Awakening in North Bengal

The introduction of Western education and the contact with the West led to the birth of Renaissance in nineteenth-century Bengal. It evoked a chain of reactions among the Bengali intelligentsia in Calcutta. It was a moderate reaction which aimed at a synthesis of the best components of the Western culture with its Indian counterpart. The impact of Bengal Renaissance beyond Kolkata becomes a distinctive feature in present-day historical research. The impact of renaissance in Kolkata and its adjacent areas have received considerable historical attention from the professional historians. S.C. Sarkar, *Bengal Renaissance and Other Essays* (People's Publishing House, New Delhi, 1981), Tapan Raychaudhuri, *Perceptions, Emotions, Sensibilities: Essays on India's Colonial and Post-Colonial Experiences* (Oxford University Press, Delhi, 1999), David Kopf, *The Brahmo Samaj and the Shaping of Modern Indian Mind* (Princeton University Press, 1997), all these works have concentrated mostly on Kolkata. However, in recent years, historians have dealt with the diverse aspects of the Renaissance. But in all these books, there is no discussion about the influence of the Renaissance in North Bengal. How this awakening spilled over almost simultaneously in North Bengal, remains an unexplored theme in modern Indian history. It is quite evident that, though, Kolkata was the seat of the Renaissance, a parallel movement, unique in its character, can be traced back to the *mofussil* areas of the northern part of Bengal.

For source materials, the present study has depended on both primary and secondary sources. Analytical method has been followed to study both the sources. Archival material as well as published government reports like district gazetteers, administrative and census reports, proceedings, official letters, newspapers, periodicals and journals have been studied in depth. Through cross-verification of archival documents, the study has sought to reconstruct the impact of Bengal Renaissance on North Bengal. But there is a major problem in getting information from official records. This is because in many government documents as one has seen, most are centred in Kolkata and surrounding areas. News and reports on this part of Bengal are hardly available. Perhaps this region was not considered important from the government's perspective. Most importantly, theoretical insights have been used from the research of previous scholars who have written on the subject earlier. One must say that one has been enriched by reading all these writings but not been able to use them directly in this work. The theme of the book is very regional and there is no discussion about the influence of the Renaissance in North Bengal. In view of this problem, much emphasis has been given to contemporary newspapers, periodicals and books.

Professor Amalesh Tripathi raised the most pertinent question in the Muzaffarpur Session of Indian History Congress (1974) as to how much the Bengal Renaissance had its impact in the far-off *mofussil* districts of colonial Bengal?[1] According to Ananda Gopal Ghosh what seems equally important is the need to examine the process through which the cultural awakening took place in North Bengal as a result of the Bengal Renaissance.[2] In this context, one might say that very little and imperative research work has been done so far on this topic the impact of the Bengal Renaissance in places in North Bengal like Jalpaiguri, Darjeeling, Dinajpur and Malda. The North Bengal zone of present Bangladesh like Rajshahi, Rangpur and Pabna was culturally, financially and educationally more advanced than the Indian part of North Bengal. Naturally, the impact of nineteenth-century Bengal Renaissance was largely prevalent in the Bangladesh part of North Bengal in comparison with its Indian counterpart. It is true that the Renaissance was first started in Calcutta by a small circle of enlightened Calcutta elite, but it soon spread to other provinces too and the impact was universalized in a way. North Bengal too experienced a similar Renaissance though much later—only in the late nineteenth century. The Debating Club Jalpaiguri, the Rangpur Sahitya Parishad, Uttarbanga Sahitya Sammilani, the Rajshahi Association, the Varendra Research Institute and others contributed largely to this cultural movement.[3]

The North Bengal region enclaves, the areas, extending from the base of the Himalayas to the bank of Ganga in the South, covering the fluvial plains of the Mahananda, Teesta, Jaldakha, Torsha, Sankosh and even reaching the Brahmaputra from the west to east. The cultural niche belongs to the ancient kingdoms of Mithila, Kamtapur and Pragjyotishpur Kamrup and also of Magadh. In writing the cultural history of North Bengal one cannot overlook the North Bengal (Pundravardhana) of ancient times. The name Pundravardhana persisted for several centuries especially from the Mauryan period to the end of the Gupta period. In the Mauryan period, Pundravardhana was an integral part of the Magadh Empire. Chandragupta Maurya, the founder of the Mauryan Empire, had to establish his predominance over this region. During the imperial Guptas, this area was a province (*bhukti*) of their empire. Several inscriptions excavated from Mahasthangarh bear the testimony of the fact that this region was under Pataliputra. After the Guptas, this region became an integral part of the Kingdom of Sashanka. During the Pala age, Pundravardhana became an important centre of Buddhist learning. A number of Buddhist *viharas* were formed in Rajshahi, Malda and Dinajpur. During the Sena period, as Nabadwip grew up as an alternative centre of politics and culture, the importance of North Bengal gradually declined.[4]

In the eighth century or later Kamtapur emerged as an important political and cultural centre of North Bengal. Kamtapur at one time was the centre for Buddhist learning but with the passage of time, Brahmanical Hinduism superseded the influence of Buddhism in this area. During the advent of Muslim rule in Bengal following the invasion of Bakhtiyar Khalji, North Bengal again turned to be politically very important because of the emergence of Gaur and Pandua in Malda.[5] During the Mughal period, the political importance of Bengal shifted from Gaur to Dhaka. But during the declining phase of the Mughal Empire, the centre of political importance again shifted to Murhsidabad from Dhaka as Murshid Quli Khan transferred the capital of Bengal from Dhaka to Murhsidabad.[6]

During the colonial rule North Bengal would include a much larger tract consisting of the districts of Dinajpur, Bogura, Pabna, Rajshahi and Rangpur—all of them in East Pakistan/Bangladesh; Jalpaiguri, Malda, Darjeeling, the princely state of Coochbehar—now in West Bengal, parts of Purnea—subsequently in Bihar/Jharkhand and then undivided Nadia—now a part of central West Bengal, Goalpara and the part of the district of Kamrup—presently in Assam. During the colonial period, a large part of the district of Murshidabad was considered an integral part of North Bengal as Berhampore—now the headquarters of the district of Murshidabad—once served as the district headquarters of Rajshahi—although it is true that Rajshahi was a separate Division since 1874. Subsequently when Rajshahi was integrated into the Coochbehar Division, the combined Division was renamed as 'Rajshahi and Coochbehar Division'. It was at this time that the Divisional headquarters was shifted to Jalpaiguri and it continued till the Partition of 1947.[7]

Generally speaking, the nineteenth-century renaissance was a natural consequence of English education as well as English rule. And as such, those places which were directly under the British rule, saw the advent of Renaissance first. Not so famous villages like Sutanuti, Govindapur and Kolkata emerged as the 'Mecca' of renaissance. Before the arrival of the British, Bengal witnessed the Renaissance of the fifteenth century. The centre of this movement was not Kolkata, rather an obscure place—Nabadwip, situated at the confluence of the Ganga and Bhagirathi. Even before this, the political and cultural seat of Bengal was Gaur in North Bengal.[8]

With the arrival of the British, there came a huge change and a village named Kolkata rose into prominence on the political stage of Bengal and in due course transformed itself from being a business and political hub to a cultural centre. Not only this, due to the patronage of the colonial rulers, Kolkata assumed an all-powerful role and brought the whole of Bengal under its influence. The Kolkata-centric renaissance of nineteenth century reached North

Bengal later on, primarily because that region came under the British rule at a later stage.[9]

The British East India Company came to Malda district first in North Bengal in 1676, and after that Rajshahi, Dinajpur and Rangpur. Jalpaiguri and Darjeeling were not in existence then. The company gained Diwani in 1765.[10] After the establishment of the British rule, keeping in view their business interests, they set up educational institutions to educate the people for clerical work. The aim of Western education was to form a class who may be interpreters between Indians and the British. But this was limited mainly to Kolkata and adjoining areas. The *mofussil* areas and North Bengal were deprived of the educational set up of the British rulers.[11]

The colonial ruler was against any decentralization of administration, and as such, they ruled with all the powers concentrated at a single power centre. It was due to this reason that Raja Rammohun Roy shifted from Rangpur to Kolkata because he knew very well that what he intended to do could not be done in any other place. Rammohun Roy's Brahmo Samaj owes its origin to Rangpur. It was at Rangpur that he first began to invite his friends to come together for evening discussions on religious subjects. In this way, the Brahmo Samaj got its auspicious start in Rangpur. Also the eighteenth-century Babu culture reached here at a much later stage—at the end of nineteenth century.[12]

During the latter half of the nineteenth century, the magazine *Aitihasik Chitra* was published by the renowned historian Akshay Kumar Maitra from Rajshahi. It was the first historical journal in any Indian language. Even Kolkata—the seat of Renaissance—could not have thought about it. But the intelligentsia of North Bengal did not only think about it but also implemented it.[13]

The North Bengal zone of present-day Bangladesh was culturally, financially and educationally more advanced compared to its Indian counterpat. The first historical research institute in the subcontinent started on private initiative, Varendra Research Institute, was set up in Rajshahi which is far away from Kolkata. During his stay in Rangpur, Raja Rammohun Roy, the father of Renaissance, had acquired knowledge from Hariharananda Tirthaswami who advocated the cause of the Hindu religion. He also translated five Upanishads in Rangpur. Historical evidence shows that the first printing press was set up by William Carey at Madnabati (then in Dinajpur district), a village in Malda district. He was supported by George Udny, a manager of a factory at English Bazar. Later Carey was transferred to Malda and set up the printing press at Hooghly. History says that the printing machine and press are the two pillars of renaissance. Thus, one may say that with the transfar of Carey to Malda, the chance of North Bengal as the first place of the nineteenth-century Bengal Renaissance had been lost.[14] This clearly shows that if Kolkata was the foundation of renaissance, a different movement with its own features came up in North Bengal.

In this discussion, one cannot overlook the contribution made by Harinath Majumder, Jaladhar Sen, Akshay Kumar Maitra and others. Asis Khastagir has observed that *Grambarta Prakashika*, one of the most leading Bengali weeklies, was edited by Harinath Majumder. It was published by the Mathuranath press in Rangpur established by him. The Bengali weekly *Kohinoor*, *Grambarta Prakashika* and *Shaibi* published in the Mathuranath press.[15] The book *Darjeelinger Itihas*, written by Harinath Majumder in 1880 (BS 1287) was also published by the same press. A group of intellectual people like Akshay Kumar Maitra, Jaladhar Sen, Mir Musharaff Hossain and Dinendra Kumar Roy helped him immensely in his publication work. However, after continuing for 22 years it was stopped due to dearth of money.[16] Professor Abul Hassan Chaudhury, the prominent folk culture researcher of Bangladesh, honoured Harinath Majumder the pioneer of rural renaissance.[17]

It is known that the main activities of the renaissance were centred in the metropolis of Calcutta. All those associated with it were the representatives of the educated professional middle class, who had availed of English education. In this context, one may honour Harinath Majumder as the father of rural Renaissance. Almost illiterate in terms of formal education, poor and deprived of the glory of image, it is surprising that despite the limitations, he established a number of cultural institutions like Kumarkhali

Sabha, Bidyotsahini Sabha and others. He stormed the minds of Akshay Kumar Maitra, Jaladhar Sen, Dinendra Kumar Roy and Sibchandra Vidyarnab. He established two schools in Kumarkhali—one in 1855 and the second for girls the next year. Jaladhar Sen was the most worthy disciple of Harinath Majumder. In his autobiography *Smrititarpan*, he wrote '*Grambarta Prakashika*, Mathuranath Press and Haranath Majumder attracted me to a large extent like a magnet. I got the inspiration for my literary pursuits from him.' Such an intellectual discourse of regional history undoubtedly deserves in depth discussion. Jaladhar Sen later took over the editorship of *Grambarta Prakashika.* He also edited *Samprakash*, one of the leading Bengali periodicals of that time. Sukumar Sen adorned him with the title of 'Sahityapremi'.[18]

Towards the end of his life, Harinath Majumder turned his attention to *Baul* songs. He formed a group comprising of his disciples to promote these songs all over Bengal. The song *Hari din to gelo sandhya holo par koro amare* gained wide popularity all over Bengal. Jaladhar Sen, the most worthy disciple of Harinath Majumder, published a volume in memory of his master named *Harinath Granthabali* in 1901. It was published by Basumati Sahitya Mandir, Rangpur. Jaladhar Sen himself was also associated with other magazines like *Bangabashi* (1899), *Basumati* (1899-1907), *Dainik Sandhya* (1907), *Hitabadi* (1907-09), *Sulabha Samachar* (1911-12) and *Bharatabarsha.* Being influenced by the literary works of Jaladhar Sen, Viceroy Lord Reading conferred him with the title of 'Ray Bahadur' in 1922.[19]

After Harinath Majumder, the one who may be called the forerunner of the Renaissance in North Bengal was Akshay Kumar Maitra. He showed his talent as a historian and archaeologist particularly on the history of Varendra or Pundravardhana (North Bengal). Ichhamuddin Sarkar thought that Akshay Kumar Maitra was a historian par excellence and his writings in history and archaeology were highly commended. He wrote a number of books like *Siraj-ud-daula, Mirqasim, Firingi Banik, Gauderkatha, A Short History of Natore* and so on. *Gaudalekhamala* written by him in 1912 provides a vivid description of the important inscriptions during the Pala age. In *Siraj-ud-daula,* he vehemently challenged the Black-Hole theory. The journal *Aitihasik Chitra* published by him was highly recommended by Rabindranath Tagore. Akshay Kumar Maitra has admitted that Pundravardhana undoubtedly represents a region of ancient heritage and civilization and at that time its glory spread far and wide. The natural beauty, excavated remains, bricks and stones lying here and there might still justify how the Hindu Kings and thereafter the Muslim rulers took special care to brighten their rule and also a tradition blended with the touches of the Hindu and Muslims vis à vis Bengalis.[20] He first showed through his writings the importance of places like Lakhnawati and Debikot where the Muslims first established their rule in Bengal. He also gave a very comprehensive account of the Iliyas Shahi dynasty, also narrated the contribution made by Sikandar Shah in laying the foundation of the Adina Mosque.[21] The environment created by Harinath Majumder impressed him overwhelmingly with its innovative ideas. He wrote many articles in some reputed journals of that time like *Bangadarshan, Prabshi* and *Sahitya.* In his book *Bharat Shilper Katha,* Akshay Kumar Maitra first mentioned Sandhyakar Nandi, the author of *Ramacharita* and the renowned poet of the Varendra region. He also highlighted the contribution of Dhiman and Bitpal in the field of art in Bengal during the Pala period.[22] It is interesting to note that till date no major research works have been published on this great son of North Bengal excepting the book *Akshay Kumar Maitra: Jiban O Sadhana* by Nirmal Chandra Chaudhury in 1984 published by the University of North Bengal. Throughout his life, he made tireless efforts to reconstruct the history of North Bengal.[23] For this reason, one may easily call him the 'Father of the history of North Bengal'.

The princely state of Coochbehar and the Christian missionaries had made immense contribution to the birth of Renaissance in the Indian part of North Bengal. The Brahmo movement gained a new lease of life in North Bengal with the marriage between Nripendra Narayan, the Maharaja of Coochbehar and Suniti Devi, the eldest daughter of Keshab Chandra Sen. Maharaja Nripendra Narayan and Princess Suniti Devi both played a crucial role in setting up educational and cultural institutions in Coochbehar and other parts of North Bengal, as well.[24] The Maharani Girls' High School and Nripendra Narayan Hindu Public Hall were both established in Darjeeling under the encouragement of Maharaja Nripendra Narayan. The Maharani Girls' High School, Darjeeling was the first Indian managed school for Indian girls in the district. It was established in 1908 by some renowned Bengali women connected with the Brahmo Samaj. Maharaja Nripendra Narayan and Maharani Suniti Devi of Coochbehar, Maharaja of Burdwan, Lord and Lady Carmichael, the Rani of Kakina, the Maharanis of Mayurbhanj and Vizanagram, Sir S.P. Sinha, B.C. Mitra, and P.N. Mukherjee all played an important role towards its foundation.[25] They made the literary sphere of Bengali literature fertile. They not only engaged in literary pursuits but also penned a large number of valuable books. Maharaja Harendra Narayan was truly a pioneer in this field. The kings of the princely state of Coochbehar were very cordial towards their Muslim subjects. The liberal attitude of Nripendra Narayan had contributed largely to enhance the numbers of Muslim students in schools. This educational development under the patronage of the princely state Coochbehar was highly praised by Sir Ashutosh Mukherjee.[26]

In Darjeeling, the main initiatives in setting up schools and colleges were taken by the British officials, European planters and the Christian missionaries. The shift of capital to Darjeeling in summer was a push factor behind the establishment of educational institutions because their children brought up from the plains suffered from anemia and were flabby, pale, and fretful. The elevation of the hill station insulated Darjeeling from most diseases. It was not only free of disease, its cool and fresh air was supposed to help Europeans to recover from their elements and fed fresh.[27]

In the context of Indian part of North Bengal, one finds the absence of any initiatives from the native *zamindar*s or landlords. Exceptions are there but very few. The *zamindar*s of Canchal, Malda and the Raikat and Rahut family of Jalpaiguri took initiatives in setting up schools and colleges in the first half of the twentieth century. Here the major part of initiatives was taken by the colonial government and the kings of Coochbehar. But in the case of Bangladesh area of North Bengal, one finds, most of the educational institutions were established by the native landlords and intellectuals. No college was established in Jalpaiguri before 1942 and in Malda before 1944. But the landlords of Dinajpur, now in Bangladesh had to set up English schools and other literary organizations in their respective *zamindari*. Churamani High School was set up by the *zamindar* of Bhupalpur in 1864. The Siddheshwari Institution was established by the *zamindar* of Canchal in memory of his mother Siddheshwari Devi in 1885. Besides school and colleges, a number of intellectual associations, drama and sports clubs were established and a number of newspapers and periodicals were published from Pabna, Bogura, Rajshahi, Rangpur and eastern Dinajpur (present-day Bangladesh) then part of North Bengal. It is quite interesting to note that being a divisional headquarter and the main tea producing zone of Bengal, the first general degree college was established in Jalpaiguri in 1942 whereas colleges were built-up in Rajshahi in 1873, Pabna Edward College in 1889 and Carmichael College Rangpur in 1916. The Nawabganj Adina Fazlul Hauque College was the second college in Rajshahi district established in 1940.[28] Here one finds a major difference between the *zamindar*s of both parts of North Bengal in regard to their response to Bengal Renaissance.

NUMBER OF SCHOOLS IN 1903

Darjeeling	05	Coochbehar	04	Malda	03
Dinajpur	01	Rangpur	07	Rajshahi	07
Jalpaiguri	01	Pabna	19		
				Total:	47

From the above Table it can be seen that out of 47 schools only 13 came up in the Indian part of North Bengal.

However, to write about the renaissance of North Bengal, one cannot ignore the three districts of Assam, that is Goalpara, Kachar and Sylhet. History says that these three districts, were once an integral part of the Bengal province. Prior to the birth of Goalpara district, it was a part of Rangpur district. Thus one cannot overlook the response of the Bengali people of these districts to the Renaissance. The first printing press in Assam was established in 1872 and named Assam Mihir. The next year, another one named Chidanand came up. In 1876, Hitabidhayani and Hitasadhani both the presses in Goalpara and Silchar (1889) and Sharadindu press (1895) both in Silchar and Balihar came into existence. The weekly *Goalpara Hitasadhani* was published from the Hitasadhani Press, Goalpara.[29]

The royal family of Gauripur had a big role in sowing the seeds of renaissance in Assam. When the Victoria College was established in the Princely State of Coochbehar, there was no college in Assam. The Cotton College of Guwahati was established in 1902. Therefore, a large number of students from Assam were admitted in Victoria College. It is true that the elite section of Assamese students went to Calcutta for higher education but the poor and middle-class students generally preferred Victoria College due to their economic hardships. So, these groups of pupils returned to their homes after completing their study also carrying with them the ideals of renaissance. This led to the birth of a cultural awakening in Assam. The same thing happened with the Carmichel College, Rangpur where a number of students pursuing their study hailed from Assam. Thus one may say with confidence that North Bengal had a big role in sowing the seeds of renaissance in Assam. The Assamese students of both the Victoria College and Carmichel College played a key role in laying the foundation of the Renaissance in Assam. Amalendu Guha too thought that the Varendra Anusandhan Samiti and Uttarbanga Sahitya Sammelan were the main sources of inspiration behind the foundation of Assam Sahitya Sabha and Kamrup Anusandhan Samiti. According to him, Assamese and the immigrant Bengali adherents of the Brahmo Samaj had a social impact in the growing administrative townships. The development of communication between Assam and Bengal through the railways brought Bengali doctors, lawyers and clerks. Most of them were Brahmos and English educated. The Assamese Literary Society was formed in Calcutta at the initiative of Assamese students. Jagannath Barooah and Manik Chandra Barooah, then studying in the Presidency College, played a significant role. Thus the so-called Bengal Renaissance left its impact on Assam. The Pradayini Sabha (society for disseminating knowledge) and the Assam Desh Hitaishini Sabha in 1857 at Sibsagar for holding study circles every Saturday, bear the testimony of the fact.[30]

The year 1878 was a memorable landmark in the history of renaissance in North Bengal. This year one saw the introduction of North Bengal State Railway (NBSR). Another important addition of railway in North Bengal was the introduction of the Bengal Duars Railway (BDR). It, no doubt, cemented the connection with Calcutta and its surrounding areas. Due to the improvement of communication, a number of educated Bengali intellectuals came to the districts of North Bengal for administrative jobs. With them, they carried the ideas of the Young Bengal movement. Similarly, the pupils who went to Calcutta for professional and higher education, returned home with the core ideals of renaissance. Therefore, the light of renaissance spread in different sub-divisional towns, thanas and villages in North Bengal. All these made the platform for the emergence of cultural awakening in North Bengal. This parallel movement was regional as well as unique.[31]

Now the most pertinent question is that, in spite of setting up the Bangiya Sahitya Sammelan, why was there the need for the intelligentsia of North Bengal to set up another one in this region with a different name—Uttarbanga Sahitya Sammelan? To cater to the single language which was predominant in a particular geographical region, why the need was felt for setting up two different identities of the Sahitya Sammelan about 100 years ago? Was this not a revelation of regional identity?[32] Steered by the Renaissance, the idea of regional identity came into being, though unconsciously.

CONCLUSION

A question lurks in the mind: how many renowned figures of nineteenth-century Bengali renaissance visited far and wide places of North Bengal? There was an exception, no doubt, but it was a small one. Some ex-students of Hindu College and followers of the Young Bengal Movement had come to the districts of North Bengal for administrative jobs. With them, they had carried the ideas of the Young Bengal Movement. For example, Harachandra Ghosh of Hooghly district and a former student of Hindu College came to Rampur-Boalia in 1844 as the superintendent of the Excise Department of Company. He had also spent eight years in Malda, Baherampur and Dinajpur districts respectively. Dr Shyama Chandra Sarkar of Hooghly district and a former student of Hindu College had joined as the physician in the Princely State of Coochbehar in 1844. Raja Kihsori Chand Mitra, brother of Parry Chand Mitra, had spent a few years in Coochbehar. Ramagopal Ghosh, Gour Chandra Basak, a friend of the poet Michael Madhusudan Dutta, had to spend a few years at Malda.[33] But one could know very little about their intellectual and social activities in North Bengal. Similarly, it is also not known how many persons from North Bengal went to study at Presidency College or how many became associated with the Young Bengal Movement. It is true that many students from Rangpur and Rajshahi went to Calcutta for higher education because the first college was set up at Rajshahi in 1873. Therefore, prior to 1873, definitely there were a few students who came to Calcutta for pursuing higher education in Presidency and Sanskrit College. A few of them might have been involved with the Young Bengal Movement. Definitely, there were a few Derozians in North Bengal at that time. If it could be ascertained, then the discussion about the Renaissance in North Bengal could have flowed with clarity in a specific direction.

NOTES

1. Professor Sushovan Sarkar, Presidential address, Proceedings of the Indian History Congress, Muzaffarpur, 1974, p. 14.
2. Ananda Gopal Ghosh and Ashim Kumar Sarkar, *Bharattirtha Uttarbanga* (Pilgrimage of India–North Bengal), Sangbedan, Malda, 2011, p. 219.
3. Supam Biswas, *Unish O Bish Shatake Uttarbanger Sabha-Samiti* (Public Associations of North Bengal during Nineteenth and Twentieth Century's), Readers Service, Kolkata, 2020, pp. 4-5.

4. R.C. Majumder, *History of Ancient Bengal,* Tulshi Prakashani, Kolkata, 2005, pp. 1-4.
5. G.E. Lambourn, Bengal District Gazetteers, Malda, Bengal Secretariat Press, Calcutta, 1918, pp. 11-13.
6. Sailen Debnath, *Essays on Cultural History of North Bengal,* N.L. Publishers, Siliguri, 2008, pp. IX-XI.
7. Samir Kumar Das, *Migrations, Identities and Democratic Practices in India,* Routledge, New York, 2018, p.2.
8. Rajanikanta Chakrabarty, *Gaurer Itihas* (History of Gauda), Rangpur Sahitya Parishad, Rangpur, Kolkata, BS 1317, p. 14.
9. Prankrishna Dutta, *Kalikatar Itibritta* (History of Calcutta), Pushtak Bipani, Kolkata, 1981, pp. 30-2.
10. Abid Ali Khan, *Memories of Gaur and Pandua,* Bengal Secretariat Press, Calcutta, 1924, p. 146.
11. Supam Biswas, *The Empire Wrote Future: The British in North Bengal,* Abhijeet Publications, New Delhi, 2024, p. 169.
12. S.D. Collet, *The Life and Letters of Raja Rammohan Roy,* ed. by D.K. Biswas and P.C. Ganguly, Calcutta, 1962, p. 12.
13. I. Sarkar, 'Akshay Kumar Moitra: His Ideas and Method of Interpretations and Reflected in His Historical Works', *Journal of the Asiatic Society of Bangladesh* (Humanities), vol. 67(1), 2022, p. 15.
14. Ananda Gopal Ghosh, 'The Syndrome of Nineteenth Century: Bengal Renaissance in North Bengal with Special Reference to the Minorities and the Non-caste People', in Shyamal Guharoy et al (ed.), *History and Thought of India: Essays in Memory of Professor P.K. Bhattacahryya,* Abhijeet Publications, New Delhi, 2022, p. 195.
15. Asish Khastagir, *Unish Shataker Bangla Chapakhana* (Printing Press of Bengal during Nineteenth Century), Sopan, Kolkata, 2014, p. 53.
16. Harimahan Sanyal, *Darjeelinger Itihas* (History of Darjeeling), ed. by Icchamuddin Sarkar, Mitram, Kolkata, 2005, p. 12.
17. Ananda Gopal Ghosh, op. cit., pp. 199-200.
18. Jaladhar Sen, *Atmajibani O Smrititarpan* (Autobiography and Memoir), ed. by Dr Baridbaran Ghosh, Jiggyasa Agency Limited, Kolkata, B.S. 1367, pp. 21-4.
19. Swapan Kumar Mandal, 'Kangal Harinath and Jaladhar Sen', in Gokul Sarkar (ed.), *Angikar,* Autumn Number, 1420 BS, Coochbehar, pp. 56-8.
20. Ichhamuddin Sarkar, op. cit., pp. 15-18.
21. Ananda Gopal Ghosh and Malay Sankar Bhattacharya, *Uttarbanger Puratattva Samgraha* (Archaeological Collections of North Bengal), Calcutta, 1984, p. 93.

22. Akshay Kumar Maitra, *Bharat Shilper Katha* (A Tale About Indian Art), Calcutta, 1982, p. 93.
23. Ichhamuddin Sarkar, *Akshay Kumar Moitra: His Ideas and Method of Interpretations and Reflected in his Historical Works*, op. cit., p. 19.
24. Shibnath Shastri, *History of the Brahmo Samaj*, Kolkata, 1993, p. 288.
25. Dick B. Dewan, *History of Education in Darjeeling Hill 1835-1985*, Indus Publishing Company, New Delhi, 1991, p. 172.
26. Harendra Narayan Chowdhury, *The Coochbehar State and its Land Revenue Settlement*, Coochbehar State Press, Coochbehar, 1903, p. 325.
27. Nandini Bhattacharya, *Contagion and Enclaves Tropical Medicine in Colonial India*, Liverpool University Press, 2012, p. 38, 29.
28. Ananda Gopal Ghosh, op. cit., p. 202.
29. Asis Khastagir, op. cit., p. 105.
30. Amalendu Guha, *Planter Raj and Swaraj*, People's Publishing House, New Delhi, 1977, pp. 23-4.
31. Ratna Roy Sanyal, 'Introduction and Impact of the Railways in North Bengal during the Second half of the Nineteenth Century', in Chandi Das Bhattacharya (ed.), *North Bengal University Review*, 2001-3, p. 13.
32. Ananda Gopal Ghosh, op. cit., p. 211.
33. Ratna Roy, 'Unish Shataker Nabajagaran O Uttarbanga' (Nineteenth Century Bengal Renaissance and North Bengal), in Kali Krishna Sutrdhar and Samit Saha (ed.), *Uttarbange Nabajagaran O Samajik-Sanskritik Andalan* (Renaissance and Socio-Cultural Movement in North Bengal), Abhijeet Publication, New Delhi, 2024, p. 17.

CHAPTER 1

History of Brahmo Samaj in North Bengal

INTRODUCTION

The Brahmo Samaj was founded in Bengal by Raja Rammohun Roy who is often described the 'Father of Modern India'. The Brahmo Samaj helped to emancipate India from Medieval feudalism to national democracy, from blind-faith and anti-social customs to knowledge and science, emancipation in every field, intellectual and religious, social, moral, and political.[1]

Much has been written on the Brahmo Samaj in Bengal but very little and imperative research works has been done on the history of Brahmo Samaj in North Bengal, especially the Princely State of Coochbehar, Jalpaiguri, Darjeeling and Rangpur. The expansion of Brahmo Samaj and its effect on spreading the Bengal Renaissance in different parts of East Bengal beyond Calcutta has been beautifully highlighted by David Kopf. According to him,

> whenever a Brahmo Samaj was established, there followed an institutional complex dedicated to social and religious reform. Whether in Mymensingh, Barishal, Chittagong, Comilla, or Sylhet, there was invariably the *mandir* or community prayer hall and meeting place, a girls' school and boys' school on various levels, possibly a college, a Sangat Sabha or discussion society for the youth, a charitable hospital, a library, a printing press for newspapers and tracts, a night school for workers and peasants, a women's society.[2]

But his work did not mention the region of North Bengal. Although there are a good number of books on Brahmo Samaj like Kenneth Jones *Socio-Religious Reform Movements in British India* (*The New Cambridge History of India*, vol. 3, University Press, 1994),

M. Borthwick *Keshab Chandra Sen: A Search for Cultural Synthesis* (South Asia Books, Colombia, 1978), A.P. Sen *Hindu Revivalism in Bengal 1872-1905* (Oxford University Press, Delhi, 1993) but these contributions have concentrated mostly on Rammohun's work and the Brahmo Samaj in Calcutta. Broadly speaking, in all these books, there is no mention of the Rangpur chapter of Rammohun's life or Keshub Chandra Sen who contributed greatly to the spread of Brahmo religion in the Princely State of Coochbehar. All these works are completely silent on this. Hence, the present study intends to fill this gap by highlighting the growth and development of the Brahmo Samaj in different parts of North Bengal.

RAJA RAMMOHUN ROY AND RANGPUR

The Brahmo Movement was first started by Rammohun Roy in Calcutta but the seeds of his reform movement in Calcutta were actually sown during his stay in Rangpur. Rammohun Roy was appointed the Dewan of Rangpur district by William Digby, the Collector there. His arrival in Rangpur was quite significant historically. From 1765 to 1829, Rangpur was the main administrative centre of the Rajshahi Division. Hence, the affluent Hindu community of East Bengal settled there for their work with the Company. The new revenue systems, setting up business in the foothills of the Himalaya were the major reasons for the influx of affluent people in this area. The administration of Sikkim and Bhutan was controlled mainly through Rangpur. During his tenure (1809-14) as the Dewan under the English East India Company, Rammohun Roy was interested mostly in setting up Dharma Sabha, Vedanta discourse, learning English and writing books in French. He also worked as an advisor to the Zamindari Estate of Rangpur. He bought three *taluk*s in Rangpur which were looked after by his relative named Gurudas. In Rangpur, Rammohun Roy was also engaged in business because it was the prominent business centre in those days. Owing to its favourable geographical location, the business spread primarily throughout the terai region and the western part of the Himalaya. In the nineteenth century, people used to come down from the mountains and reach Rangpur through the terai region mainly for business purpose. At Mahiganj, the Bhutia businessmen had to set up their establishment. So, it is easily discernible that beside his job as the Dewan of Rangpur, Roy earned a lot because of his business initiatives. This material affluence of Rammohun helped him to establish himself in Calcutta after his return and also set up different socio-religious centres there.[3]

During his stay in Rangpur, Roy started studying English. With Digby's help, he also got the opportunity to read different newspapers and magazines from England. As a result, he became acquainted with the liberal movements, humanism, democratic ideals and above all, the scientific point of view prevailing in Europe at that time. These studies influenced him a lot and he began thinking about freedom and welfare of his countrymen. Moreover, Roy wrote the *Vedantasutra* in Rangpur. Every evening, he used to arrange a religious discourse at his house in Mahiganj, in which people from different religions took part. In these discourses he opined against idol worship and promoted the need for achieving brahmajnana (knowledge). The discussion-meetings which he used to hold with friends and orthodox Hindu and Muslim critics in Rangpur, indicate that his characteristic attitude to religion had already taken a definite shape and these may be accordingly regarded the earliest foundation of the future Brahmo movement. He studied the modern Tantric works with the help of Hariharananda Vidyabagish and learnt about Jainism and studied the Jaina texts borrowed from the Marwaris of Rangpur. He also studied Vedantic monism in Rangpur. During the period, he was part of the delegation to Bhutan to settle border disputes between Bhutan and Coochbehar.[4]

It is believed that the evening religious discourse of Rangpur pioneered the establishment of the Brahmo Samaj. Rammohun Roy's campaign against the practice of Sati was also started in Rangpur. Sibnath Shastri has opined that the ideals of Rammohun Roy preceded him much before his arrival in Calcutta. His residence in Rangpur was a fruitful one. He is said to have made a careful study of modern Tantric works with the aid of Harihara Nanda Tirtha Swami—a Bengal Tantric mendicant.[5] So, it is clear that the seeds of the reformation movement in Calcutta were actually sown during his stay in Rangpur. His stay in Rangpur was, undoubtedly, a historical milestone which cannot be overlooked. But it is quite strange that such an important episode had remained quite ignored and major focus had always been on Rammohun Roy's work after his return to Calcutta.

Rammohun Roy returned to Calcutta in 1815 and founded an organization named Atmiya Sabha at his Maniktala residence with a number of friends like Dwarakanath Tagore, Brajamohan Majumder, Haladhar Basu, Nandakishore Basu, Raja Kalishankar Ghoshal, Rajnarayan Sen, Brindaban Mitra, Baidyanath Mukherjee and others. Regular meetings were held alternately in the houses of different members. The meetings were ended with religious songs. The Atmiya Sabha remained active in Calcutta from 1815 to 1828 and probably became extinct after the foundation of the Brahmo Samaj of which it was in very real sense a precursor. The Brahmo Samaj was launched on 20 August 1828 in Calcutta in a rented house belonging to Ramkamal Basu at 48 Upper Chitpore Road, Jorasanko. About two years later it shifted formally to its new building at 55, Upper Chitpur Road.[6]

After the death of Rammohun Roy, the leadership of the movement was taken over by Debendranath Tagore who provided the movement the best organizational structure. But the movement was actually taken out of the limited elite circles of Calcutta into the district towns of East Bengal led by Bijoy Krishna Goswami and Keshub Chandra Sen in the 1860s. Goswami bridged the gap between Brahmonism and the popular religious tradition of Vaishnavism, while Sen's specific focus was to reach out to the larger number members of non-Westernized Bengalis in the eastern Gangetic plains and take the movement outside Bengal to other provinces of India.[7] In this backdrop, one will attempt to highlight the growth and course of the Brahmo movement in different districts of North Bengal.

HISTORY OF BRAHMO SAMAJ IN NORTH BENGAL

The famous Brahmo leader Shibnath Shastri has mentioned a list of 54 Brahmo temples of Bengal in his book *History of the Brahmo*

Samaj (1866). But there is no mention of any Brahmo temple established during that period in the northern part of Bengal. It proved that prior to 1866, not a single Brahmo temple was established in North Bengal. However, despite the temples, the branches of Brahmo Samaj grew there.[8]

In the northern part of Bengal, the Brahmo Samaj was first established in Englishbazar, Malda in 1861. The number of Brahmos in Malda was very low. In a report of the District Collector Malda (1870), it is mentioned that the number of followers of the Brahmo Samaj was only six. All of them have come here from different parts of Bengal to serve the colonial administration. For example, the Brahmo leader Madhusudan Sen joined the District Collector office in 1872 and stayed there for a few years. Dr Annada Charan Khastagir arrived in Malda as Civil Surgeon. Charu Chandra Bandopadhyay, a *zamindar* of Canchal, adopted the Brahmo religion. He was a famous writer and had close connection with Rabindranah Tagore. In west Dinajpur, the foundation of the Brahmo Samaj was laid by Bhuban Babu, a homeopath by profession. Kali Shankar Das helped him a lot in his job. In a report of the District Collector West Dinajpur (1870), it is said that a few Brahmos inhabited Balurghat though there was no Brahmo temple or worshipping centre there.[9]

THE BRAHMO SAMAJ IN DARJEELING

For administrative purposes, the British government appointed a number of Bengali Hindus to act as government officials in Darjeeling. Many of them were Brahmos. They laid the foundation of the Brahmo Samaj in Darjeeling in January 1879. Shibnath Shastri, a prominent Brahmo leader went twice to the Brahmo Samaj of Darjeeling in 1908 and 1909 respectively. During his stay, he paid a visit every Sunday to the Brahmo temple for worshipping. His daughter Hemlata Sarkar was the headmistress of Maharani Girls High School. During that period, a number of prominent personalities like the princesses of Burdwan, Mayurbhanj, Suniti Devi of Coochbehar and others, contributed financially in setting up the foundation of the school. Maharani

Suniti Devi once wrote 'Some of the Governors of Bengal have been most kind to my school at Darjeeling where sixty or seventy children of all castes are taught in the Kintergarden and I am glad to say it does very well indeed'.[10] To acknowledge her contribution, Hemlata Sarkar named it the Maharani Girls School. The famous poet Lila Majumder was a student of the school. She also tried her best for the cause of women's education in Darjeeling. Dr Bijali Sarkar, the court physician of the Nepal royal family was her husband. Though the Samaj was founded in 1879, the Brahmo temple was established after few years. Radhanath Roy, the Land-revenue officer of the district, arranged for land where the first Brahmo temple was built in 1888. However, the temple, under the initiative of Hemlata Sarkar, later shifted to its present address near Lal Dighi in 1919.[11]

With the establishment of the Brahmo Samaj, a number of Brahmo leaders paid regular visits to Darjeeling. For example, Srinath Chanda and his brother Prakash Deb came in October 1898. Srinath Chanda came the second time on 27 September 1910 to attend a conference organized by the Brahmo Samaj Darjeeling in the memory of Raja Rammahun Roy. He chaired the conference as the president. Many other Brahmo leaders like Sashibhushan Dutta and Debendra Prasad Das gave speeches on many important topics of the Brahmo religion. The building could accommodate a congregation of 100 persons where a meeting was held every Sunday morning at 8.30 a.m. in Bengali, occasionally in English. The building was constructed with the great interest and strenuous efforts on the part of Troilokyonath Chakrabarty, the then headmaster of the Government Bhutia Boarding School and the president of the Brahmo Samaj, Darjeeling. Motilal Haldar helped him a lot in his mission. It was consecrated on 15 April 1880. During the period of Troilokyonath Chakrabarty, a number of Brahmo leaders had come several times to Darjeeling. Harimahan Chanda, the Deputy Magistrate, Parbati Charan Roy, the Deputy Collector and most importantly, Keshub Chandra Sen delivered a series of lectures there many times. Keshub Chandra Sen attended a programme in Brahmo temple in 1882 where he delivered a speech on 'Brahmo Dharma O Buddher Jibon' (Brahmo religion and the life of Buddha). It was so enchanting that the audience was absolutely overwhelmed. Among them those prominent were Maharaja Nripendra Narayan and his wife Suniti Devi, Maharani Sucharu Devi of Mayurbhanj, Acharya Jagadish Chandra Bose, his wife Lady Abala Basu and Dr Nilratan Sarkar. Sir Jadunath Sarkar delivered a very nice lecture in the Brahmo Samaj hall on 27 September 1937. Since 1932 a large number of Brahmo families residing dwindled in Darjeeling.[12]

The Brahmo temple was set up in Kurseong, mainly under the initiative of Motilal Haldar and Girish Chandra Guha. Sibnath Shastri had a close connection with this place. He came several times to Kurseong (1886, 1910 and 1911) and wrote his famous novel *Himadri Kusum* there. The eminent Brahmo preacher Krishna Kumar Mitra wrote in his autobiography that a branch of the Brahmo Samaj was set up by Dr Ganga Govinda Sarkar, a railway physician, near the railway station in Tindharia. In the plains, the Brahmo Samaj was established near the Siliguri Station by Dr Ananda Chandra Roy. Bipin Chandra Pal in his autobiography also wrote a brief account about Dr Ananda Chandra Roy and his service towards the Brahmo Samaj. He further added that a few Brahmo families lived in Phansidewa and Bipin Chandra Pal came there in 1879 to spread the Brahmo religion. Though the Brahmo Samaj established its offshoot in Darjeeling hill and plains and a number of Brahmo leaders came regularly with a mission, but it had no profound impact among the hill people. Only two hill persons (*paharia*) adopted the Brahmo religion.[13]

THE BRAHMO SAMAJ IN JALPAIGURI

Since it was the administrative headquarter of the Rajshahi division, a number of educated Indians, mainly Bengali Hindus were brought by the British government from different parts of eastern Bengal for administrative jobs in Jalpaiguri town. Many of them later started tea gardens and invested in timber business. A large section of them were Brahmos. In the administrative report of the District Collector (1870), it has been mentioned that most of the high officials and government employees were Brahmos.

Among eighteen Brahmos three were the teachers of government schools.[14]

With the arrival of Keshub Chandra Sen, a branch of Sanagta Sabha was established in 1863 in Dhaka. In 1881 there were around 34 Brahmos, among them 26 were men and 8 were women. At that time the total number of Brahmos in different districts of East Bengal like Jessore, Rangpur, Dhaka, Faridpur, Bakharganj and Chittagaong was high. Munshi Jalaluddin was influenced by the ideas of the Brahmo religion, attended a conference held in Dhaka in 1869 where he converted to Brahmonism. The other leading Brahmo leaders of the Sabha were Babu Rajanikanta Ghosh, Kalinarayan Roy, Ambika Charan Sen, Kailash Chandra Nandi, Prasanna Kumar Roy and Bhuban Mahan Sen. They endeavoured to a great extent to develop women's education. This resulted in establishing a girl's school in 1870. Pyari Bibi was a student of the school.[15] She married Jalaluddin who had become a Brahmo. This religious conversion sparked huge reaction among the Muslim society in Dhaka. At that time the Brahmo leaders of Calcutta stood with him and made all arrangements for his evacuation from Dhaka to Jalpaiguri overnight. Both of them later played a key role in spreading the Brahmo religion and women's education in Jalpaiguri and beyond. They both taught in a girls school founded by Dr Recket, the then Commissioner of Jalpaiguri. At present, this school is known as Sunitibala Sadar Girls' High School.[16]

One may mention here another example of Muslim persons who later became Brahmos. In 1889 Nilmani Chakrabarty, a famous Brahmo leader, arrived in Guwahati to preach the Brahmo religion. He saw two Muslims there named Akbar Mukunda and Akbar Yogindra who came from Calcutta and initiated into the Brahmo philosophy. They used to sell books in Guwahati. They could not survive there for long due to their religious conversion. From this example one can easily understand how long the religious conversion of both Jalal and his wife were highly opposed by the orthodox Muslims in Dhaka.[17]

Bhagwan Chandra Bose, father of renowned scientist Acharya Jagadish Chandra Bose, was the Deputy Magistrate of Jalpaiguri town. The Bengali entrepreneurs of Jalpaiguri town, being influenced with his ideas, opened many tea gardens in the teari-duars region during the British Raj. However, Bhagwan Chandra Bose was a Brahmo and very close to Sibnath Shastri. The prominent Brahmo leader Bipin Chandra Pal arrived in Jalpaiguri town in December 1879. He stayed at the household of Chandi Charan Sen who devoted his whole life to spread the Brahmo religion in different parts of North Bengal and beyond. The eminent Brahmo preacher Anath Krishna Shil delivered a speech on 'Bharater Karmadhara' in the Brahmo congregation hall of Jalpaiguri town. Dwarakanath Ganguly, a prominent Brahmo leader, came to Jalpaiguri town in 1882. The main purpose of his advent was to collect news about tea garden labourers in the Duars region.[18]

Harimahan Chakrabarty was the Secretary of the Brahmo Samaj, Jalpaiguri town. After him, Dr Indu Bhushan Majumder, the principal of Ananda Chandra College and a resident of Rangoon, took charge in 1944. Jyotirindra Das was the joint secretary. Other prominent Brahmo leaders of the town were Sunitibala Chanda, Sadhana Basu, Nalini Dutta, Debaprasad Dutta, Sudhindra Nath Sarkar, Shanti Majumder, Gyan Chandra Roy, Sushil Dey, Harimahan Chakrabarty, Matilal Barua, Jamini Mahan Chanda, Hem Prabha Chanda, Ashrukana Dasgupta, Karuna Basu, Aruna Dasgupta and others. A small hamlet, popularly known as 'Samaj Para', grew up where the Brahmos of the town lived. The Bengali tea entrepreneurs, both Hindus and Muslims, had a generous view towards the Brahmos of the town.[19]

The nineteenth-century movements to reform Hindu society and religion like the Brahmo movement also left their impact in Jalpaigui town. The Brahmo congregation hall of Jalpaiguri town was established in 1923 where they generally met twice in a week for worshipping purposes. They had a large-scale contribution to the spread of modern education, especially women's education and a general upliftment of society. Brahmos, however, made an attempt to detribalize the Meches by educating some of them. The result was that the Brahmos, succeeded in Hinduizing some of them. These Meches were mainly the inhabitants of Kamakhyaguri and their leader was Prabhau Dayal Moshahari.

All of them later took the title 'Brahmamandal'.[20] Despite the establishment of a Brahmo congregation hall in Jalpaiguri town and advent of Bramho leaders on several occasions, it could not leave a major impetus in contemporary society. The Brahmo families who resided permanently in Jalpaiguri town numbered only three to four. Their influence and sphere of activity were limited to the educated middle classes of the urban areas.[21]

THE BRAHMO SAMAJ IN COOCHBEHAR

Keshub Chandra Sen provided the movement with a better organizational structure and ideological consistency. The growth and development of Brahmo Samaj in Coochbehar was started before the marriage of Suniti Devi in 1878. The Coochbehar Brahmo Samaj was established more than fifty years ago, when late Ray Kalikadas Dutta Bahadur was the Dewan of the Coochbehar State. The British Deputy Commissioner of Coochbehar had submitted a report to W.W. Hunter that 'there were a few followers of the Brahmo Samaj, although no regular Samaj has been established in Kuch Behar'. However, the Brahmo movement gained a new lease of life in North Bengal with the marriage between Nripendra Narayan, the Maharaja of Coochbehar and Suniti Devi, the eldest daughter of Keshub Chandra Sen.[22]

In a letter written to Max Müller, Keshub Chandra Sen expressed his view that 'The marriage was a political marriage, a whole kingdom was to be reformed'. Though it was an inter-caste marriage between two persons, who both received Western education, but it brought about a schism in the Samaj as Keshab Chandra Sen himself violated the Brahmo Act III of 1872. The radical Brahmos, led by Sibnath Shastri, Ananda Mahan Bose, Dwarakanath Ganguly and others, finally broke away from Keshub Chandra Sen and founded the Sadharan Brahmo Samaj in 1878. Hereafter, Keshub Chandra Sen lost his grip and the movement centred round the Sadharan Brahmo Samaj.[23]

The central figure behind the founding of Sadharan Brahmo Samaj in Coochbehar was Ray Kalikadas Dutta Bahadur, the Dewan of the Coochbehar State. During his tenure, Brojendra

Nath Sil became the president of Sadharan Brahmo Samaj for few days. The other founding members of Brahmo Samaj in Coochbehar were Babu Nandalal Madak, Babu Siddheshwar Ghosh, Babu Rajanikanta Ray, Kedarnath Mukhopadhyay, Ray Bahadur Manmaham Bakshi and Lalit Mahan Bakshi. The first worshipping temple of Sadharan Brahmo Samaj (New Dispensation Church) led by Keshub Chandra Sen was set up in Coochbehar in 1880. In no time, the Brahmo religion became the state religion in Coochbehar.[24]

After the death of Maharaja Nripendranarayan, Kumar Gajendranarayan led the Brahmo movement and founded the Keshub Ashram in 1888. A Bengali periodical popularly known as *Surukha* was published by Ramchandra Singha. Its main aim was to spread the ideas of Brahmo religion among the general people. Victor Nityendranarayan became the secretary of Sadharan Brahmo Samaj in Coochbehar in 1915. Nirupama Devi also made a major contribution. The movement had little impact on the Muslims of the region. It was heard that Iyantullah, an inhabitant of Haldibari, willingly converted himself to Brahmo religion.[25] In no time, it sparked a fire among the native Muslims and as a consequence, he was summoned to a Sabha held by the religious preachers of the Muslim community. Both Babu Gaur Govinda Ray of Calcutta and Babu Prankrishna Dutta of Coochbehar the Brahmos stood with him.[26]

CONTRIBUTION OF THE BRAHMO MOVEMENT

The influence of the Brahmo movement in North Bengal was greately felt in the Princely State of Coochbehar. It had a very notable bearing on the education and cultural development of the state. A major outcome of the movement was felt in the field of literature and the forerunners were the people who belonged to the middle-class intelligentsia. Shakespeare, Milton, Bentham, Macaulay, and Mill shaped their mentality and outlook. The installation of the printing press in 1875 in Coochbehar, announced the dawn of a new age in the world of writing. The number of monthly magazine and periodicals named *Kulashastra* (1855),

Sukatha (1893), *Kangal* (1895), *Paricharika* (1916) and *Coochbehar Darpan* (1940) are those literary pieces which remained focused towards economic, social and cultural progress of the state.[27]

Nirupama Debi's poetic creations helped the verses to acquire their own unique place in the realm of Bengali literature. She was probably the first accomplished modern writer of Coochbehar. Janki Ballabh's *Sobha* didn't leave a lasting impression on the reader's mind, though it entertained the readers particularly of that time. A good number of books like *Coochbeharer Itihas* (1883) by Jadav Chakrabarty, *Kuchbihar Rajchitra* (1915) by Ghanashyam Dalai, *Coochbeharer Itihas* (1936) by Amanatullah Ahmed, *Bishwaketu Chandrabali* (1912) by Shafatulla Sarkar and others, provided Bengali prose and poetry with lucidity and clarity. Birja Charan Gupta, Bhagawati Charan Bandopadhyay, Kokileshwar Bhattacharya, Sharat Chandra Ghoshal, Bimal Chandra Chakrabarty, Nihar Bala Devi, Khan Chaudhury Amanat Ullah Ahmed, Ashruman Dasgupta, Birendra Nath Bhattacharya, Akhil Chandra Palit, Devi Prasad Sen, Jiban Krishna Mukhopadhyay, were all torch bearers of the renaissance movement of the Bengali intelligentsia of Coochbehar. Their efforts improved Bengali language and literature in Coochbehar greatly.[28]

In 1915, Sahitya Sabha was established in Coochbehar. It became a prized possession of the people as far as Bengali language, literature and culture was concerned. Victor Nityendra Narayan made the Sahitya Sabha a medium for publication of various literary works ranging from epic, novel to music. His wife, Nirupama Debi took the initiative to publish an illustrated version of the monthly magazine *Paricharika*. 'Under your Highness order a monthly magazine named *Paricharika* edited by Rani Nirupama Devi, wife of Maharaja Victor Nityendra Narayan, is being published regularly from the State press from November last.' She was also a prolific writer. *Basantamalaika* (1916) and *Dhup* (1918) were two notable creations of the period.[29]

Paricharika first took its birth in Calcutta. It was edited by Pratap Chandra Majumder, brother of Nirupama Devi. Later Mohini Devi, wife of Keshub Chandra Sen's eldest son, Sucharu Devi, Maharani of Mayurbhanj and Manika Devi took the responsibility to publish it. Later, it started to be published from Coochbehar. After 1924 the publication of *Paricharika* became irregular from Coochbehar as Nirupama Devi later shifted to Shantiniketan.[30]

Paricharika in turn helped Sahitya Sabha to discharge the role which it was meant to play. Many stalwarts like Rabindranath Tagore, Kalidas Roy, Kumudranjan Mallick, Karuna Nidhan Bandopadhyay, Priyambada Devi, Savitri Prasanna Chattopadhyay, Nagendra Nath Basu, Akshay Kumar Maitra contributed to the growth of the magazine *Paricharika* with their valuable writings. A large number of poetic pieces reveal an amalgamation of the east and the west, and this paved the way for creation of far more refined literature. Thus, the Sahitya Sabha began to grow as a permanent asset of Bengali culture. In 1918, Sir Ashutosh visited Coochbehar and was felicitated warmly by the Sahitya Sabha. At the ceremony, Sir Ashutosh commented that nowhere in British India had education spread at such a pace as in Coochbehar. Renowned rebel poet, Nazrul visited Coochbehar and sang a number of patriotic songs.[31]

Despite the ups and downs, the contribution of the Brahmo movement in the modernization of Coochbehar was immense. It, undoubtedly, opened a new era of Brahmo movement in Coochbehar and modernized the royal state with Western ideas and thought. Endeavours were made for women's education and publication of Bengali periodicals like *Sukatha, Paricharika, Dharmatattwa, Tattwa Kaumadi, Pracharak.* These periodicals contributed a lot to propagate the Brahmo ideas and modernize thinking on issues like women's education, women's emancipation and widow remarriage. During the period of Nripendra Narayan, a number of primary schools were set up. Ishwar Chandra Vidyasagar's campaign in Bengal for social reform in 1850s must have had a deep impression on the young generation. Philanthropic works or humanitarian services like Surapan Nibarani Sabha (alcohol ban society) were the most significant features of the movement.[32]

The Renaissance movement in Coochbehar had active participation from people belonging to different professions like landholders, *dewan*, deputy magistrate, pleaders, physicians and teachers. Their cultural outlook was mostly a blend of the East and the West. This golden era saw a flourishing of talent in every field and the prominent figures among singers were Chinta Haran Roy, Dwijendra Nath Banerjee, Tarapada Banerjee, Lalit Mahan Bakshi, Himadri Ballabh Biswas, Ashruman Dasgupta and many more. In the field of theatre, Tara Prasanna Dasgupta, Suresh Chandra Mustafi, Bimal Kumar Chakrabarty, Indubhushan Mukhopadhyay, Kumar Kanak Narayan, Lalit Mahan Bakshi, Nagendra Nath Sarkar, Jogesh Chandra Singha and others. Pyari Mahan Das, Kedar Chakrabarty, Keshab Barman, Ganga Charan Biswas, Nayeb Ali and Abbasuddin were prominent figures in the field of folk songs. There was not so much of artistic endeavour in the Princely State of Coochbehar, whatever artistic creation there was, was mainly due to the rural artists. The Khagrabari Dramatic Club was established in 1870 and it was patronized by Maharaja Nripendra Narayan. Later it came to be known as 'Young Men's Theatrical Club'. A number of Bengali plays were staged there like 'Ratnabali', 'Chandragupta', 'Sita', 'Debala Devi', 'Draupadi Parinay' and so on. In 1919, the Coochbehar Musical Club was set up. A number of leading personalities of that time was associated with this literary institution. The Lansdowne Hall was constructed in 1894 in commemoration of the visit of lord Lansdowne, Viceroy and Governor-General of India. It played a key role as a place of public meeting and reading room. On 2 February 1895, a State Library was opened there by Maharaja Nripendra Narayan.[33]

Art and architecture reached great heights during the Mughal reign but there was a gradual wearing away with the decline of Mughal rule. Some mosques in Coochbehar, still bear glimpses of those artistic creations. When the British began to rule the country, many artists travelled to India, in search of work. In 1876, the Coochbehar kings appointed Major Mont for designing the royal palace based on the Moorish architecture. Later on, an Italian architect made a design based on the architectural styles of Rome, Venice, and Florence. This was implemented for the building of the palace by F. Berkeley in assistance with a building firm named Marilier and Edwards. The palace was an exhibition of ornamental design of the West. The native artistic culture had no connection with this imitated western culture. The rulers of Coochbehar promoted the native cultural art and tried for its resurgence. The Madan Mahan Temple, the Shiva Temple at Baneswar, and Devi Bari Temple bears the testimony of the fact. In early twentieth century, Bengalis in Coochbehar became more and more interested in science. The learned Europeans engaged in scientific endeavour in different subjects. Two students from Victoria College, Bhola Chakraborty and Taraprasad Chattopadhyay, must be mentioned here as persons who dedicated themselves towards the advancement of science education. Again, there were many other renowned personalities who were equally sincere in their efforts to work for scientific achievement, like Madan Mahan Saptashashtri in Ayurveda, Indu Bhushan Majumder in agricultural science, Harinarayan Bandopadhyay, Birendra Nath Bhattacharya, Pramila Majumder, Bharati Chakrabarty and others in medical science.[34]

In 1904, the then Governor-General Lord Curzon visited Coochbehar at the invitation of the kings. He participated in the game of hunting of leopard in the jungle of Jaldapara. There were many other renowned persons like kings and *zamindar*s who visited Coochbehar from time to time. They were Bijay Chand Mehtab the Maharaja of Burdwan, Pravat Chandra Barooah and Pramathesh Barooah of Gauripur, Prasanna Deb Raikat of Jalpaiguri, Sawai Man Singh of Jaipur and the kings of Baroda, Patiala and Mahishadal.[35]

The middle-class people of Coochbehar were generally religious. The strict views of religion gave way to more open-minded attitude and this led to the weaning away of dogmatic racial and caste attitude. The middle-class Bengali Hindu, enlightened by the Renaissance, was not so keen to understand the underdeveloped status of the middle-class Muslims. They were not so sympathetic towards their aspirations. Whereas, the Coochbehar rulers were very much concerned about them and as such this prevented any political discord in the Raj estate. Moreover, the unequal progress did not hinder their coexistence.

In Coochbehar, the movement against the drinking of alcohol led by Kumar Gajendranarayan and other Brahmos was a new phenomenon in socio-reform movements in nineteenth-century

Bengal. Such an endeavour was first seen in Medinipur in 1861 led by Rajnarayan Basu. For this reason, he was criticized by a group of people, mainly the alcohol sellers and they even tried to kill him. A parallel association was formed in Dhaka by the Brahmo leader Brajasundar Mitra. The movement against the drinking of alcohol took a new turn with the establishment of 'Bengal Temperance Society' in 1863 by Pyari Charan Sarkar, the Head Master of Hare School and editor of the *Education Gazette.* A number of students like Keshub Chandra Sen and Shibnath Shastri, being influenced with his views, widely participated in the movement. *Hitasadhak* and *Well Wisher* published monthly were the mouthpieces of the organization. Their main objective was to propagate the harmful effects of alcohol on health among the youths.[36]

The Bharat Sanskar Sabha (Indian Reform Association) was established in Calcutta by Keshub Chandra Sen in October 1870. It had five branches. Among them the alcohol ban branch was the most prominent. The object of this section was to redress the growth of intemperance among the native population, especially among the better educated classes. In April 1871, a monthly magazine popularly known as *Mad Na Garal* came into light. It was edited by Sibnath Shastri and Keshub Chandra Sen was the main figure behind it. In 1878, the 'Band of Hope' was established in the house of Keshub Chandra Sen 'Lily Cottage' where the members openly took the oath to ban the use of alcohol in society. They had a close connection with the 'United Kingdom Alliance', established in London, with the same objective.[37]

Keshub Chandra Sen's mission against the use of alcohol was not confined to Calcutta; it also left its impact in other parts of Bengal. In the northern part of Bengal, it was felt greatly in the Princely State of Coochbehar. From the beginning, Keshub Chandra Sen had a close relation with this state in connection to his daughter's marriage with Maharaja Nripendra Narayan Bhup Bahadur. Naturally, after Calcutta, Coochbehar ranked first in this noble object. Kumar Gajendranarayan of Coochbehar and Maharaja Sri Ramachandra Bhanjadeo of Mayurbhanj were both overwhelmingly impressed with his work. Sri Ramachandra once said 'I am in favour of a reasonable restriction on the use of opium, but

I am unutterably opposed to liberty in the selling of liquor'. In Coochbehar, the movement against the drinking of alcohol was first launched by Kumar Gajendranarayan who was assisted by a group of officials namely Dewan Kalikadas Dutta, Babu Narayan Chaudhuri, Kunjabihari Majumdar, Jadunath Bhattacharya, Narendranath Sen, Priyanath Ghosh and others. Sabitri Devi, wife of Kumar Gajendranarayan, gave an elaborate description of their activities in her book.[38]

Maharaja Nripendra Narayan generously supported their activities as he lost his father at a very early stage due to excessive drinking. In a conference of the Temperance Society attended by around 250 people, Nripendra Narayan openly addressed them, asking them to come forward for this great social cause. Being overwhelmingly impressed with his call, around 52-3 boys signed a pledge where it was written 'Touch not, taste not and smell not that intoxicates the brain'. In a conference of the 'Band of Hope' held at Jenkin's School in 1889, Sri Kunjabihari Sen, brother of Keshub Chandra Sen, warned the attendees about the ill effects of alcohol. The conference was attended by a large section of government employees, lawyers and officials of the state where a group of 10-12 youths took the oath against drinking. They arranged conferences and workshops in the neighbouring villages like Gughumari, Doderhat and Baneswar. In 1916, the Brahmo leader Gopal Chandra Guha and Troilokyonath both organized a conference on temperance and anti-smoking at Baneswar, the place of Shiva Temple. Lectures were also delivered at several places in eastern Bengal, Coochbehar, Tangail and Gauripur, Assam.[39]

Thus one might say that the spread of British administration and its associated infrastructure, the cultural activities of the Brahma Samaj, particularly by Maharaja Nripendra Narayana and Suniti Devi as well as the direct and indirect impact of the Bengal Renaissance sowed the seeds of renaissance in Coochbehar. What was more important about them was that they posed an intellectual challenge to the religious and social orthodoxy of Hinduism. But the movement was actually taken out of the limited group of people of Coochbehar and other district towns of North Bengal. It could not form the basis for the emancipation of the exploited. The economic interests of the working class could not be linked with the reform movement and it failed to cause the total awakening among the people. The leaders failed to bring the Muslim community.

DECLINE OF BRAHMO MOVEMENT IN NORTH BENGAL

The impact of the Brahmo movement started to decline after the period of Indira Devi, the wife of Maharaja Jitendra Narayan Bhup Bahadur. After his death, a Regency Council was formed of which Indira Devi was the central figure. She had no affection for Brahmo religion at all. Immediately after being the head of the Regency Council, she stopped sanctioning money totally to the Brahmo Samaj, Coochbehar. As a consequence, the Brahmo religion lost its status as the state religion and the employees who were Brahmos were debarred from their professions. A number of professors of Victoria College, Brahmos by religion, left Coochbehar permanently. This degradation disheartened Suniti Devi to a large extent and as a consequence, she left the royal palace and settled permanently at Calcutta. She spent the last days of her life in Ranchi.[40] The Neo-Hindu movement had a big role in descreasing the popularity of the Brahmo movement in Coochbehar. Sashadhar Tarkachuramani, the founder of Neo-Hinduism, arrived in the royal state for the resurrection of Hinudism among the people of Coochbehar. He had to organize a number of conferences in 1884 against the practice of Brahmo religion which had a major impact among the common people in general. Shankaradeva's philosophy had a great impact among the common people. All these factors made the background in redressing the influence of the Brahmo movement in Coochbehar.[41]

Finally, most of the Brahmos who lived in Coochbehar hailed mainly from Calcutta and its surrounding areas for their profession. After retirement they did not stay there and returned to their birth place. As a result, the Brahmo movement lost its importance in Coochbehar due to the dearth of its preachers.[42] If they settled permanently in Coochbehar after retirement the history of Brahmo movement would be written in different forms?

NOTES

1. Sugata Bose and Ayesha Jalal, *Modern South Asia History, Culture, Political Economy,* Oxford University Press, New Delhi, Second Edition, 2004, p. 65.
2. David Kopf, *The Brahmo Samaj and the Shaping of Modern Indian Mind,* Princeton University Press, 1997, p. 226.
3. Ananda Gopal Ghosh, 'Brahmo Andolon O Tar Parinati' (Brahmo Movement and Its Evolution), in *Mukhapatra,* First Issue, Malda, December 1984, p. 25.
4. Ananda Gopal Ghosh and Soumendra Prasad Saha, *Uttarbanga Itihas O Samaj* (History and Society of North Bengal), vol. II, Sangbedan, Malda, 2015, pp. 110-12.
5. Ajit Kumar Ghosh, *Rammohan Rachanabali* (Essays on Rammohan), Haraf Publication, Calcutta, 1973, p. 584.
6. Dilip Kumar Biswas, 'Brahmo Samaj', in Narendra Krishna Sinha (ed.) *History of Bengal 1757-1905,* University of Calcutta, Calcutta, Second Edition June 1996, p. 564.
7. Sekhar Bandyopadhyay, *From Plassey to Partition,* Orient Longman, New Delhi, 2004, p.152.
8. Shibnath Shastri, *Ramtanu Lahiri O Tatkalin Brahmo Samaj* (Ramtanu Lahiri and the Contemporary Brahmo Samaj), New Age Publishers, Calcutta, Third Edition 2009, p. 170.
9. Ananda Gopal Ghosh, 'Uttarbange Brahmo Dharma O Samaj Andalan' (Brahmo Religion and Socio-religious Movement in North Bengal), in Mayukh Das (ed.), *Itihascharcha* (Studies in History), vol. I, Calcutta, 2016, p. 59.
10. Biswanath Das, *Autobiography of an Indian Princess* (Memory of Maharani Suniti Devi), Vikas Publishing House, New Delhi, 1995, p. 212.
11. Dick B. Dewan, *History of Education in Darjeeling Hill 1835-1985,* Indus Publishing Company, New Delhi, 1991, p. 172.
12. E.C. Dozey, *A Concise History of Darjeeling since 1835,* N.L. Publishers, 2011, Siliguri, p. 78.
13. Ananda Gopal Ghosh, 'Uttarbange Brahmo Dharma O Samaj Andalan', op. cit., p. 61.
14. W.W.W. Hunter, *A Statistical Account of Bengal,* vol. X, 1876, London, p. 260.
15. Muntasir Mamun, 'Banglay Brahmo Samajer Itibritto' (History of Brahmo Samaj in Bengal), in Atanu Sashan Mukhopadhyay (ed.), *Dashdishi Patrika,* Calcutta, 2014, p. 178.

16. Wakil Ahmed, *Unish Shatake Bangali Musalmaner Chinta-Chetonar Dhara* (Stream of Thoughts of Bengali Muslims in Nineteenth Century), (vol. II.), Bangla Academy, Dhaka, Bangladesh, First Edition, 1983, p. 76.
17. Umesh Sharma, 'Jalpaigurir Shatabarshiya Brahmo Samaj' (Centenary History of Brahmo Samaj in Jalpaiguri), in Arabinda Kar (ed.) *Kiratbhumi* (Land of Kiratas), vol. XXIX, Jalpaiguri, 2015, p. 29.
18. Sibsankar Mukherjee, 'Emergence of Bengali Entrepreneurship in Tea Plantation in Jalpaiguri Duars 1879-1933', unpublished PhD thesis, University of North Bengal, 1978, pp. 80-2.
19. Umesh Sharma, op. cit., p. 30.
20. Charu Chandra Sanyal, *The Meches and the Totos* (Two Sub-Himalayan Tribes of North Bengal), Calcutta, 1973, p. 18.
21. Ananda Gopal Ghosh, 'Uttarbange Brahmo Dharma O Samaj Andalan', op. cit., pp. 67-68.
22. *Administrative Reports of Coochbehar for the year of 1916-1917*, Coochbehar State Press, Coochbehar, 1917, pp. 24-5.
23. Sekhar Bandyopadhyay, op. cit., p. 153.
24. Sanjay Saha, 'Jharer Pakhi-Nirupama Devi (Storm Bird-Nirupama Devi)', in Debashish Das (ed.), *Coochbehar Rajnagarer Andarmahal* (In the Inner Palace of Coochbehar Royal Palace), Bibrita Sahitya Prakashani, Malda, 2015, pp. 93-4.
25. Dhananjay Roy, *Uttrabanga Unish O Bish Shatak* (North Bengal: Nineteenth and Twentieth Century's), Dip Prakashan, Calcutta, 2002, p. 31.
26. A.P. Sen, *Hindu Revivalism in Bengal 1872-1905,* Oxford University Press, Delhi, 1993, p. 46.
27. Bhagwati Charan Bandopadhyay, *Kuchbiharer Itihas* (History of Coochbehar), Coochbehar State Press, Coochbehar, 1882, p. 27.
28. Nirupama Devi, *Ekkhan*, Autumn Number, 1401 B.S., Coochbehar, pp. 24-6.
29. Subodh Chandra Das and Biman Chakrabarty, 'Kuchbehar Rajye Brahmo Andalan' (Brahmo Movement in the Princely State of Coochbehar), in Ajitesh Bhattacharya (ed.), *Madhuparni, Kuchbehar Jela Sankhya* (Special Volume on the District of Coochbehar), BS 1396, p, 374.
30. Wakil Ahmed, op. cit., p. 77.
31. *Sudhakar*, 23 Kartik, 1926, pp. 6-7.
32. *The Annual Administration Report of the Department of General Administration and Criminal Justice of the Coochbehar State for the year 1921-2*, Coochbehar State Press, Coochbehar, 1922, pp. 3-4.

33. Centenary Souvenir, Khagrabari Dramatic Club, Coochbehar, 1971, pp. 12-14.
34. Dhananjay Roy, *Uttarbanga Unish O Bish Shatak,* op. cit., pp. 32-3.
35. *Annual Administrative Report of Coochbehar for the year of 1904-5,* Coochbehar State Press, Coochbehar, 1905, p. 12.
36. Shibnath Shastri, *Ramtanu Lahiri O Tatkalin Brahmo Samaj,* op. cit., pp. 359-60.
37. Sophia Dobson Collect, *The Brahmo Year Book for 1878,* Brief Record of Work and Life in the Theistic Churches of India, Williams and Nor Gate, London and 20 South Frederick Street, Edinburgh, 1878, p. 36.
38. Sabitri Devi, *Swargiya Kumar Gajendranarayan* (Late Prince Gajendranarayan), Calcutta, 1928, p. 156.
39. *Dharmatattwa,* 1 chaitra, BS 1323, p. 55.
40. Ananda Gopal Ghosh, 'Uttarbange Brahmo Dharma O Samaj Andalan', op. cit., p. 67.
41. Bipin Chandra Pal, *Memories of My Life and Times,* Modern Book Agency, Calcutta, 1973, pp. 271-2.
42. Subodh Chandra Das and Biman Chakrabarty, op. cit., p. 373.

CHAPTER 2

Press, Periodicals and Libraries

INTRODUCTION

The social and political movements of the nineteenth century gave a fresh impetus to journalism. The old *Hindu Patriot* was then the leading Indian paper in Bengal, under the editorship of Kristo Das Pal, exercising great influence over the educated middle-class and government. *The Indian Mirror*, founded by Keshub Chandra Sen in August 1861, quickly rose to fame and popularity for its liberal, social and political views. The *Bengalee* (1862) under the editorship of Surendranath Banerjee was turned into a powerful weapon of political propagandas. The weekly *Brahmo Public Opinion* (1878) had considerable impact on the young Brahmos during that period.[1]

While some of the old veterans were continuing their existence, quite a number of new Bengali periodicals appeared in the field. Of these the weekly *Somprakash*, first projected by Vidyasagar and published on 15 November 1858, attained the foremost place among the Bengali newspapers. It was followed by the *Sulava Samachar* in November 1870, the *Bangabasi* in December 1881 and the *Sanjibani* in April 1883. These three Bengali weeklies had a profound impact in the contemporary social and political field of Bengal to a great extent. The *Bangadarshan,* founded and edited by the famous novelist Bankim Chandra Chatterjee in 1872 and the *Bharati* in 1877 edited by Dwijendranath Tagore, Swarnakumari Devi, Rabindranath Tagore and others, became the harbinger of the new literary and cultural Renaissance in Bengal.[2]

Two pillars of the Renaissance such as the setting up of the presses and the publication of books were not confined to Calcutta only, rather they extended to other areas too. Not only did printing and publishing increase greatly in Calcutta, but presses were set up in many other district towns and villages. A good number of periodicals came out, of which the *Sadharani* of Chinsurah (Hooghly), the *Grambarta Prakashika* of Kumarkhali (24-Parganas), the *Bharatmihir* of Mymensingh, the *Dacca Prakash,* the *Hindu Hitaishini* and the *Garib* of Dacca and the *Grambasi* of Uluberia (Howrah) had god local circulation.[3]

There are a good number of books on the history, growth, and development of press, periodicals and libraries in colonial India nay Bengal. Among the earlier works, B.S. Kesavan's *History of Printing and Publishing in India* (New Delhi, 2004), Graham Shaw's *Printing in Calcutta To 1800* (London, 1981) mentioned the history of printing and press in colonial India. The history of press and libraries has in recent years drawn more attention of historians. Muntasir Mamun in his works like *Unish Shatake Purbabanger Mudran O Prakashana* (Dhaka, 2006) and *Unish Shataker Bangladesher Sambad-Samayik Patra* (Dacca, 2004) has highlighted the details of various press, newspapers and periodicals that developed in different districts of East Bengal. Ramananda Chattopadhyay's book *Boi Bybsa O Panch Purusher Bangali Pariwar* (Kolkata, 2002) has a long chapter on the list of books published in nineteenth and twentieth centuries Bengal. Barun Kumar Mukhopadhyay's book *Bangla Mudrita Granther Itihas,* (vol. 1, Kolkata, 1985) did not get any separate mention. Broadly speaking, these contributions mentioned above have concentrated mainly on Calcutta and other districts of East Bengal. The northern part of Bengal mainly the districts of Rajshahi, Rangpur, Jalpaiguri and the Princely State of Coochbehar did not lag behind much in this area. But none of them has probed so deep in this field. Hence an attempt has been made to make a study in this field.

PRESS AND PERIODICALS IN NORTH BENGAL

The first printing press of North Bengal during the British period was established in Rangpur in 1846, popularly known as the Rangpur Bartabaha Press. The weekly *Rangpur Bartabaha* was first published from this printing house under the editorship of

Gurucharan Roy, a government employee. After his untimely death, his wife Bhagirathi Devi sold the press to Nilambar Mukhopadhyay. After ten years of publication, the press closed down due to the introduction of the Press Act of 1857. Although closed, this press was not completely finished. Sambhu Chandra Roychaudhury, the *zamindar* of Kakina bought it and named it Digdarshan Press from where *Rangpur Digprakash* was published. He was so enthusiastic about the publication that he invited everyone in the village to eat there for three days. In this mission, he was assisted by Raja Rajmohun Roychaudhury, the *zamindar* of Kakina to a great extent. Since 1860, it was edited by Madhusudan Bhattacharya of Burdwan and Tarashankar Maitra of Nadia. *Behardanta,* written by Brindeshwari Devi, wife of Maharaja Narendra Narayan of Coochbehar was first published from this press.[4]

However, Sambhu Chandra's interest in the printing world did not end here. He donated a printing machine to Bhagwati Charan Chattopadhyay, the editor of the weekly *Samachar Chandrika.* Apart from the Digdarshan Press, a number of presses were established in Rangpur at various times. For example, Lakaranjan Sakha Press (1883) at Haridebpur, Padmabati Press (1886) and Mahiganj Press (1894) at Mahiganj, Bibhakar Press (1894) at Kurigram and Parijat Press (1896) at Barai Bari. The weekly *Chatra Sahachar* edited by Ramcharan Deb and Manmathnath Singha was published from the Bibhakar Press. And the weekly *Bhikshukh* edited by Saradakanta Maitra was published from the Parijat Press. Perhaps the weekly *Utsaha* edited by Abinash Chandra Chakrabarty was published from the Parijat press. Two more printing presses named Saraswati (1899) and Joy (1900) were established in Rangpur towards the end of the century.[5]

The printing press in Rajshahi grew mainly because of Bengali weeklies. The Rajshahi press was established in 1870 because of the weekly *Rajshahi Sambad.* The number of printing presses in Rajshahi was about eleven. Among them six were established in Boyalia like Girish Chandra (1868), Rajshahi Binod (1891), Bani (1897), Tamaghna (1868) and Boyalia (1867). The *Aitihashik Chitra* edited by Akshay Kumar Maitra was published from the Bani Printing House. The others were Sudhakar (1879) in

Dighapatia, Tattwaprakash (1884) in Taherpur, Rajshahi Samiti (1893) and Hindu Ranjika (1872). The Tattwaprakash Press was set up by Kumar Sashi Sekhareswar Roy, a *zamindar* of Rampur Boyalia from where the weeklies *Shilpa Krishi* and *Krira O Kautak* were published. The weekly *Baishayiktattwa* edited by Banku Bihari Khan was also published from the press.[6]

Hindu Ranjika, a monthly newspaper published in 1866 under the patronage of the Rampur Boaliya Dharmasabha, Rajshahi, was edited by Srinath Singha Roy, the president of the association. It was the mouthpiece of the conservative Hindu society and stood against the Brahmo ideas. It was written in the weekly *Purnachandradoy* that it would publish all the books related to Hinduism in Sanskrit. The printing machine of this association was donated by Haranath Roychaudhury, the *zamindar* of Dubalhati in 1872.[7]

In the same year, *Gyanankur* of Rampur Boaliya Dharmasabha by Srikrishna Das and *Gyanprabha* by Chandranath Sengupta from Sirajganj, Pabna came into existence. Several issues of the famous novel *Swarnalata* were consecutively published in *Gyanprabha.* The weekly *Rajshahi Samachar* was first published from Natore in 1875. These were some of the outstanding Bengali periodicals published by the new generation of Bengali intellectuals which set a new tone and standard of Bengali journalism in Bengal.[8]

Udyog Bidhayani, the mouthpiece of Udyog Bidhayani Sabha, Pabna was edited by Barada Prasad Roy and published first in 1863. It was printed from Dhaka and the annual price was one and a half *taka.* It survived only for two and half years. *Rachanabali* was first published in 1864 from the Shambhu Chandra Printing Press, Rangpur in 1864. *Pabna Darpan* first published in 1864, was edited by both Ramasundar Roy and Kashinath Mitra. In 1873, *Pallidarshan* edited by Ishan Chandar Chakrabarty was published in Pabna and *Suhriday,* the mouthpiece of Bhatpara Unnatisadhani Sabha, Dinajpur and edited by Tarabandhu Sharma came into existence. The monthly *Gyanbikashini* was published under the patronage of Gyandayini Sabha, Pabna in 1873. It was the mouthpiece of all sections of people, and contained brief expositions on literary, historical, social and legal topics. In the last phase of the nineteenth century a number of printing presses were established in Pabna like Arya (1890), Mahamudia (1891), Dibakar (1882), Nababikash (1888) and Nababibhakar (1883). In Bogra two presses named Chaudhury and Roy (1882) came into existence.[9]

During 1885-8, two Bengali periodicals namely *Dinajpur Patrika* by Brajendra Chandra Singha and *Krira O Kautuk* by Radesh Chandra Seth initiated a favourable atmosphere for the growth of national press. In 1890, the weekly *Ashalata* edited by Kunja Bihari Dey was brought out from Pabna in which *Asha,* the first poem written by Rajanikanta Sen was published. In the course of a few months in 1897-8, two bilingual periodicals namely 'Hour Bond' in English from Pabna and *Utsaha* in Bengali edited by Suresh Chandra Saha from Rajshahi were published. Numerous writings of Rabindranath Tagore and Akshay Kumar Maitra were published several times there. Akshay Kumar Maitra brought out a Bengali periodical named *Aitihasik Chitra* in 1899 from Rajshahi. The advent of this periodical opened a new arena in studying the archaeology and culture of ancient Bengal. It tried to make the Bengalis, conscious of their ancient past irrespective of caste and class.[10]

In 1859, Maharaja Narendra Narayan took an initiative to set up a press in Coochbehar. The main purpose behind its establishment was to publish the rare *puthis*, manuscripts in book form. For this reason, he brought a printing machine from Calcutta, the capital of British India. But it could not open due to the untimely death of Maharaja Narendra Narayan on 6 August 1863. Therefore, Dewan Nilkamal Sanyal and others took the initiative to fulfil the long-cherished dream of Maharaja Narendra Narayan. They earnestly requested Beveridge, the then Deputy Commissioner of Coochbehar to take immediate steps for this purpose. In a letter to J.C. Haughton, the Commissioner of Coochbehar, he wrote that 'there is ample room for a press in Coochbehar for the purpose of printing receipts, forms, circular-orders of the commissioner and if the jail prisoners were made to work it, the cost would not be heavy'. In the meantime, the British government took steps to prepare the land according to survey reports of the royal state of Coochbehar. Therefore, the setting up of a printing press in Coochbehar was highly needed to print the land-survey documents at low cost. As a consequence, a printing machine was bought from the Wiseman Brothers & Company, Calcutta. At the initial stage, it was installed at the office of the Divisional headquarter, Jalpaiguiri. Later it was shifted to Coochbehar in 1875.[11]

The most noteworthy publications of the Coochbehar printing press were the *Kuchbihar Patrika,* a monthly magazine by Rangila Narayan in 1877 and *Coochbehar Select Records* (vol. 1) by Babu Rajani Kanta Roy comprising with 359 pages. This book throws light mainly on the Anglo-Koch treaty (1772) and several records and letters from 1777 to 1815. *Kochbiharer Itihas* written by Bhagawati Charan Bandopadhyay was first published from Coochbehar State Press in 1882. During that period, there were no other places in North Bengal except Coochbehar and Kakina, which had their own printing press. Raja Rajmohun Roychaudhury of Kakina first established the printing press in 1846. The weekly *Rangpur Bartabaha* first published from this press in 1847. It was later renamed as *Rangpur Digprakash* under the patronage of Shambhu Chandra Roychaudhury of Kakina in 1859.[12]

In the same year, *Beharadanta* written by Brindeswari Devi, the Princess of Coochbehar was also bought out by the same press. In 1883, *Kochbihar Rajyer Sankhipta Bibaran* (A Short History of Coochbehar) written by Jadav Chandra Chakrabarty was published. The first volume of *Gitasutrasar*, a book on classical songs, written by Krishnadhana Bandopadhyay was published. The accession of Maharaja Nripendra Narayan to the throne also took place in the same year. In 1884, the second volume of *Coochbehar Select Records* containing with 279 pages provides an elaborate description on the letters written between 1816 and 1864. On 3 March 1884, the *Coochbehar Gazette* was published. It was the first official Gazette and was published by the Superintendent of the Coochbehar State Press. The *Calcutta Gazette* was taken as model in preparing it. At first, it was published every Monday after two weeks but later every week. All important decisions of the council, orders relating to appointment of officers, municipal notices, weather and crop reports, current price rates and other important reports were published.[13]

In 1887, a Bengali periodical *Sukatha* was published under the patronage of the Maharaja. The Administrative Report of 1890-1 has referred it as the 'Organ of the New Dispensation'. However, the circulation of *Sukatha* was stopped in 1897 due to the heavy earthquake. It also affected the Nababidhan Brahma Temple of Coochbehar adversely to a great extent. In 1895, the weekly *Kangali* by Krihsna Sundar Sen came into light. In 1897, a monthly journal relating to the sanitization of the royal state came into circulation and its editor was Durgadas Gupta, a physician by profession. But it was short lived due to the retirement of Durgadas Gupta on 18 February 1898.[14]

Beside the Bengali periodicals and administrative reports, a number of books on literature and circular orders were published. For example, *Ananda Lahari* by Pandit Dinanath Majumder and *Handbook of Circular Orders* by Babu Chandar Mahan Guha in 1889 and *Kumudini* by Babu Ramachandra Singha was published in 1890 by the Coochbehar State Press. In 1892, *Janma Brittantam* written by Bikramananda Mishra in Sanskrit was published on the occasion of birth of Prince Raj Rajendra Narayan. In the same year, *A Statistical Account of the Independent and Feudatory Princes of India* written by Jadav Chandra Chakrabarty was published. In 1894, another famous work *Correspondence Relating to the Settlement of Cooch Behar* came into light. Several reports, pamphlets and books of Nababidhan Brahmo Samaj, Coochbehar were published in Coochbehar State Press between 1895 and 1896. In 1903, the famous book *The Coochbehar State and Its Land Revenue System* written by Harendra Narayan Chaudhury, a land-revenue officer by profession, was published.[15] The *Banaushadhi Darpan* written by Kabiraj Birjacharan Gupta in 1908 was the most useful book relating to the use of indigenous medicinal plants. It was published under the guidance of Maharaja Nripendra Narayan and the preface of the book was penned by Bijayratna Sen Kaviranjan, the famous Ayurvedic practitioner during that period. It was said that Maharaja Nripendra Narayan endeavoured to publish a comprehensive history of Coochbehar but it was not fulfilled due to his untimely death in 1911. His long-cherished dream was later fulfilled by Khan Chaudhury Amanatullah Ahmed. The name of the book was *Kuchbiharer Itihas* (History of Cooch Behar) published by Coochbehar State Press in 1936. It was translated into English by Sarat Chandra Ghoshal in 1939.[16]

The reign of Maharaja Harendranarayan and Nripendra Narayan Bhup Bahadur was truly the golden age of Bengali literature. The royal court was the main centre of the scholars' meet. The poets, educationists and servants have all received patronization widely from there. It is not known whether the publication of books, administrative records and composition of rare *puthis*, the *Ramayana*, the *Mahabharata*, and Puranas have taken place in any other royal court of Bengal or Assam. A detailed list of the scholars during that period can be found from the manuscripts or books kept in the libraries. The monthly *Paricharika* published by Nirupama Devi, wife of Prince Victor Nityendranarayan in 1916, was circulated from Kuchbihar Sahitya Sabha. It continued for eight years only. Free discussion of social problems were regularly published in it, which helped in the creation of a kind of public opinion on such social and religious problems like idolatry, polygamy, child-marriage and women's education.[17] The monthly *Kuchbihar Darpan* published by Coochbehar State Press, came into circulation in 1937. A number of notable figures of contemporary Bengal like the 'rebel poet' Kaji Nazrul Islam, Balai Chand Mukhopadhyay popularly known as 'Banphul' was associated with its publication. *Sahitya Bastobota*, one of the outstanding articles written by poet Bibhuti Bhushan Bandopadhyay was first published in it. It was more of a literary magazine but journalism was also an inseparable part of it. It was first edited jointly by Janaki Ballava Biswas and Sarat Chandra Ghoshal. Later, it was edited by Satyendranath Niyogi and after him; Amulya Ratan Gupta took its publication charge. After 1947, its publication was stopped.[18]

Dinajpur Patrika published from Dinajpur district, came into circulation in 1885. It was more of a literary magazine but journalism was also an inseparable part of it. Brojeshwar Singh was its founder editor. Next came Bishnucharan and after him Joginchandra, an ardent congressman and a renowned lawyer became the editor. The British government penalized the owner of the press with a fine of Rs. 500 under section 3(3) of the India Press Ordinance. Not only this, in 1940, the same newspaper was once again alerted by the district administrator of Rajshahi.[19]

In 1924, *Satyagrahi* appeared to spread news, views and information related to *satyagraha*. It was published by Abdullah Kafi of Dinajpur, a Gandhian. It was published from Calcutta but its area of focus was rural Bengal. The paper, under bold and able guidance of Abdul Kafi, infused strong nationalism in the minds of the youths. This paper had strong nationalist fervour coupled with relentless anti-imperialistic struggle. But it could not survive long. It became a sore in the eyes of the British government. As such, its publication was stopped and the editor was sent to jail. In October 1942 another Bengali periodical, *Manashi,* was brought out by Baradabhusan, a renowned politician of Dinajpur. It was driven by communist ideals. It was taken out of circulation because of the high handedness of the British government. The magazines published from the districts served as a mouthpiece for the people inhabiting miles away from the capital. They acted as agents of voicing their demands and grievances. They also created public opinion against British imperialist rule.[20]

In 1894 *Gourbarta* was published by Radesh Chandra Seth from Malda. He was a renowned politician who had attended the third session of the Indian National Congress held in Madras. He had to set up the Krishnakali Press with the help of a group of leading personalities of the town. Most of them were lawyers and teachers by profession. However, *Gourbarta* did not last long due to the dearth of money and lack of enthusiasm among the people. Soon afterwards, Radesh Chandra Seth began to publish another newspaper *Gourdoot.* He wrote several articles in it on numerous issues like landlord-peasant disputes, maladministration of the municipalities, the district board and the local boards. However, the publication of *Gourdoot* comes to an end in 1897 when the Krishnakali Press collapsed due to a strong earthquake. Thereafter he joined the *Maldaha Samachar* as a regular columnist.[21]

Maldaha Samachar published by Rangalal Ghosh from Malda was a weekly magazine. The British government came down heavily on it as Radhesh Chandra, brought to light various illegal activities indulged in by British government employees through this magazine. Binoy Kumar Sarkar of Malda published a monthly magazine named *Grihastha*. He was in charge of its publication from 1911-15. When he was abroad, *History of Russian Revolution* was published in this magazine. All of a sudden, it was discontinued after the publication of just four issues—on the order by the British government. Later on, a few essays like *Paribar* and *Dhan Daulater Rupantar* were also published in this magazine. The publication of these two essays annoyed the British government in such a way that they stopped its publication once and for all. Here it is worth mentioning that the magazine was published from Calcutta but its focus was on *mofussil* areas.[22]

As one of the leading Bengali newspapers of North Bengal, the name of *Gambhira* is particularly noteworthy. The founders of the newspaper took the name *Gambhira* probably thinking of the traditional folk song of the district 'Gambhira'. Kalicharan Sarkar, a *zamindar* by profession, was the publisher and editor. He was a well-educated and prolific writer, too. He had a rich library comprising of rare books, monographs and *puthis*. He was the in-charge of the National School of Kaligram. At one time it was one of the seats of Sanskrit language practice in North Bengal. This village had the largest number of educated people in the district. For example, Pundit Purushottam Goswami, Ishai Lahiri, Krishnaratna and Krishna Keshav Goswami the famous scholar of Nyayashastra were very well-known personalities to the contemporary literary world of North Bengal. No other districts in North Bengal had such a large number of educated people. Villages measuring up to this one existed only in East Bengal during that time. It was published thrice in a year and survived for three years only (1914-16). During these years, Kalicharan Sarkar had to spend a total of five thousand rupees. Its subscription was only one rupee. This newspaper featured poetry, essays and discussions on science. More essays were published than poems. All those who wrote in the newspaper were well-educated. Some of them were, Professor Binay Kumar Sarkar, Professor Tarakeswar Bhattacharya, poet Rajanikanta Sen, Krishna Chandra Roychaudhury, Suresh Chandra

Roychaudhury and Haridas Palit. Apart from them, the writings of writers from other parts of Bengal were also included. Its main objective was to promote the culture of North Bengal like folk songs and music in Calcutta and also to introduce the young talented writers of the region.[23]

The twentieth century witnessed the beginning of the publication and printing of the newspapers and journals in Jalpaiguri, the divisional headquarter of North Bengal. In the first half of the twentieth century, a modern Bengali middle and upper-class society emerged which played a key role in developing the literary and cultural environment of the town. The first printing press in Jalpaiguri was set up in 1895 by Purna Chandra Ghosh, popularly known as Jalpaiguri Press. In 1912, during the period of Swadeshi movement, the Royal Printing Workers Limited came up in Jalpaiguri town. The key figures behind it were Nagendra Nath Sikdar, a pleader by profession and Tarini Prasad Roy and Jogesh Chandra Ghosh, two famous tea industrialists of Bengal. This printing house was established mainly for the interests of the Bengali tea planters of Jalpaiguri town. Similarly, the Planters' Press Limited was founded in 1927 with the same objective and the key figures behind it were a group of tea planters of Jalpaiguri town like Purna Chandra Roy, Rajen Niyogi, Taranath Ghatak and Bhabakinkar Banerjee. *Trisrota*, a popular Bengali periodical of the town, was published from there.[24]

In 1920, the Bina Printing House came into existence and a group of Bengali intellectuals cum pleaders of Jalpaiguri town like Jyotish Chandra Sanyal, Satish Chandra Lahiri, Jagabandhu Sarkar and Shanti Bidhan Roy stood behind it. *Janamat*, a popular Bengali newspaper published by Jyotish Chandra Sanyal, first bought out from this printing house. The publication of this printing house was totally anti-British and therefore, came under vigilance of the detective department. Next to it, the Kohinoor Printing Workers Limited was set up in 1926. The Nawab family of Jalpaiguri town was the main inspiration behind it. They had a huge name and fame as tea industrialist in India and abroad. *Nishan,* a popular monthly of the Muslims tea entrepreneurs of Jalpaiguri town, was published from this printing house. In 1934, the Modern Art

Printers Private Limited was set up under the guidance of Santosh Kumar Basu, a pleader by profession. A number of leaders of Jalpaiguri District Congress like Abani Dhar Guha Niyogi, Sourin Basu, Atul Roy, Pabitra Kumar Chakrabarty and others played a key role behind its establishment. In 1939, the Alipurduar Press came into existence.[25]

Trisrota, published in 1900 by Sashi Kumar Niyogi and Bhujangadhar Roy, heralded the coming of the periodical in Jalpaiguri. After a few years its publication was stopped. But in 1925, under the editorship of Suresh Chandra Paul, it started its journey again. After him, a group of intellectuals of Jalpaiguri town like Bhabaranjan Ganguly, Bishwanath Karmakar, and Kalyan Sikdar took the responsibility to carry it on. *Trisrota* had always been ever daunting in showcasing everything from the farmer's anguish, to the Sabha-Samiti activities as well as the stories of local markets (hats) or village fairs. Market price of tea leaves, Company profit and loss statements, description of women organization (Mahila Samiti) and schools for handlooms and *charkha*s have all been described in its issues. Beside *Trisrota*, there were other Bengali periodicals like *Janamat, Varendra, Muktibani, Deshabandhu, Nishan, Nawjawan, Bharatbani* and others. These periodicals consisted mostly of provincial news, at the same time included articles on the socio-economic and cultural conditions of the nation. They also included with short stories, poems and essays penned by the local residents.[26]

The weekly *Janamat*, published by Jyotish Cahndra Sanyal, a pleader by profession on 14 January 1924, welcomed the Bengali press as useful and beneficial to the interests of the local people. The first autumn issue of North Bengal was published in this Bengali weekly in 1934. A number of leading pleaders of Jalpaiguri town like Pritinidhan Roy, Satyendra Mallick, Jyotish Chandra Sanyal, Aruna Dasgupta, Taraprasad Biswas, and Birendranath Majumder contributed to this issue.[27] Pritinidhan Roy opened a branch of 'All India Rabindra Sangha' in the town. The weekly *Varendra* was sponsored and patronized by Jyotish Chandra Sanyal. He got the whole-hearted economic and moral-support from his close friend and associate Tarini Prasad Roy. He helped to raise the moral tone of the press above the level of the contemporary English periodicals and also tried to make the people irrespective of caste and class, and conscious of their political, social and human rights. However, all these periodicals could not survive for a long period as they were considered anti-British and became an eyesore to the colonial rulers.[28]

Muktibani, edited by Khagendranath Dasgupta, was published from Sarala Printing House, Jalpaiguri in 1928. Its fiery editorials about the oppressive rule of the British government ignited in the minds of the youth's nationalistic zeal during the Civil Disobedience Movement. Khagendranath Dasgupta's *The Sedition Case at Jalpaiguri* and Bhabaranjan Ganguly's *Bichar* raised question against the British rule in India. So, from its onset, the magazine was under the vigilance of the detective department. Ultimately in 1931, the British government stopped its publication, on the ground of anti-British government activities, and arrested both the editor and publisher. *Deshabandhu* (1937) edited by Pritinidhan Roy and patronized by Santosh Kumar Basu, was the mouthpiece of the educated intellectuals of the town. Being a lawyer by profession, Santosh Kumar Basu was a prolific writer too. He wrote several articles on the history and culture of Jalpaiguri. Through his writings, he was the first to throws light on the Totos, the most primitive tribe of the district. He had to set up a press namely Modern Art Printers in 1937. An intellectual group grew in Jalpaiguri town centering round the magazine.[29] The Brahmo leaders of Jalpaiguri town, like Indubhushan Majumder, Suniti Bala Chanda, Dr Ashrubala Dasgupta and Debaprasad Dutta were attached with such magazine, journal and Bengali weeklies.[30] The weekly *Ahwan,* edited by Bhabaranjan Gangopadhyay, was the mouthpiece of the Bengali tea industrialists.[31]

Jalark, was one of the most renowned literary magazines not only in Jalpaiguri or North Bengal, but of the entire Bengal. In the 1950s no prosperous town outside Calcutta seems to have produced such a high quality magazine. It was the mirror of the literary atlas of the town. Its first issue was published in 1359 B.S. with the financial assistance of Dr Ashrubala Dasgupta, a renowned physician of the town. Several Brahmo families of the town were associated with this magazine. The magazine was named after poet Premendra Mitra. Sunil Chandra Sarkar's poetry was published in the first issue of the magazine. Amalendu Bose, Professor of English language and culture, has written two of his articles there—one was about Parimal Roy and the other on Jibananda Das. Srikumar Bandopadhyay, Professor of Bengali language and literature, has written a long article on Bengali novels. The last issue of the magazine was published in 1954.[32]

The weekly *Nishan* (1931) by Abdul Khalek, a pleader by profession had always been the first to propagate the ideas of the Muslim League. It stimulated the writings of the Muslim youths. *Nawjawan* published by Nasiruddin, a full-fledged organ of the orthodox Muslims, thundered vehemently, provoking the anti-Hindu slogan more violently.[33] The most striking feature of the period was the emergence of Muslim intellectuals. Many of them were prolific writers. *Waqafnama* by Rahim Baksh (1904), *Tahakaye Ahawab* by Nehatullah Ahmed (BS 1320), *Islam Sangit* by Muhammad Abdurrab (BS 1319), *Islam Rtana* by Idrish Ahmed (BS 1325), *Kirat Banglar Math* by Taskinuddin Ahmed (1947) deserved to be mentioned. Taslimuddin Ahmed, a lawyer by profession, was the first to translate the Quran into Bengali.[34]

GROWTH AND DEVELOPMENT OF LIBRARIES IN NORTH BENGAL

The establishment of Calcutta Public Library in 1836 had an immense impact in nineteenth-century Bengal. This paved the way of establishing a number of libraries in different parts of Bengal. The northern part of Bengal did not lag behind in this field. The Rangpur Public Library, established in 1832, was the oldest library in Bengal. Other libraries in several districts of Bengal like Barisal, Jessore and Bogra were set up in 1834. The Calcutta Public Library was established in 1835. The Rangpur Public Library was first inaugurated in the building of the Rangpur Landholders Association. In 1858, a temporary building was set up on the land donated by Sambhu Chandra Roychaudhury, *zamindar* of Kakina. After his death, Ramani Mahan Roychaudhury of Tushbhander and

Mahima Ranjan Roychaudhury of Kakina patronized the library. During the period of Rajmahan Roychaudhury, it came under the flag of Rangpur Sahitya Parishad. In 1912, the library started to function as an independent institution after the construction of the Edward Memorial Hall on a piece of land donated by Mahima Ranjan Roychaudhury of Kakina. The library was, however, taken over by the Government of India in 1935.[35]

The *zamindar* of Tushbhandar, Rangpur was someone who was famous for caring about the welfare of his subjects. Ramanimohan Roychaudhury of this family was a worshipper of culture and literature. He set up a school for girls. During the Bengal famine, he collected food from various sources with his own money and distributed it to the famine affected general public. For his generous act, he was conferred the title Roychaudhury by the British. In the memory of his mother, he established a library called Bhagabati Devi Pathagar in 1875 which was open to the general public. This library was looked after by poet and scholar Jadavchandra Banibhushan. After Ramanimohan's death, 'Ramanimohan Memorial Public Institution was set up in Tushbhandar, Rangpur. His successors donated the valuable books of Bhagabati Devi library to this institution. Madhu Sudan was Kundi's *zamindar* and his youngest son Suresh Chandra was an ideal person among the *zamindars* of Rangpur. He was attached to social, educational and cultural societies. In a programme at Rangpur town hall, Rangpur Sahitya Parishad was created as a branch of Bangiya Sahitya Parishad. The programme was presided over by Ashutosh Lahiri, the then district engineer of Rangpur. Suresh Chandra was elected as the secretary of this branch. Suresh Chandra himself was a great scholar and he donated a huge number of informative books and writings to the Parishad from his own collection. This included many books in Sanskrit as well. Another literary personality in Rangpur was Janaki Ballava Sen, the *zamindar* of Dimla, Rangpur. He first established the Rangpur Municipality in 1869. He was an active member of Rangpur Sahitya Parishad and a key figure behind the foundation of Rangpur Public Library where he donated a number of precious books from his own collection. Raja Gopal Roy, the *zamindar* of Tajhat, Rangpur was the founding member of Varendra Anusandhan Samiti, Rajshahi. He donated many books and archeological items to Varendra Anusandhan Samiti and Rangpur Sahitya Parishad. Ramrudra Roy Chaudhury, the *zamindar* of Kaina had his own library full of numerous rich books. It was said that Francis Buchanan visited the library in 1909 and was highly enriched.[36]

The Rajshahi Public Library came into existence in 1844. The land was gifted by Pramadnath Roy, the *zamindar* of Dighapatiya and the building was constructed under the tutelage of Kaliprasanna Lahiri. Sarat Kumar Roy was the president of the library from 1925-41. The Victoria Public Library was established in 1901 by a group of leading personalities like Subir Chandra Roy, Narendranath Lahiri and others. The library received patronization from Raja Jagadindranath Roy of Natore to a great extent. The Northbrook Public Library was set up by Anandanath Roy, the Raja of Natore in 1882. The Shah Makdum Institute and Public library was established in 1891.[37]

In Pabna, Ananda Govinda Roychaudhury, the *zamindar* of Tantibanda, established a library in his own name in 1890. The Woodburn library, Bogra was established in 1900 under the initiative of T.P. Larkins I.C.S., the Collector of the district. It was set up in the memory of Sir John Woodburn, the then Lieutenant Governor of Bengal. Abdus Chaudhury, Nawab of Bogra and Altaf Ali Chaudhury, the *zamindar* of Bogra financially assisted to lay the foundation of the library.[38]

William Carey had a profound relation with Dinajpur. He arrived in Dnajpur in 1793. He founded the Baptist Mission Church at Dinajpur in 1796 to carry out missionary activities.[39] Two vernacular boarding schools (one for boys and the other for girls) were established under the initiative of this mission. He established a library at Madnavati, a little place on the Tangan River in Banshihari Thana, possessed with rare Indian classical books. It was said to have been the first printing press in Bengali and edited a religious journal from there. During his stay at Madnavati, he wrote an article named 'Remarks on the State of Agriculture in the District of Dinajpur'.[40] A number of persons like Ramram Basu, Golaknath Sharma, Kahsinath Mukherjee and others helped him to lay the foundation of the library. John Thomas, a missionary of contemporary Dianajpur, helped him immensely to set up the library. Mr. Ward, the first printer in India, visited Dinajpur at that time.[41] Carey also started his first school there with a few local boys, teaching them reading, writing and arithmetic. On 10 January 1800, Carey left Dinajpur and permanently settled in Sreerampur where he worked relentlessly for the spread of modern education and translated many Indian classical books form Sanskrit to Bengali. He once said 'Our labors at Dinajpur have not been in vain . . . we hope to visit these places once or twice a year besides corresponding'.[42]

Another famous library of Dinajpur was Ramananda Vaishnava Sahitya Pith. Francis Buchanan in his famous work *Geographical, Statistical and Historical Description of the District, Dinajpur* gave a vivid description of the library. It had comprised of many rare collections on Vaishnavism like *Brihat Bhagavatamritam* by Sanatan Goswami, *Laghu Bhagavatamritam* by Rup Goswami, *Vidagdhamadhava, Lalita Madhavam, Hanshadutam, Ujjwal Nilmani* and so on. Maharaja Girijanath Roy was a notable social reformer and educationist of contemporary Dinajpur. He had his own library enriched with precious collections like Sir William Sleeman, *A Journey through the Kingdom of Oude* (2 vols., London, 1858), E.H. Hilton, *The Tourist Guide to Lucknow 1858-1913*, Meer Hassan Ali, *Observation on the Mussalman of India (1917),* W.K. Firminger (ed.), *Bengal District Records Dinajpur 1787-9* (vol. 1), Durgadas Lahiri, *Bangalir Gan* (1905). The contemporary Bengali periodicals and magazines in the library like *Marmabani* and *Manahsi, Sanjibani, Bharat Mihir, Bharatvarsha, Narayan, Sabuj Patra* and *Prabashi* added another attraction to the readers. The library was supervised by Pandit Mahesh Chandra Tarka Churamani, a renowned fellow in Sanskrit of contemporary India. A large number of educationists cum researchers like Rakhakdas Bandopadhyay, Nihar Ranjan Roy were highly enriched to study the collections of the library. They highlighted the importance of the library through their writings. F.O. Bell and Francis Buchanan both studied the reports and books of this library meticulously to prepare their research works. Beside being a venue for reading the books, it was also a venue for cultural discussions. H. Bidon the Collector,

Bhuvan Mahan Kar, Sunil Chandra Guha Khasnawis, Jogindra Chandra Chakrabaty a pleader by profession and other leading intellectuals were some important participants of such cultural gatherings.[43]

Sushil Chandra, the then sub-divisional Officer of Dinajpur, played a key role in establishing a library in Kaliyaganj. In this mission, he was assisted by a group of people of the town like Sharat Majumder, Hiralal Karmakar and Gyanendra Guha Roy. In 1885, the Arya Library was founded and the key figures behind it were Jogindra Nath Chakrabarty, Trailakya Sen, Ramachandra Sen, Kumudnath Sen, Madhav Chandra Sikdar, Haricharan Sen and others. In 1934, the Dinajpur Khwaja Najimuddin Muslim Hall and Public library was set up in memory of Khwaja Najimuddin, the Education Minister of undivided Bengal. The founding members were Hemayat Ali, Hasan Ali, Delwar Khan. In 1909, the Edward Memorial Library and club were established in memory of Edwards VII.[44]

A distinctive feature of Bengali language, literature and culture is observable in the Coochbehar state. The Rogers library which was set up at the initiative of Colonel Haughton is the first library of Coochbehar state. At that time, books were collected from M/S Rozario & Company, a renowned book stall in London and transported to the study room of this library. A Sanskrit scholar, Brajanath Ghosh looked after this library in 1870. This library, became known as the Coochbehar State Library later. The library commenced its operations in a room of 'Neelkuthi' in 1895 but later it was shifted to Lansdown Hall by Maharaja Nripendra Narayan, the modernizer of Coochbehar. Statistics show that there were about 8,000 books in different languages at that time. The Maharaja used to collect books from Gauriya Samaj and Vernacular Translation Society of Calcutta for this library. Different *puthi*s, manuscripts and rare royal documents were transferred to this library. In 1938, Maharaja Jagdipendra Narayan opened the gates of this library for the general masses. This library is a rich source of different subjects.[45]

In the second decade of the nineteenth century, Coochbehar saw the setting up of a number of libraries, like 'Coochbehar Sahitya Sabha' which was set up in 1916. Maharaja Jitendranarayan and

Princess Indira Devi were the forerunners of the Sahitya Sabha which started its journey with just 69 books.[46] At that time, Haldibari PVN library was established in 1916. Moreover in 1937, Nripendra Narayan Memorial Library at Mekhliganj, Raj Rajendra Narayan Library at Tufanganj and Maharaja Nripendra Narayan Library at Dinhata in 1938 were set up. The Pioneer Club Library was established in Dinhata by Jyotish Paul and Kshitish Ghosh. Among all the above-mentioned libraries, special mention must be made about Victor Narayan and Jagadipendra Narayan regarding the establishment of the three libraries. The Raj Rajendra Library of Tufanganj owes its origin to the efforts of educationist like Sharat Chandra Ghoshal, Manabendra Bhattacharya and Lalit Mahan Bakshi. The library building was stocked with many rare books of the *zamindar* family of the nineteenth century.[47] The college library of Victoria College established in 1888 was rich in a collection of books on subjects taught in the college. Jenkins school was established in 1861 and its library also has a rich collection to be proud of. The same goes with the Suniti academy established in 1881. The Muhammadan Literary Society Coochbehar, established by Abdul Latif had a rich library. The Maharaja was a patron of this society. After Independence, the district library of Coochbehar came into being in 1957. In 1969, the district library and Coochbehar State Library merged to form the 'Uttarbanga Rashtriya Granthagar' (North Bengal State Library). Not only in Coochbehar but all over North Bengal, this library is looked up with high regard.[48]

At the beginning of nineteenth century, a large number of Bengali youths from different parts of Eastern Bengal migrated to Jalpaiguri in search of better occupation and livelihood. They settled there permanently and many of them later became successful entrepreneurs, businessmen and traders in various fields like tea, timber and jute. Mainly due to their desire and efforts, a unique literary and cultural circle grew up among them. In the last decade of this century, a renowned educationist of the town, Dinabandhu Bandopadhyay set up a library at Dinbazar. At the beginning of the twentieth century, due to the efforts of Sharat Sen, a library attached to the union club was established. In 1902, the Arya Natya Samaj was set up. The management of the Samaj had to establish a library which was taken care of by them.[49]

In order to inspire the youths who were attached with the revolution movement, distinguished citizen of the town, Kalimohan Niyogi set up a library in 1906. In 1910 the Radhika library and in 1911, the Harendra Hall and Dramatic Club were set up at Maynaguri. It also had a library attached to it. In 1915, the Edward Memorial Library was set up at Alipurduar in memory of Edward VII. In initial stages the library consisted of only donated books. The first president of the library was E.T. Coats, the then subdivisional officer of Alipurduar. A number of leading businessmen of the town like Tarachand Jethmal, Shova Chand Nahata, Orang Bahadur, Ramratan Agarwala, Haridas Gabur, Ramrup Singh and many more, contributed largely to its foundation. The weekly *Alok* was published from this library under the initiative of a group of educated people of the town like Sunil Bhowmick, Jagannath Biswas, Shantipada Gangopadhyay, Ganesh Sanyal and so on. Various cultural programmes were organized there. It produced a favourable atmosphere for the growth of libraries in the town. The background for the next stage of development of libraries was provided mainly by the young generation. The movement reached its climax by the end of the 1940s. Various types of libraries emerged in different parts of the town like Pragati, Jagriti, Gandhi and Subhash Pathagar. In 1944, Newtown Library was also set up in Alipurduar. The first reading room library of Jalpaiguri town was established in 1918.[50]

The Brahmo leaders of Jalpaiguri town like Chandi Charan Sen and Harimahan Chakrabarty first established a library of their own association in 1922. The library was very rich and had a number of rare and precious books.[51] In 1931, the Sangram Pathagar came into being. But the British government closed this library during the August Revolution. The library for the Muslims of the district was first established in 1924 under the patronization of Muhammad Sonaulla and Moulavi Nur Ahmed, two outstanding literary figure of contemporary Jalpaiguri town. This district had a good number of personal libraries such as the Congress Pathagar (1931), Aravinda Pathagar (1939), Marawari Sangha Pathagar

(1933), Raikat Para Boys Pathagar (1944), Bangabashi Pathagar, and Gandhi Pathagar (1949).[52] The Bengali *babus* of tea gardens, beside their professional life, had a cultural world of their own. For recreation, they had to develop dramatic clubs and theatres in their gardens. Some of them also wrote diaries or other branches of literature like poems, poetry, stories and so on. As a result, the library movement started gaining grounds in the neighbouring tea gardens. The Rajendra Smriti Pathagar in Nimtijhara tea estate, Netaji Pathagar in Needam tea estate, Jogesh Chandra Club Pathagar in Jogesh Chandra tea estate and Subhashini Pathagar in Subhashini Tea Estate bear the testimony of the fact.[53]

The Azad Hind Pathagar was established in 1942 by a group of members belonging to Forward Bloc party, Jalpaiguri like Sashadhar Kar, Jatish Chandra Lahiri and Sushil Basu. The library of the Jalpaiguri Cultural Institute was very rich which had modern English and Bengali periodicals like *Desh, Prabashi, Shanibarer Chithi, Chaturanga, Arthik Jagat* and newspapers like *Ananda Bazar Patrika*, *Amrita Bazar Patrika*, and *Modern Review*. The library was open for two hours every morning and afternoon.[54] A painting exhibition was held there on 30 April 1944 on the occasion of Rabindranath Tagore's birth anniversary. This was the first painting exhibition organized in the town.[55] The first women's library was founded by a group of members of Mahila Atmaraksha Samiti (Women Self-Protection Society) such as Aruna Sanyal, Dipti Roy, Kalpana Niyogi, Rina Chanda and Prafulla Bala Banerjee in 1946. The magazine *Shyamali* edited by Rina Chanda was published from there.[56]

There were fifteen public libraries in the district of Darjeeling. Most of which were located in the chief towns like Kurseong, Kalimpong and Darjeeling. All were fairly well equipped and provide satisfactorily for the needs of the reading public, some offering additional recreation to subscribing members. The total number of members of those libraries was 1909 in 1943.[57]

In Kurseong, there was the Bengali Association that had stemmed from the Kurseong Amateur Club established in 1908 by the local Bengalis. Many of them were Brahmos who established the Brahmo Samaj in Darjeeling hill in 1879. Besides practising

DISTRICT-WISE GROWTH OF PUBLIC LIBRARIES IN NORTH BENGAL (1901-1940)

Districts	*1901-10*	*1911-20*	*1921-30*	*1931-40*	*Total*
Coochbehar	–	07	–	01	08
Jalpaiguri	02	02	07	04	15
Darjeeling	–	02	03	05	10
Malda	–	03	05	25	33
Dinajpur	03	05	07	31	46
Rajshahi	03	02	02	06	13
Rangpur	04	01	02	15	22
Pabna	–	06	09	16	31
Bogra	–	–	03	10	13

Source: Bhakti Pada Jana, Evolution of Public Libraries in Colonial Bengal: 1800-1947, unpublished PhD thesis, Vidyasagar University, 2020, pp. 7-8.

religion, they were also active in developing literary culture. For this purpose, they had opened a library which was rich in Bengali and English literature and books on various subjects. The Deshbandhu District Library was first started in 'Step Aside', the house of C.R. Das, the most leading political leader of British India who breathed his last there. With the contributions of a group of elites from the hills like Dharanibir Sharma, D.S.E.O. Darjeeling, Surya Bikram Giyali, retired Head Master of Darjeeling Government High School, T. Manlen, the prominent Congress leader of the town, Dr Kaji and J.C. Talukdar, the library was set up. The first librarian was K.B. Mothe who later joined the Department of Library Science, University of Calcutta. The other libraries of the hills started in the buildings of Nripendra Narayan Public Hall, Planters Club, Nepali Sahitya Sammelan of Darjeeling and Gymkhana Club, Kurseong.[58]

In the plains, the first library that came into existence was called Tarai Library which was built up on the land of D.I. Fund. Surendranath Bhattacharya was the key figure behind its foundation. The first librarian was Sharat Chakrabarty, a railway employee by profession. The library was later shifted on to the land of Haricharan Majumder and renamed Tarai Harasundar Library in the memory of his father. The library of Bangiya Sahitya Parishad,

Siliguri was started on 21 February 1951 in the building of Deshbandhupara Arya Samiti. Kalibrahma Mukhopadhyay, Bhawani Charan Guha, Shibprasad Chattopadhyay, Satyaranjan Majumder and others were the key figures behind setting it up.[59]

CONCLUSIONS

It shows that most of the newspapers and periodicals were published with the financial assistance of the landlords and tea industrialists. A few were also brought out under the initiative of a group of middle-class professionals like teachers, writers and lawyers. A detailed discussion or opinions on any topic or news were printed. They exerted an overwhelming influence on the new educated Bengali middle class. Views on social reforms and British rule were also published. Some of the outstanding Bengali weeklies conducted by the new generation of Bengali intellectuals set a new tone and standard of journalism in North Bengal. It is true that the publication of many newspapers were stopped due to the financial crisis or sometime by the British government as they expressed anti-British feelings. But they succeeded in making a large section of the society aware about their motherland. It was growing more and more indignant through the decades against the pernicious policies and measures of the British government.

In the nineteenth century, the printing presses became the main point of attraction to many businessmen as they easily understood that the rapid development of education would soon make their business profitable. Without the existence of the press, publication of books, newspapers and weeklies would be impossible. In addition to the Hindus, the Muslim community also showed their interest in this business, albeit to a lesser extent. It is true that not all the Bengalis were successful in this venture. Many presses could not survive for long due to lack of experience and financial capacity. A number of printing presses, as a result, changed hands several times, with changes in name and ownership as well. Again the address changed frequently. Therefore, it is quite impossible to collect the lifetime data of the printing presses properly.

The public libraries established in different town and villages in North Bengal by the active initiative of the common people, played an important role to spread mass education. Most of the libraries were established in Rajshahi division during that period were the product of voluntary services. Throughout North Bengal, especially in the districts where English education spread first, the need of libraries was felt greatly. Rajshahi, Rangpur, Dinajpur and Jalpaiguri ranked first in this field. In these districts, the *zamindars* and educated middle-class people played the primary role in setting up libraries, though the representation by the people of the minority community and women were very limited. The period between 1910 and 1940 was that of national awakening. Imbibed with the ideas of nationalism, the Bengali youths came forward to set up public libraries for the educational development of the common people. The Rangpur Public Library established in 1832 prior to the birth of Calcutta proves that Rangpur, was culturally, financially and educationally more developed than Calcutta in those days. With the arrival of the British, there came a huge change and a village named Kolkata rose into prominence on the political stage of Bengal and in due course of time transformed itself from being a business & political to a cultural centre. Not only this, due to the patronage of the colonial rulers, Kolkata put on an all-devouring role and brought the whole of Bengal under its influence.

NOTES

1. Muntasir Mamun, *Unish Shatake Dhakar Mudran O Prakashana* (Press and Publications of Dhaka during Nineteenth Century), Dhaka, 2004, p. 36.
2. Brajendranath Bandopadhyay, *Bangla Samayik-Patra* (Bengali Periodicals), vol. I, Kolkata, BS 1379, pp. 189-91.
3. Benoy Ghosh, 'Press in Bengal', in Narendra Krishna Singha (ed.), *The History of Bengal 1757-1905*, University of Calcutta, 1996, pp. 228-30.
4. Dr Muhammad Maniruzzaman, *Rangpurer Itihas* (History of Rangpur), Gatidhara, Dhaka, Bangladesh, 2012, pp. 376-7.

5. Muntasir Mamun, op. cit., p. 36.
6. Asish Khastagir, *Unish Shataker Bnagla Chapakhana* (Printing Press of Bengal during Nineteenth Century), Sopan, Kolkata, 2014, p. 66.
7. Brajendranath Bandopadhyay, *Bangla Samayik-Patra* (Bengali Periodicals), vols. I & II, Karuna Publication, Kolkata, 2013, pp. 1-8.
8. Muntasir Mamun, op. cit., p. 42.
9. Asish Khastagir, op. cit., pp. 67-70.
10. Muntasir Mamun, *Varendra Theke Prakashita Sambad Samoyikpatra* (Newspapers and Periodicals Published from Varendra), in Icchamuddin Sarkar (ed.), *Aitihye O Itihase Uttarbanga* (North Bengal-Its History and Heritage), NL Publishers, Assam, 2002, pp. 218-29.
11. Bhagwati Charan Bandopadhyay, *Kuchbiharer Itihas* (History of Coochbehar), Coochbehar State Press, Coochbehar, 1882, p. 27.
12. Proceedings of the Rangpur Sahitya Parishad Patrika, Rangpur, BS 1315, p. 7.
13. Swapan Kumar Roy, *Prachin Kochbihare Mudran Jantrer Abirbbhav O Pragatir Unmesh* (Growth and Development of Printing Press in Coochbehar), *Kochbihar Jela Sankhya* (Special Volume on the District of Coochbehar), Government of West Bengal, BS 1413, pp. 191-6.
14. Nirupama Devi, *Ekkhan*, Autumn Number, 1401 BS, Coochbehar, p. 25.
15. Swapan Kumar Roy, op. cit., p. 194.
16. Mrinal Kanti Dam, 'Kochbihar Raj Amalae Sahitya Charcha' (Literary Practice of Coochbehar during the Royal Period), *Kochbihar Jela Sankhya* (Special Volume on the District of Coochbehar), Government of West Bengal, BS 1413, Kolkata, p. 169.
17. *Paricharika,* vol. IV, Autumn Number, BS 1326, Coochbehar, p. 2.
18. *Kuchbihar Darpan,* vol. V, 1 Ashad BS 1351, Coochbehar, pp. 46-7.
19. *Dinajpur Patrika,* Dinajpur, 9 Magh BS 1291, p. 14.
20. Dhananjay Roy, *Uttrabanga Unish O Bish Shatak* (North Bengal: Nineteenth and Twentieth Century's), Dip Prakashan, Kolkata, 2002, pp. 192-3.
21. Ashim Kumar Sarkar, *Nationalism, Communalism and Partition in Bengal: Maldah 1905-53,* Readers Service, Kolkata, 2013, pp. 29-30.
22. Haridas Palit, *Maldaher Radeshchandra* (Radeshchandra of Malda), BS 1318, Calcutta, pp. 18-19.
23. Ananda Gopal Ghosh and Ratna Roy Sanyal, 'Growth of Public Opinion in North Bengal: A Case Study of Newspapers and Periodicals (1870-1947)', *North Bengal University Review,* Journal of Humanities and Social Science, University of North Bengal, 1993, pp. 22-4.
24. Ananda Gopal Ghosh and Soumendra Prasad Saha, *Uttarbanger Itihas O Samaj* (History and Society of North Bengal), vol. II, Sangbaden, Malda, 2015, pp. 34-6.

25. Ananda Gopal Ghosh and Sumana Das Barman, *Uttarbannger Itihas O Sanskriti* (History and Society of North Bengal), vol. VIII, Sagnik Books, Kolkata, 2022, pp. 163-5.
26. Soumendra Prasad Saha, 'The Literary Atlas of Jalpaiguri District (1869-2019)', in Ananda Gopal Ghosh et al., (ed.) *Sesquicentennial Commemoration Volume of Jalpaiguri District (1869-2019),* Kunal Books, New Delhi, 2020, p. 376.
27. *Janamat,* Jalpaiguri, 17 Aswin 1341 BS, p. 67.
28. *Janamat,* Jalpaiguri, 18 May 1945, p. 42.
29. Ranajit Kumar Mitra, 'Jelar Samayik Patra Patrika' (Contemporary Newspapers and Periodicals of the District), in Ajitesh Bhattacharya (ed.), *Madhuparni,* Jalpaiguri Jela Sankhya, BS 1394, p. 343.
30. Subir Roy, 'Jalpaigurite Brahmo Samaj' (Brahmo Samaj in Jalpaiguri), in Ajitesh Bhattacharya (ed.), *Madhuparni,* op. cit., p. 142.
31. Bhabaranjan Gangopadhyay, 'Jalpaiguri Jelar Sambadpatrer Sankhipta Itihas' (A Concise History of the News Dailies in the District of Jalpaiguri), in Charu Chandra Sanyal (ed.), *Jalpaiguri District Centenary Volume,* Jalpaiguri, 1970, p. 197.
32. Ananda Gopal Ghosh, *Jalpaigurir Sahityalekha O Anyanya Prabandha* (Cultural History of Jalpaiguri and Other Essays), Sangbedan, Malda, BS 1417, p. 35.
33. *Trisrota,* A Bengali Weekly, Jalpaiguri, 13 May 1931, p. 31.
34. Ali Ahmed, *Bangla Muslim Granthapanji* (Index of Muslim Books in Bengali Language), Bangla Academy, Dhaka, 1985, pp. 40-50.
35. Rangpur Sahitya Parishad Patrika, Rangpur, 1324 BS, p. 24.
36. Maniruzzaman, *Rangpurer Itihas* (History of Rangpur), Gatidhara, Dhaka, Bangladesh, 2012, pp. 392-8.
37. *Bengal District Gazetteers,* Rajshahi, Bengal Secretariat Press, Calcutta, 1923, p. 26.
38. *Bengal District Gazetteers,* Bogra, Bengal Secretariat Press, Calcutta, 1913, p. 20.
39. F.W. Strong, *Eastern Bengal District Gazetteers,* Dinajpur, Allahabad, 1912, p. 24.
40. Report of Dinajpur Mission by Rev. Greene, Calcutta, 1953, p. 28.
41. Shaktibrata Ghosh, *William Carey er Sahitya Sadhana* (Literary Pursuits of William Carey), Burdwan, 1980, p. 21.
42. Chittaranjan Acharya, 'Carey Dinajpure Chay Bachar' (Six Years of William Carey in Dinajpur), in Dhananjay Roy (ed.), *Anchalik Itihas Charchay Dinajpur Jela* (Study the Regional History of the District of Dinajpur), Sanskrit Pushtak Bhandar Publication, Kolkata, 2009, p. 194.

43. Dhananjay Roy, *Uttarbanga (Unish O Bish Shatak),* Dip Prakashan, Kolkata, 2002, pp. 64-5.
44. Abul Kalam Azad, *Khwaja Najimuddin Muslim Hall and Public Library,* Granthatirtha, Dinajpur, 1970, pp. 2-4.
45. Swapan Kumar Roy, op. cit., pp. 191-3.
46. *Coochbehar Sahitya Sabha Patrika,* First Issue, No. 1, 1380 BS, Coochbehar, p. 14.
47. Amarendra Basak (ed.), *Centenary Volume,* Tufanganj Subdivision, Coochbehar, 1992, p. 18.
48. Durgadas Majumder, *West Bengal District Gazetteers,* Coochbehar, Government of West Bengal, Calcutta, 1977, pp. 176-7.
49. *Tristota,* Jalpaiguri, 15 April 1928, p. 16.
50. Pramad Nath, 'Alipurduar Mahakumar Granthagar Andalan' (Library Movement in the Subdivision of Alipurduar), in Pabitra Bhushan Sarkar (ed.), *Matir Choya* (Touch the Ground), vol. 21, No. 15, Alipurduar, 1995, p. 116.
51. Subir Roy, *Jalpaigurite Brahmo Samaj* (Brahmo Samaj in Jalpaiguri), op. cit., p. 142.
52. Dhananjay Roy, op. cit., p. 72.
53. Supam Biswas, *Uttarbanger Bangali Cha Udyagpatider Bikash O Bilay,* Readers Service, Kolkata, 2016, pp. 132-3.
54. *Trisrota,* A Bengali Weekly, Jalpaiguri, 21 May 1944, p. 28.
55. Ibid., 30 April 1944, p. 36.
56. Ananda Gopal Ghosh, *Jalpaigurir Sahityalekha O Anyanya Prabandha,* op. cit., p. 29.
57. A.J. Dash, *Bengal District Gazetteers,* Darjeeling, Bengal Secretariat Press, Calcutta, 1947.
58. Dick B. Dewan, *Education in the Darjeeling Hills An Historical Survey: 1835-1985,* Indus Publishing Company, New Delhi, First Edition 1991, p. 200.
59. Dilip Chaudhury, 'Darjeeling Jelar Sadharan Granthagar O Granthagar Andalan' (General Library and Library Movement in the District of Darjeling), in Ajitesh Bhattacharya (ed.), *Madhuparni,* Darjeeling Jela Sankhya (Special Volume on the District of Darjeeling), November 1996, pp. 266-9.

CHAPTER 3

The Zamindars and their Cultural Contribution

INTRODUCTION

Among the many changes brought about in North Bengal as an outcome of the Renaissance was the development of education in both English and Bengali. In the second half of the nineteenth century, the *zamindar*s offered adequate grants and scholarships for the development of education. The introduction of Western education was perhaps the most important single factor behind the cultural awakening. Western education did not, however, spread solely at the initiative of the government and Christian missionaries. A large number of *zamindar*s contributed to a great extent in this endeavour. Many historians have sketched their exploiting character but none of them has probed deep into their role in setting up educational institutions, establishment of press and publication of periodicals which paved the way behind the actual beginning of the cultural awakening in North Bengal. Seeds of the Renaissance were sown that were to germinate in due course. The focus of study in this chapter is based on the *zamindar*s of three regions like Rajshahi, Rangpur and Dinajpur during the early phase of the Bengal Renaissance.

Ancient North Bengal has had a rich tradition in the sphere of education. Both elementary and higher education in India has been developing impressively since time immemorial. Higher education for Hindus was imparted in the *tol*s. It was the customary duty of the teachers in Bengal and the Mithila *pandit*s who conformed to the Bengal tradition, to lodge and feed their students. Such generous practice did not prevail in the neighbouring province of Bihar and Orissa. Rent-free lands were assigned to the Brahmins to maintain these institutions. Maharaja Krishna Chandra of Nadia and Rani Bhawani of Natore played an important role in this field.[1] Buchanan found 119 *tols* in Purnea, 34 professors in Rangpur, while in Dinajpur 7 out of 22 thanas kept 16 schools of Sanskrit learning. These schools attracted students from Assam, Nepal. The Bengali students went out of their province to supplement their education. The course of studies in these schools included literature, grammar, law, logic, philosophy, the Puranas, the Tantras and medicine.[2]

Adam came across 38 *tols* in Rangpur with 397 pupils in 1836. The students entered the schools between the age of 9 to 15 and most of them were Brahmins with a sprinkling of Vaidyas, Kayasthas or Vaishanvas. Buchanan reverently noted that the Brahmins, generally speaking, have an intelligence and acuteness far beyond other Hindus. In 1836 Adam visited the district of Rajshahi where he came across only one *madrassa* at Kusbeh Bagha with no organization or discipline, while 40 schools of Hindu learning existed.[3]

THE ZAMINDARS OF RANGPUR

The *zamindari* districts of Bengal comprised primarily of some noted places like Rajshahi, Rangpur and Dinajpur and just one or two *zamindars* exercised their authority throughout these districts. Rangpur, in this field, was an exception to this. It was an assemblage of many renowned *zamindars* and was not under the rule of one or two *zamindars*. In the middle of the nineteenth century, these *zamindars*, apart from their subject oriented welfare, began to promote cultural and literary endeavours. Their efforts were fruitful and as a consequence of this, Rangpur Sahitya Parishad, Rangpur Public Library and Uttarbanga Sahitya Sammilini came into being. The *zamindars* of Rangpur also tried their hands in different literary activities and ultimately came up as noted novelists and prolific writers. A great event in the history of North Bengal was the establishment of Rangpur Sahitya Parishad, a notable Bengali literary society in early twentieth-century society. Several *zamindars* were directly involved in establishing it and had to extend their hands with financial and other help. Two notable *zamindar*s of Rangpur namely Surendra Chandra Roy Chaudhury and Mritunjoy Roy Chaudhury were closely associated with it. In a literary conference held on 16 Falgun 1311 BS, both of them took the initiative to form the literary branch of Bangiya Sahitya Parishad in Rangpur. As a consequence, the foundation of Rangpur Sahitya Parishad was laid down in a conference held at Rangpur Town Hall on 12 Chaitra 1311 BS. It served as a centre for historical research as well as a forum for contemporary writers of Rangpur district. It had two organs—*Rangpur Sahitya Parishad Patrika and Uttarbanga Sahitya Sammilani.*[4]

Surendra Chandra Roy Chaudhury was the first secretary of Rangpur Sahitya Parishad. A committee consisting of 28 members was formed, among them 12 belonged to Rangpur. Most of them were *zamindar*s of Rangpur like Mahima Ranjan Roy Chaudhury of Kakina, Abdul Majid Chauhdury of Mahipur Estate, Bhabani Prasanna Lahiri of Naldanga Estate, Manindra Chandra Roy Chaudhury of Kundi Estate, Radharaman Majumder of Dewanbari Estate and others. Beside the landowning classes, the pleaders of contemporary Rangpur like Rajani Kanta Bhatacharya, Kunja Bihari Mukhopadhyay, Rashbihari Mukhopadhyay and Rashbihari Ghosh had a prime role in laying the foundation of Rangpur Sahitya Parishad. However, apart from Rangpur, a number of *zamindar*s from other parts of North Bengal and beyond, like Maharaja Girijanath Roy Bahadur, Sharadindu Roy of Dinajpur, Jagadish Narayan Mushtafi, Pramada Ranjan Bakshi of Coochbehar, Jagadindra Narayan Raikot of Jalpaiguri and Prabhat Chandra Barua of Gauripur Assam, did not lag behind for this great cause. Rangpur Sahitya Parishad had a museum that contained rare and precious artefacts from Bengal, Assam and Tibet.[5]

Rangpur Sahitya Parishad Patrika was the mouthpiece of this institution. It was published quarterly and was the first ranked Bengali weekly during the period. It had two parts—first, the articles based on the past and untold history of North Bengal and Assam and second, news and reports of annual conferences. A group of intellectuals and prolific writers like Pravat Kumar

Mukhopadhyay, Bhabani Prasanna Lahiri, Jadunath Ghosh, Panchanan Sircar, Keshablal Basu and others enriched its status through their valuable write ups. The Muslim writers did not lag behind in this field. Hamid Ali, Khan Bahadur Taslim Uddin and Abdul Ali wrote many articles there. The landholders of Rangpur had a key role, both financially and culturally, in setting up the institution. Mahima Ranjan Roy Chaudhury, being the first president of this institution, donated 1.20 acre of land for the construction of the buildings. He also introduced the practice to honour the writers with whose article on Rangpur would be selected as the best, with 50 rupees. This system, no doubt, glorified the history and culture of Rangpur to the readers. Both Mahendra Ranjan Roy Chaudhury, the *zamindar* of Kakina and Surendra Chandra Roy Chaudhury patronized the first and ninth annual conference of *Uttarbanga Sahitya Sammilani* (North Bengal Literary Conference), a regional branch of Rangpur Sahitya Parishad. Surendra Chandra himself wrote nine articles based on Rangpur which was published in various number of *Rangpur Sahitya Parishad Patrika*. Sumeru Giri Gossain, the *zamindar* of Mahimganj Estate, honoured Kalipada Bagchi with a silver memento in 1914 for his outstanding article 'Swadesh Hitaishana' based on Raja Rammohun Roy, the acclaimed modernizer of India. Hara Gopal Das Kundu was a prolific writer. Two articles 'Karatoya' and 'Sherpurer Itihas' written by him, received wide acclamation form the contemporary intellectual society.[6]

Kali Chandra Roy Chaudhury, a *zamindar* of Kundi was the harbinger of English education in Rangpur. The publication of 'Rangpur Bartabaha' in 1847 under his leadership heralded a new age in the literary world of North Bengal. The Bengali play *Kulin Kula Sarvaswa* written by Pandit Ramayan Tarkaratna Chattopadhyay was first published in 1853 under his patronage. It was the first social drama in Bengali attacking Brahmin polygamy. For this notable creation, Kalichandra honoured him with 50 rupees. Kalichandra was a champion of women's education in Rangpur. He started the first women's school and founded the women's text book society.[5] Surendra Chandra Roy Chaudhury was very famous for his cultural achievements. He was the lifetime president of

North Bengal Landholders Association, Rangpur Sahitya Parishad and Uttarbanga Sahitya Sammilani. He was honoured with the title 'Dharmabhushan' by Banaras Hindu University.[7] The Rangpur Sahitya Parishad was closed in 1950 when the *zamindari* system was abolished by the Government of Pakistan.

The contribution of *zamindar*s for the cause of women's education in Rangpur was highly praiseworthy. Kalichandra Roychaudhury of Kundi founded a girl's school. It was assumed, that it was the first Girl's School in Rangpur. He was said to have edited the historical journal *Rangpur Bartabaha* and wrote many articles for women emancipa-tion where he strongly protested against religious and social orthodoxy of Hinduism. The first book on women's education was published from Rangpur under his patronage. Raja Sambhu Chandra Roychaudhury, the *zamindar* of Kakina, stood up for women's education. He held discussions every week, imparted educations among his sons and believed that women could be liberated only through education. The real beginning of women's education took place in Rangpur during his period. Two vernacular elementary schools and one girls' school were established.[8] The girls' school survived till the period of *zamindar* Mahimaranjan Roychaudhury (1868-1909). After him, the students of the school were admitted to Mahimaranjan English High School and thus the history of the first English School in Rangpur came to an end. Raja Janaki Ballav Sen of Dimla established a girls' school namely Rani Brindamayee Girls' School in his wife's memory. In 1913, it came to be known as Dimla High School. The expenses were met from the personal repository of Rani Brindamayee.[9]

HISTORY OF UTTARBANGA SAHITYA SAMMILANI

The *zamindar*s of Rangpur, beside the creation of Rangpur Sahitya Parishad and publication of several Bengali periodicals, had also contributed largely in organizing the conferences of Uttarbanga Sahitya Sammilani for about ten years (BS 1314-23). It was the branch of Rangpur Sahitya Parishad and meeting place of writers, archaeologists, historians, researchers from North Bengal and Assam for cultural and literary discussions. Justice Ashutosh

Chaudhury was the President and Surendra Roy Chaudhury was the Secretary. The first conference of Uttarbanga Sahitya Sammilani took place at Rangpur Town Hall on 13 Ashar 1315 (27 June 1908). It was presided over by the renowned historian Akshay Kumar Maitra. A number of delegates from different parts of North Bengal like Panchanan Sircar, Pandit Kokileshwar Vidyabhushan, Amir Uddin Ahmed and Mahendra Nath Adhikary from Coochbehar, Jagadindradeb Raikat and Umapati Roy from Jalpaiguri, Rajanikanta Chakrabarty, Radesh Chandra Seth and Tarakeshwar Bhattacharya from Malda, attended the cultural gatherings.[10] Akshay Kumar Maitra, in his presidential address, stated that

> Once North Bengal was so much popular for its tradition of literary criticism. North Bengal has observed the process of transcreation of the earliest Indian epic the *Ramayana* and the work is hailed for making the incidents of the epic popular among the Bengali people. Narottam Das inculcates the idea of sacrifice and divinity in the trajectory of Bengali literature. In modern times, Raja Rammohun Roy, who introduced the framework of contemporary Bengali literature and propounded the idea of love for the nation, stayed in Rangpur for few years.[11]

The second conference took place at Bogra from 31 January to 1 February 1909 and was presided over by Pandit Jadaveshwar Tarkaratna of Rangpur. The presence of Akshay Kumar Maitra and Rajendralal Acharya, the renowned archaeologist enriched the cultural discussions. Dipesh Chakrabarty has aptly remarked 'Akshay Kumar Maitra was one of the most leading figures whose contribution to making history a researchable subject in Bengal is undeniable'.[12]

The third conference took place at Gauripur, Assam on 9-10 January 1910 and patronized by Prabhat Chandra Barua. It was presided over by Pandit Padmanabha Bhattacharya Vidyabinod, the renowned Sanskrit scholar of Syhlet. It proved that Gauripur, though an integral part of Assam, had a close cultural contact with North Bengal.[13]

The fourth conference took place at Malda on 9-10 January 1912. Krishnalal Chaudhury, a *zamindar* by profession and Radesh Chandra Seth were the president and secretary of the reception committee. There were other members such as Binay Kumar Sarkar of Calcutta University, Pandit Rajani Kanta Chakrabarty and Munshi Abid Ali Khan. All of them were eminent in their fields and sons of Malda. The conference was presided over by Sir Jadunath Sarkar, the son of Rajshahi and renowned historian of all time. The conference was attended by Justice Ramesh Chandra Mitra, archaeologist Rakhaldas Bandopadhyay, journalist Ramananda Chattapadhyay, poet Barada Charan Mitra and Nalini Pandit I.C.S.[14]

The fifth conference held at Guwahati on 6-7 April 1913 was presided over by Sashadhar Roy, the great son of Pabna and a pleader by profession. Amanatullah Ahmed of Coochbehar, Binay Kumar Sarkar, Haridas Palit, Kumudnath Lahiri and Pandit Bidhusekhar Shastri of Malda, Nalini Bhushan Adhikary of Balurghat and others attended the discussions. Many literary societies like the Rangpur Sahitya Parishad and Uttarbanga Sahitya Sammilani cropped up in various parts of North Bengal which produced many eminent scholars of Indology. As a result, the proposal of establishing Kamrup Anusandhan Samiti was first rose in the fifth conference by *zamindar* Mrityunjoy Roychaudhury of Kundi and Amanatulla Ahmed of Coochbehar.[15] The next year, Kamrup Anusandhan Samiti was formed in Guwahati. Its main purpose was to produce a vast literature encompassing almost all aspects of history and antiquity of Assam.[16] The book titled *Kamrup Shasanabali* was published and it dealt mainly with the history of Kamrup and the ancient and political history of the region. Though the list of scholars who enriched the Samiti from its beginning is quite long, some of the distinguished personalities like Mahamahopadhyaya Dhireswaracharyya Kaviratna, Padmanath Bhattacharya Vidyavinod, Khan Chaudhury Amanatulla Ahmed of Coochbehar, Maharaja Jitendra Narayan, Sir Edward Gait, Raja Prabhat Chandra Barua, Mahamahopadhyaya Hara Prasad Shastri, Nagendra Nath Basu, Rai Bahadur Kalicharan Sen should be mentioned, along with many more.[17]

The sixth conference was held at Dinajpur on 14-15 June 1914. Maharaja Girijanath Roy and Jogindranath Chakrabarty, the pleader cum Congress leader of Dinajpur were the President and

Secretary of the reception committee. The presidential address was delivered by Justice Ashutosh Chaudhury. But he could not complete the address due to sudden health problem. Therefore, it was later completed by Panchkari Bandopadhyay. A vivid description of the conference was given by Jaladhar Sen through his article 'Uttarbanga Sahitya Sammilani' published in *Bharata-barsha*. Sajanikanta Das in his book *Atmasmriti* gave a vivid description of the conference.[18]

The seventh conference was held at Pabna on 27-28 March 1914. It was presided over by Jagadindranath Roy, the Maharaja of Natore. Justice Ashutosh Chaudhury was the president of the reception committee. The most outstanding landmark of the conference was that Rabindranath Tagore was welcomed there with great honour for winning the Nobel Prize. He stayed at the palace of Jogendranath Mitra, the Zamindar of Pabna. The welcome address in honour of Rabindranath Tagore was read out by *zamindar* Kishori Mahan Roy, the editor of *Suraj*. Jaladhar Sen, Akshay Kumar Maitra, Rakhaldas Bandopadhyay, Pramath Chaudhury and Professor Panchanan Niyogi of Rajshahi College also participated in the conference. Sudhir Chandra Sarkar in his book *Amar Kal Amari Desh* gave a vivid description of the conference.[19]

The eighth conference was held at Rajshahi on 1-2 March 1915. Rabindranath Tagore gave his consent to preside over the conference. But due to personal reasons, he could not do so. Therefore, it was later presided over by Pramath Chaudhury. In his welcome address, he expressed his love for North Bengal. The ninth conference was held at Rangpur on 4-5 April 1916. The president of the reception committee was Gopal Lal Roy, the *zamindar* of Tajhat and Mahendra Chandra Roychauduhry, the Raja of Kakina. The presidential address was delivered by Sir Ashutosh Mukherjee. The tenth conference was held at Bogra on 12-13 August 1917. The president of the conference was Deshbandhu Chittaranjan Das and Nawab Altaf Hossain Chaudhury of Bagra was the president of the reception committee. He was the only representative from among the Muslim intellectual community who first chaired as a president in a conference of Uttarbanga Sahitya Sammilani. On 29 July 1928, a conference took place and it was presided over by Sir Debaprasad Sarbadhikari. Perhaps this was the last conference of Uttarbanga Sahitya Sammilani. After that one could not hear the news of any conference of Uttarbanga Sahitya Sammilani held at any places of North Bengal.[20]

THE ZAMINDARS OF DINAJPUR

The intellectual revolution and the flowering spirit of enlightenment influenced the *zamindars* of Dinajpur to a great extent. As one knows, in Jalpaiguri and Darjeeling districts, the main initiative in the socio-cultural field were taken by the British officials, Missionaries in general and Bengali tea industrialists in particular. But in the case of Dinajpur, it dealt mainly with by the local *zamindars*. With the spread of education, an enlightened public opinion emerged and began to demand social reforms. From the year 1801 to 1857 there was a watershed in the sociocultural history of Dinajpur. With the spread of Western education and the consequent rise of a new middle class, there developed a new urge to develop education and enhance culture. As a consequence, a number of school and colleges and other cultural institutions built up and the main role in this direction was that of the *zamindars*. Pransundari Devi, wife of Radhanath Roy of Dinajpur Estate and her two sons Govindanath Roy and Taraknath Roy had immense contribution in this field. Again, the *zamindars* of Raisaheb Estate and Haripur Estate of Dinajpur contributed to this spirit to a very great extent. According to Dhananjay Roy, the spread of Western education brought about sociocultural changes in the district of Dinajpur.[21]

The first landmark in this field was the foundation of Churaman Dramatic Society. Ghanashyam Chaudhuri, the first *zamindar* of Churaman Estate, made a sincere attempt to lay its foundation. F.W. Strong wrote 'This is an excellent dispensary maintained by the Estate at Churaman, a boy's middle school and a model girl's school'. Raja Krishna Chandra Roy and Bhupal Chandra Roy made a noteworthy contribution in this direction. They opened schools and colleges to impart modern education. The Marnai School was established in 1868 and later renamed Prahlad Chandra

Vidyalaya. Bipul Chandra Roychaudhury, the *zamindar* of Bhupalpur, established the Bhupalchandra Vidyapith in 1955. Mahendra Narayan Chaudhury established the Marnai F.E. School in 1899 and he was financially helped by Sarat Chandra Roychaudhury. Upendra Kishor Nandi was the first head master of this institution. The Upendra Memorial library was formed in his memory. The Bidhumukhi library, presently known as Vandemataram library, was formed by Harendra Nath of Bahin *zamindari*, Raiganj. In this great work, he was assisted financially by Uday Chandra Roychaudhury. The Kishanganj library was established by Kalimuddin Sarkar of Goagram *zamindari*.[22]

There was a great desire among the parents to provide their sons with the best education. The need of a well-organized institution was first felt by Girijanath Roy of Dinajpur Estate. He devoted his time and energy to the cause of spreading education in Dinajpur. As a consequence, the Raiganj Coronation High School was established in 1911. A landmark in the history of cultural awakening was the foundation of Raiganj Institute by Jagadish Nath Roy, son of Girijanath Roy in 1939.[23]

The women of the *zamindar* families did not lag behind in this field. In the second half of the nineteenth century, they offered adequate grants for education. Maharani Shyam Mohini Devi of Dinajpur was the central figure and had a close relationship with Ishwar Chandra Vidyasagar. She knew that the spread of education among women was necessary to develop a rational attitude in society. For this object, she formed the Dinajpur Girls School in 1869. She was very keen to elevate the position of women in society. She strongly opposed polygamy and other prevailing practices against the interest of women in society.[24] It would not be an exaggeration to say that she was the chief architect of women's education in Dinajpur. F.W. Strong said 'In 1875, the year of the great famine, the Rani earned great gratitude of Government by her generous contribution towards the relief of distress and received the title Maharani'. Her son Girijanath Roy established a vernacular school and named it as 'Jubilee School'.[25]

The movement which was launched against the oppression of women was later carried on by Hemprabha Devi, wife of Maharaja

Girijanath Roy. She rose by dint of her own merit to become a social reformer. She waged a long struggle to imbibe them with nationalism. For this purpose, she formed the 'Saraswati Samiti'. Snehalata Devi, wife of Maharaja Jagadish Nath Roy, played an important role to lay the foundation of Arya Library where she offered adequate grants, nearly ten thousand rupees for purchasing books. She also laboured hard for education. She realized that education would be the chief instrument required for the emancipation of women. She had to set up schools for women's education. She had a good relationship with Urmila Devi, sister of Deshbandhu Chittaranjan Das. Both of them formed the 'Narikarma Mandir' the main aim of which was to raise a consciousness among the women.[26]

Maharani Siddheswari Devi of Canchal Estate, commonly known as Second Annapurna, was very popular for her benevolent activities. Dakshayani Devi, wife of Sarat Chandra Roychaudhury of Cachal started 27 Pathshalas and offered grants for establishing the National School in Malda. She helped the freedom fighters secretly. Being influenced by her patriotism, Sarat Chandra Roychaudhury responded to Gandhi's call for *swaraj*.[27]

THE ZAMINDARS OF RAJSHAHI

Rajshahi was one of the leading districts of undivided North Bengal. In the beginning of the fifteenth century, this region was ruled by Raja Ganesh. It is said that the Raja, after dethroning the Sultan of Gaur, became the ruler of Bengal and came to be known as 'Raja-Shah', i.e. a Hindu Raja who occupied a Muslim throne and thus the territory got its name as 'Rajshahi'. During the period of permanent settlement, it was one of the most important administrative divisions of undivided Bengal. The *zamindars* of Rajshahi, like the *zamindars* of Puthia, Natore and Puthia had an important position in the atlas of the *zamindari* system of colonial Bengal. Dubalhati was the oldest one but it was not as large as those of Natore and Puthia. They had an important role in the collection of revenue of Bengal.[28]

The *zamindars* of Rajshahi played a significant role in the economic transformation of Bengal. Side by side, they had a pivotal role in enriching the socio-cultural atlas of the region. The history of the *zamindars* of Rajshahi is so fascinating that it links up the history of the *zamindari* system introduced by the Mughals which blossomed during the British period.

The *zamindari* of Puthia was established during the age of Akbar the Great. Maharaja Harendranath Roy helped Shibchandra Siddhanta in setting up a school at Puthia. Maharani Sharatsundari played a key role in establishing the school and other cultural institutions in Rajshahi. She set up schools in Lalpur and Zhaoil villages and introduced stipends for the students of Puthia. She helped Pratap Chandra Roy immensely for the publication of the Bengali translation of the *Mahabharata*. She also helped the Rajshahi College financially for the construction of its building. After the death of Maharani Sharatsundari, the *zamindari* was put in charge of the Court of Wards. At that time Hemantakumari was a minor. When she took charge from the Court, she was only eighteen years old. She made sincere attempts to lay the foundation of Hemantakumari Sanskrit College in July 1904. Initially the classes began at Rajshahi College. Later, the structural development took place under the patronage of Maharani Hemantakumari. The Maharani Hemantakumari Hostel, Maharani Hemantakumari English High School at Zhawal and Maharani Hemantakumari School at Nandina of Mymensingh bear the testimony of her dedication towards education. Her most significant contribution was the foundation of Bhuban Mahan English High School in memory of her father in 1919. She introduced water projects for the supply of drinking water in Rajshahi. Later it came to be known as 'Maharani Hemantakumari Water Works'. For her benevolent activities, the British government honoured her with several titles. She was awarded the title of 'Rani' during the reign of Lord Curzon in 1901 and 'Maharani' during the reign of Lord Irwin on 1 January 1927. Maharani Manamahini Devi had a great contribution in the field of education. She introduced Law classes in Rajshahi College and all the expanses were met by her. She donated five thousand rupees in laying the foundation of the Diamond Jubilee Industrial School at Rajshahi.[29]

The Natore Raj family, established by Ramjiban during the reign of Murshid Quli Khan, flourished actually during the period of Rani Bhawani. During her reign of about fifty years, the boundary of the Estate was extended up to Dinajpur, Bogra, Pabna, Kusthia, Jessore, Rangpur, Murhsidabad, Birbhum and Malda. She devoted her whole life to the cause of education. For this purpose, she had to set up many Pathshalas and offered scholarships.[30] For example, Sripati Vidyalankar of Tajpur, Rudrakanta of Chougram, Ramnath Talukdar of Matikopa, Kaliprasad Chakrabarty of Amhati, Kashikanta, Panchanan and many others received scholarships. Professor Rudrakanta Bhattacharya of Bariagram Chatuspathy received an annual scholarship of 60 rupees from Rani Bhawani. In 1752, Gadadhar Siddhanta established a Chatuspathy at Amhati where she granted scholarship of 10 rupees. Hindu law and logic were taught there. Rani Bhawani and Raja Ramakanta established 33 centres for Vaishnava teachings and nearly 83 Pathshalas. She also introduced stipends for both the Brahmin and Muslim saints. The centres, well known for Sanskrit teachings like Basudevpur, Kalam and Baidyabelghoria also received her generosity to a large extent.[31]

The period of Maharaja Jagadindranath Roy witnessed a revolution in art and literature. During his tenure, a literary conference was held at Natore Court Compound. He was the president of the literary conference held in Pabna on 22 February 1914. He also presided over the meeting of literature held at Muktagacha, Mymensingh. Regular meetings of men of letters generally took place at Victoria library, Natore.[32] Maharaja Jagadindranath Roy himself was a prolific writer. Two books *Nurjahan* and *Sandhatara* written by him attained wide recognition from the intellectual society of the contemporary period. He dedicated the book *Sandhyatara* to Ramesh Chandra Majumder, a doyen of Indian history. He also composed a number of Bengali poems like 'Atit Smriti', 'Abhiman', 'Asamay', 'Akutala', 'Duti', 'Sangbad', 'Padaprakkhalan', 'Minati' and so on. He also composed travel stories 'Hyderabad' and 'Secendrabad'. The Maharaja wrote prefaces to many books like *Brihatbanga* by Dinesh Chandra Sen, the famous historian and *Bangalir Bal* by Rajendra Lal Acharya both in 1328 BS *Manasi-O-Marmabani,* a Bengali newspaper published every month came into light under his patronage. Prabhat Kumar Mukherjee helped him to a great extent in this field. Maharaja

Jagadindranath Roy had good relations with Rabindranath Tagore. He added the music of 'Pakhwaj' with Rabindra Sangeet and sometimes played on 'Pakhwaj' in many occasions. He was very much fond of sports and games. He formed a cricket team in Natore. He established the Maharaja J.N. High English School and assisted the Natore Girl's High School financially for its construction. He also founded a school in Calcutta in name of Rani Bhawani.[33]

Beside the cultural world, the Maharaja established his name in politics too. He was a dedicated member of the Bengal Provincial Congress. In 1897, the meeting of the Bengal Provincial Congress was held in Natore and the Maharaja was the President of the Reception Committee. He was an elected member of the new council for the Montego-Ford Scheme for the third time. His most significant contribution was the establishment of the 'Bengal Land Holder's Association' in 1901. A group of *zamindar*s like Maharaja Surya Kanta Roychaudhury and Pramadnath, the Raja of Dighapatia helped him to a great extent. Jagadindranath Roy was the fifth President of the Rajshahi Association, established in 1872. Lord Lytton, the then Viceroy of India conferred him with the title of 'Maharaja' in 1877 in the 'First Darbar of Delhi'. He died on 5 January 1926.[34]

Kalinath Chaudhury shows that the Dighapatia Estate established by Dayaram, the Dewan of the Natore Raj, contributed largely to the development in education, infrastructure and culture of North Bengal. They were especially famous for their generosity and public spirit. He was a devotee Hindu and constructed a number of temples at Jessore. He also set up *pathshala*s to impart education in Sanskrit language.[35]

Raja Prasannanath Roy had an immense contribution in the field of education. In 1851, the Deputy Magistrate of Natore established a school which was later merged with the Prasannanath Academy. The Deputy Magistrate applauded Prasannanath highly for this notable work and described this institution as a harbinger of better days for Rajshahi. In 1841, the Magistrate of Natore sub-division had to establish a hospital and Dighapatia English School in Natore. Raja Prasannanath Roy issued a government promissory note of rupees one lakh including one-year interest to government through the commissioner. For this immense contribution he was applauded highly by the government.[36]

Prasannanath Roy was also famous for his welfare activities. He constructed a number of roads within the Estate. The existing capital road from Dighapatia to Rampur Boila (Rajshahi) was extended previously up to Natore. Later on the road was extended further up to Dighapatia and was connected with the road to Bogra. He established the Prasannakali Temple and arranged lunch and dinner for the devotees. For his great achievements, the government conferred him with the title of 'Raja Bahadur'. The title was handed over to him by Lord Dalhousie, the then Viceroy at a Public Darbar in Government House which was graced by the Maharaja of Patiala and a number of the elite. Next to him, Raja Pramathnath Roy was famous for his contribution in the field of education. He was highly fond of women's education and founded the Rajshahi Girls High School singlehandedly. He arranged three scholarships for the development of the school and donated an annual government promissory note amounting 180 rupees only for its expenditure. He also contributed one and half lakh rupees to develop the Rajshahi College. His son Pramadanath Roy had a great passion for education. He took over the charge of both the Dighapatia School and Noukhila School and constructed a building for P.N. School, Rajshahi. For the welfare of students of Rajshahi College, he donated 25 lakh rupees and introduced scholarships for the students pursuing Master degree there. For the development of the silk industry he established the Diamond Jubilee Industrial School in 1898. The foundation of the Rajshahi Library and Museum was contributed largely by him. He donated twenty thousand rupees to Lady Duffrin Fund. He was the president of the Rajshahi Association in 1901. In the same year, the 'Bengal Land Holders Association' was formed and he was a founding member along with other dignitaries like Raja Jagindranath Roy, Maharaja Surya Knata Acharya Chaudhury and Ashutosh Chaudhury. For his social and educational contribution, the British government awarded him with the title 'Raja Bahadur'. Basanta Kumar Roy, the most worthy son of Pramadanath Roy, largely contributed in setting up the Hemantakumari Sanskritik College in Rajshahi. During his period, the P.N. Girls School turned into a High School and a library was formed in the Dayarampur Rajbari.[37]

Sarat Kumar Roy ranked higher in the field of education and culture in comparison with other members of the Dighapatia *zamindar* family. He had a close relationship with the Tagore family. He made a great contribution towards the establishment of the Bharatiya Sangeet Samaj in 1897. Rabindranath Tagor was the main inspiration behind it.[38] Sarat Kumar Roy built a school namely Basanta Kumar M.E. School, in the memory of his elder brother. Sarat Kumar Roy was the President of the reception committee of the Bangiya Sahitya Parishad which was established in Rajshahi in February, 1909. The session was attended by a number of renowned personalities like Maharaja Manindra Chandra Nandi, Ramendra Sundar Trivedi and Acharya Prafulla Chandra Roy, the great scientist. The third session of the Bangiya Sahitya Parishad was held at Bhagalpur in 1910 where Sarat Kumar Roy, Akshay Kumar Maitra and Ramaprasad Chanda participated. Sharat Kumar Roy wrote books such as *Tailik Jati* and *Mahan Lal.* His wife Rekha Roy was a prolific writer. She wrote two books *Varendra Randhan* and *Varendra Jalkhabar.* For the development of agriculture, he constructed the Rani Drabamai Farm in his mother's memory. He developed the irrigation system by constructing a canal from the Baral River.[39]

Hemandra Kumar Roy was the youngest brother of Sarat Kumar Roy. He donated 1,500 rupees to Rajshhai College for the apparatus of chemistry and 10,000 rupees to Rajshahi P.N. Girls High School for the construction of its building. He developed the Haricharan Child School immensely and renamed it as Sabitri Siksha Vidyalaya.[40]

CONCLUSION

Thus it appears that the *zamindars* contributed to a great extent to enrich the education and culture of their estates by establishing a number of schools, colleges and other cultural institutions. It helped the people to come to terms with the cultural awakening of nineteenth-century Bengal. With the passage of time, they became aware of the cultural enlightenment and their cultural awakening later reflected with the setting up of two literary organizations namely Rajshahi Association (1872) and Varendra Research Museum (1912). Dipesh Chakrabarty has rightly commented 'if Varendra Anusandhan Samiti had not been created, we would not have known about the historical facts of many places in Bengal'.[41] They received Maharaja and Rai titles of honour from the Mughal Empire and Raja Bahadur and other titles from the British crown. Raja Sarat Kumar and Basanta Kumar Roy of Dighapatia, Prasannanath Roy are worthy of mention. In the development of education, the women of these estates such as Maharani Sharatsundari, Rani Bhawani, Rani Manamahini Devi and others contributed enough by setting up educational institutions in their *zamindari*. Besides the expansion of education, they stood for a number of social reforms. The local *zamindar*s did not lag behind in this great endeavour. They helped them financially in this great cause.

The voice which emerged from the *zamindar*s was overwhelmingly that of the upper-caste Hindu. The number of Muslim *zamindar*s was very few. It is true that their ceaseless efforts led to the birth of a small group of educated middle class who helped the *zamindar*s in their work. To them, education was a means of survival in difficult times, a tool for achieving economic prosperity and getting power, rather than just a pathway to intellectual enlightenment. But the fruit of their movement did not reach out to common people, mainly rural. Above all the message of their efforts could hardly penetrate deep into society. Their total faith in British and English education set them apart from the general masses and as a result, they never succeeded in organizing any social movement.

NOTES

1. Dr. Ramesh Chandra Mitra, 'Education', in Narendra Krishna Sinha (ed.), *The History of Bengal (1757-1905),* University of Calcutta, 1996, p. 431.
2. Buchanan Hamilton, *The History, Antiquities, Topography and Statistics of Eastern India*, vol. II, p. 705 and vol. III, 1801, Calcutta, p. 708.

3. Adam, *Reports on the State of Education in Bengal,* Calcutta, 1836, p. 293.
4. *Rangpur Sahitya Parishad Patrika*, Rangpur, BS 1324, pp. 23-4.
5. Maniruzzaman, *Rangpurer Itihas* (History of Rangpur), Gatidhara, Dhaka, Bangladesh, 2012, pp. 330-1.
6. Ibid., pp. 394-8.
7. J.A. Vas, *Bengal District Gazetteers Rangpur,* Allahabad, 1911, p. 135.
8. Maniruzzaman, op. cit., p. 363.
9. J.A. Vas, op. cit., p. 135.
10. *Proceedings of the First Conference of Uttarbanga Sahitya Sammelan,* Rangpur, 27 June 1908, pp. 12-15.
11. Maniruzzaman, op. cit., pp. 299-300.
12. Ananda Gopal Ghosh, *Jalpaigurir Sahityalekhya O Anyanya Prabandha,* (Cultural History of Jalpaiguri and Other Essays), Sangbedan, Malda, W.B., BS 1417, p. 82.
13. *Proceedings of Uttarbanga Sahitya Sammilani, for the year 1910-11,* Rangpur, 1911, pp. 24-5.
14. Introductory part, in Samir Patra and Sekhar Bhowmik (ed.) *Akshay Kumar Maitra Smarak Grantha,* Ashadip, Kolkata, 2012, p. 3.
15. *Annual Proceedings of Uttarbanga Sahitya Sammilani, for the year 1912-13,* Rangpur, 1913, pp. 42-4.
16. Maniruzzaman, op. cit., p. 346.
17. *Centenary Volume of Kamrup Anusandhan Samiti,* Guwahati, 2010, pp. 8-9.
18. *Bharatabarsha,* Monsoon Issue, BS 1320, Kolkata, p. 21.
19. Maniruzzaman, op. cit., p. 350.
20. Ananda Gopal Ghosh, *Jalpaigurir Sahityalekhya O Anyanya Prabandha,* op. cit., pp. 82-5.
21. Dhananjay Roy, *Dinajpur Jelar Itihas* (A History of Dinajpur District), K.P. Bagchi, Kolkata, 2006, p. 255.
22. F.W. Strong, *Bengal District Gazetteers Dinajpur,* Bengal Secretariat Press, Calcutta, 1911, p. 20.
23. Kamalesh Goswami, *Raiganjer Itihas* (History of Raiganj), Dibaratrir Kabya Publication, Kolkata, 2008, p. 24.
24. Sukumar Barai, *Dinajpurer Anchalik Itihaser Nana Diganta* (Various Horizons of the Regional History of Dinajpur), Pragatishil Prakashak, Kolkata, 2015, p. 57.
25. F.W. Strong, *Bengal District Gazetteers Dinajpur,* Bengal Secretariat Press, Calcutta, 1911, p. 21.
26. Dhananjay Roy, 'Uttarbanger Mahila Jamidarder Kahini', *Dainik Basumati,* Siliguri, 22 August 1999.

27. Bhupendranath Das, *Canchal Rajbari* (The Royal Palace of Canchal), *Uttar Malda Sambad,* Autumn Number, BS 1411, Malda, pp. 117-22.
28. S.M. Rabiul Karim, 'Rajshahi Zamindars: A Historical Profile in the Colonial Period' (1765-1947), unpublished PhD thesis, University of North Bengal, 2006, pp. 1-2.
29. Ibid, pp. 60-70.
30. Moksudur Rahman, *Natorer Maharani Bhawani* (Queen Bhawani of Natore), Rajshahi, 1988, p. 5.
31. Ibid, pp. 114-15.
32. Fazlul Hauque, *Maharaja Jagadindranath Roy* (King Jagadindranath Roy), Bangla Academy, Dhaka, 1992, p. 12.
33. S.M. Rabiul Karim, op. cit., pp. 124-7.
34. Ibid, pp. 130-2.
35. Kalinath Chaudhury, *Rajshahir Sankhipta Itihas* (A Short History of Rajshahi), Calcutta, BS 1308, p. 202.
36. Bimal Prasad Ray et al., *Natorer Katha O Kahini* (Words and Stories of Natore), Calcutta, 1981, pp. 74-8.
37. S.M. Rabiul Karim, op. cit., pp. 161- 5.
38. Saifuddin Chaudhury, *Kumar Sharat Kumar Roy* (Prince Sharat Kumar Roy), Bangla Academy, Dacca, 2002, p. 08.
39. S.M. Rabiul Karim, op. cit., pp. 165-7.
40. Ibid, p. 171.
41. Dipesh Chakrabarty, *Itihaser Janajiban O Ananya Prabandha* (History, Public Life and Other Essays), Ananda Publishers, Kolkata, 2011, pp. 118-19.

CHAPTER 4

Changes in Educational Scenario

INTRODUCTION

The most outstanding outcome of Renaissance in North Bengal was the introduction of Western education. It was perhaps the most important single factor behind the cultural awakening. There was a positive demand by this time for Western education. There were schools under private management where children were taught by missionaries or individual Englishmen. In Darjeeling, the schools started by Christian missionaries prospered. The waves of Western education surfaced, not just in Darjeeling hill but also in other mofussil towns like Rajshahi, Dinajpur, Jalpaiguri, Malda, and the princely state of Coochbehar. Western education did not, however, spread solely at the initiative of the British government. The *maharajas*, *zamindars*, tea industrialists and a group of educated people have contributed to a great extent for the development of education in North Bengal. The local *zamindars* and philanthropists sponsored the founding of schools, supported the local initiatives for providing education and patronized numerous associations that were formed to initiate and implement reforms.

THE PRINCELY STATE OF COOCHBEHAR

The advent of English education in Coochbehar began with the establishment of a school in 1831 during the period of Maharaja Harendra Narayan. Maharaja Sivendra Narayan had an immense contribution behind its growth and development. For this purpose, he wrote a letter to Colonel Jenkins. In reply, it was stated:

The Governor-General in Council is disposed to encourage the proposition of the Rajah for the establishment of a school and when arrangements shall have been completed for the appropriating sufficient funds for its maintenance, the subject of supplying teachers from the Presidency will be taken into consideration.

Maharaja Sivendra Narayan, however, could not see its full-fledged development due to his untimely death in 1861.[1]

The Brahmo movement had an immense contribution in the field of education in Coochbehar. During that period two educational institutions, namely Jenkins School and Victoria College were set up and that led to the actual beginning of the cultural awakening in Coochbehar. A regional language medium school was started in the town of Coochbehar in 1857 for the education of Maharaja's kinsmen. In 1859, the medium of instruction in this school became English. Colonel Jenkins had a big role in laying the foundation of this school. He advised Maharaja Narendra Narayan (1847-63) to start an English school with the money offered to him and accordingly an English school was established in 1861. The Maharaja named the school 'Jenkins School' after his name. Being overwhelmed with this honour, Colonel Jenkins wrote a letter to Maharaja Narendra Narayan where he stated 'I am obliged to you for laying the foundation of the school in my name and I hope you will take measures to provide for its being a prosperous institution. . .'. Kalikadas Bagchi was the first headmaster of this intuition. On every Saturday, the meeting of the Coochbehar Hitaishini Sabha took place generally in the school premises.[2]

Victoria College, established in 1888, under the encouragement of Maharaja Nripendra Narayan Bhup Bahadur, was the pride in higher education not just all over Bengal but north-eastern India. Maharani Suniti Devi wrote in her autobiography 'the Maharaja took a keen interest in matters pertaining to education and founded a college of which he was very proud'.[3] The first principal of the college was J.C. Goodley. During the period when Brojendra Nath Shil was the Principal of the Victoria College (1896-1993), the institution reached its apex of glory. He first started his professional career in Morris College, Nagpur in the Department of Philosophy.

Later he joined the Krishnanath College, Murshidabad from where he was appointed as the principal of the Victoria College in 1896. During his tenure, the first students' hostel was set up in the college. A large number of students from outside Bengal, who hailed mainly from Assam, used to come there for higher education. Many of them later earned name and fame in their professional life. Annada Charan Bhattacharya, the recipient of Bihsnu Priya Devi award from University of Calcutta in 1898, Panchanan Sircar BA MA in Sanskrit LLB from University of Calcutta, Abbasuddin the famous Bhawaiya Singer, Kumud Bandhu Chakrabarty, the recipient of Hemanta Kumar award and Panchanan Barma BA MA in Sanskrit studied there. A number of teachers who had nationwide fame, served the college for a period of time. In those days, according to Kumud Chakrabarty, Coochbehar had a galaxy of teachers.[4] Acharya Brojendra Nath Shil got various scholars to help him in the development of education in the State of Coochbehar. Every Sunday and on other holidays as well he used to arrange discussions. Eminent political personality Bipin Chandra Pal used to participate in some of these discussions.[5]

Panchanan Sircar passed the ME Examination in first division from Mathabhanga School and stood first in the general list of the Rajshahi division. Panchanan Barma was the founding member of Rangpur Sahitya Parishad, established in 1905. He was the editor of the *Rangpur Sahitya Patrika* for about seven years (1905-7) and had the credit to publish twenty volumes. He was a prolific writer, too.[6] He wrote three articles on Govinda Mishra's *Gita* and these were published in several volumes of the *Rangpur Sahitya Patrika*. One of his most outstanding literary creations was 'Kamtabihari Sahitya' which he proposed in the third conference of Uttarbanga Sahitya Sammelan in Gauripur, Assam. He also attended the fourth conference of Uttarbanga Sahitya Sammelan held at Malda between 9 and 10 January 1911. This conference was presided over by Sir Jadunath Sarkar, a doyen in Indian history.[7]

With the efforts of Brojendra Nath Shil, almost every branch of literature attained its height in Coochbehar. There were news regarding education, rights of civilians and the world war. It was in Coochbehar that he completed his outstanding creations like

New Essays in Criticism, Quest Eternal and *Positive Sciences of the Ancient Hindus.* He had a very good relationship with Maharaja Nripendra Narayan who made arrangements for Brojendra Nath Shil to attend a number of conferences abroad. For example, he attended the 'International Congress of Orientalises' in Rome in 1906 and delivered the inaugural speech for the 'First Universal Race Congress' in London in 1911. His writings acted as a bridge between Bengali readers and European literature. He adapted the theme and style of European writings in such a way that the Bengali readers were enthralled by his prose pieces when he served it to them in the native language.[8]

He served on various committees aimed to promote the educational scenario of British India. He was the member of the Simla Commission formed under the guidance of Lord Curzon, the then Governor-General of India, for the development of universities. But his contribution to the development of *swadeshi* education was memorable. In 1906, Satish Chandra Mukherjee, Gurudas Banerjee, Rashbehari Ghosh, Ransundar Trivedi, Binay Kumar Sarkar and Brojendra Nath Shil established the National Council of Education. In 1902 Swami Vivekananda wrote to him, seeking his help for chalking out a plan and programme for social work. Brojendra Nath could not meet him that time but he sent a message through Swami Vivekananda's second brother Mahendra Nath Dutta promising to chalk out a plan as devised by Swami Vivekananda. Unfortunately Swami Vivekananda passed away soon afterwards. In this connection he said that if Swami Vivekananda were alive, he would have given him a plan for social reform on the lines of Rammohun Roy and Vidysagar. He further said that his wife had given him a great impetus for the educational uplift of the Indian women.[9] However, Brojendra Nath Shil, responded to the invitation of Sir Ashutosh Mukherjee, joined the University of Calcutta as a professor of Philosophy. Later he was awarded an honorary doctorate degree from this university. In 1921, he was appointed the vice-chancellor of Mysore University. He was awarded an honorary knighthood in 1925. Victoria College, under the guidance of Acharya Brojendra Nath Shil, became the venue of the Renaissance in Coochbehar nay North Bengal. He was the friend of Swami Vivekananda, the great monk and disciple of Ramakrishna Paramhansa, the great Indian philosopher. A majority of students of this college hailed from Assam, many of whom later initiated socio-political movements there. From this point one may argue that the Victoria College served as the main ideological basis to them in launching the political movements against the British Raj in Assam. The professors of the college inspired their students with the ideas of nationalism and they later sowed the seeds of revolutionary movements in the place of their birth or the places where they worked.[10]

During the anti-partition movement, Kalimahan Ghosh, a student of the college, joined the anti-circular society. Being overwhelmingly impressed with the teachings of Brojendranath Shil, a number of students opened *swadeshi* schools in different parts of Bengal. Ambika Charan Roy established the National School in Behrampur during the non-cooperation movement. Satyendranath Majumder, the editor of *Ananda Bazar Patrika*, was a student of Brojendranath Shil. Pulin Bihari Das, one of the leading figure of Anushilan Samiti, was the student of the college. In his autobiography he wrote, 'in Coochbehar boarding school, students had to pay Rs. 5 per month in winter and Rs. 5 in summer. This provided two meals in a day, reading material, anointing oil and a bedroom'. The Dhaka Anushilan Samiti opened its branch in Coochbehar. A number of students of Jenkins School like Ananta Kumar Roy and Debabrata Mukherjee joined and became members of this revolutionary society, distributing its activities secretly around the whole state. In a government report it was stated, 'the Dacca leaders appointed Braja Govinda Guha to be in charge of the North Bengal Anushilan Samiti and Niranjan Ghosh for Dhubri in Assam'. The students of Victoria College had a close relationship with students in different parts of Bengal. For example, Suresh Chandra Acharji, a student of the Victoria College sent a 'Swadeshi Bharat' leaflet to a student of the Brajamahan College, Basirhat in 1912. When the waves of the non-cooperation movement created discontent among the students of the college, Maharaja Jitendra Narayan addressed the students in a conference telling them that they were free to go elsewhere for their desired education. The Maharaja also issued strict order to suppress the non-cooperation movement in his state. In a conference of the State Council he stated, 'His Highness does not propose to review the argument for or against non-cooperation. It is sufficient to deserve that the movement can have no *raison d'être* in Coochbehar, where *swaraj* had long been an established fact'. However, it is interesting to note that although the Coochbehar State administration adopted a strict attitude against the movement, it did not take such strict steps against Kazi Nazrul Islam when he was invited by the students of both the Jenkins School and Victoria College. He gave strong speeches against the British rule. The royal administration only monitored his movements but did not take any action against him.[11]

The reign of Maharaja Nripendra Narayan Bhup Bahadur (1863-1911) was truly the age of Renaissance in Coochbehar. He had an immense contribution towards the modernization of the Coochbehar State. For the first time, he had to set up a 'Local Committee of Public Instruction' in 1865. The post for the Superintendent of School Education was introduced in 1870. He introduced the grants-in-aid system in Coochbehar to improve the state of education.[12]

Maharaja Nripendra Narayan had to establish three sub-divisional schools at Mathabhanga, Dinhata and Mekhliganj; twelve model schools in his state. His reign was the golden age of

LIST OF GRANTS-IN-AID IN COOCHBEHAR
FROM 1871-1900

Year	*In Govt. Sector*	*In Private Sector*	*Total Amount*
1871-2	22,233	6,273	28,506
1875-6	82,591	22,357	64,948
1879-80	60,685	33,213	93,898
1892-3	56,863	15,832	72,695
1895-6	57,995	18,212	76,167
1897-8	59,433	18,236	77,669
1899-1900	63,710	19,819	83,529

Source: Harendra Narayan Chowdhury, *The Coochbehar State and Its Land-Revenue Settlement,* Coochbehar State Press, Coochbehar, 1903, pp. 325-6.

women's education. It is true that the first endeavour to promote women's education in Coochbehar was started under the leadership of Brindeswari Devi, the wife of Maharaja Sivendra Narayan. In 1865, Tribhanga Mukhopadhyay, the Assistant Secretary of Hitaishini Sabha and headmaster of Jenkins School, first raised the proposal to establish a girls school in Coochbehar. This attempt took a new dimension during the time of Maharaja Nripendra Narayan and his wife Suniti Devi. The foundation of Suniti Academy in 1881 was a landmark in this field. It was upgraded as a Middle English (ME) School in 1884 and was affiliated to the University of Calcutta in 1928.[13] During his period, the number of girls school was 23 in 1875. In 1868-9, it was only 6 whereas the numbers of boy's schools was 25. At the end of 1878, nearly 560 girls studied in 43 girls' schools. In 1879 the number of educational institutions and students increased to 50 and 651.[14]

The Maharani Girls' High School was the first Indian managed school for Indian girls in the district of Darjeeling. It was established in 1908 by some renowned Bengali women connected with the Brahmo Samaj the Maharaja Nripendra Narayan and Maharani Suniti Devi of Coochbehar, Maharaja of Burdwan, Lord and Lady Carmichael, the Rani of Kakina, the Maharanis of Mayurbhanj and Vizanagram, Sir S.P. Sinha, B.C. Mitra and P.N. Mukherjee all played an important role in its establishment.[15]

THE DISTRICTS OF RAJSHAHI, RANGPUR AND DINAJPUR

In the second half of the nineteenth century, the *zamindars* of Rajshahi, Rangpur and Dinajpur offered adequate grants and scholarships for the development of education. The introduction of Western education was perhaps the most important single factor behind the cultural awakening in North Bengal. Western education did not, however, spread solely at the initiative of the government and Christian missionaries. A large number of *zamindars* contributed to a great extent in this endeavour. Many historians have talked about their exploiting character but none of them has probed so deep into their role in setting up educational institutions, establishing presses and publishing periodicals which paved the way the actual beginning of cultural awakening in North Bengal. Thus, seeds of the Renaissance were sown and these were to germinate in due course of time.

Kalichandra Roychaudhury, a *zamindar* of Kundi was the pioneer of English education in Rangpur. He started the first girls school and founded the women textbook society. The landlords of Rangpur had the dream to establish colleges for fostering the spirit of education there. Both Manindra Chandra Roychaudhury and Surendra Chandra Roychaudhury donated 419 acres of land for its construction. Local *zamindar*s also came forward for this great cause. This resulted in the formation of a college in Rangpur. Lord Thomas David Carmichael, the then Governor of Bengal laid the foundation stone of the college on 10 November 1916 and it was named after him. It got its affiliation to University of Calcutta in July 1917. A trustee board was set up, of which Raja Gopal Ray, the Zamindar of Tajhat and Rai Bahadur Ananda Mohan were the members, and Gyanendra Mohan Gupta, the collector of Rangpur (1913-1916) was the president. A sub-committee comprising of eighteen other members was set up to undertake the work of construction of the college building. Initially four lakhs was collected for this purpose, and the amount eventually went up to seven lakhs. Among the twenty-four donors, eighteen persons who top the list were mostly Zamindars and Jotedars. Ananda Mohan was the highest contributor with Rs.1 lakh. In July 1917, classes started in the building of Rangpur District Board. In the meantime, 900 bighas of land was made available by way of donation for the college campus-out of which Manindra Chandra Roychaudhury and Surendra Chandra Roychaudhury themselves donated 419 bighas of land. Rest was collected from different persons belonging to the Zamindar and Jotedar class of Rangpur. In 1918, newly appointed governor Ronaldsay disbursed a government grant of Rs 90,000 in two instalments for the new campus which is now located in Lalbagh. In this way, Rangpur Carmichael College came into existence with the sincere efforts of different zamindars and well-to-do persons of Rangpur district.

Since then, till the middle of the twentieth century, the Carmichael College had been a leading light for the spread of higher education far and wide in North Bengal as well as in Assam. On being granted the permission by Calcutta University, the college which started in 1917 with BA class had become a full fledged honours college within a span of eight years. After Lord Lytton's visit in 1922, the college was granted further permission for starting honours courses in 11 other subjects. Thereafter, in 1925, B.Sc. course was introduced. Till the partition, this heritage educational institution functioned under the University of Calcutta.[17]

In Dinajpur, Raja Krishna Chandra Roy and Bhupal Chandra Roy both opened schools and colleges to impart modern education. The Marnai School was established in 1868 and later renamed Pralhad Chandra Vidyalaya. Bipul Chandra Roychaudhury, the *zamindar* of Bhupalpur, established the Bhupalchandra Vidyapith in 1955. Mahendra Narayan Chaudhury established the Marnai F.E. School in 1899 and he was financially helped by Sarat Chandra Roychaudhury. Maharaja Girijanath Roy of Dinajpur Estate devoted his time and energy to the cause of spreading education in Dinajpur. As a consequence, the Raiganj Coronation High School was established in 1911. A landmark in the history of cultural awakening was the foundation of Raiganj Institute by Jagadish Nath Roy, son of Girijanath Roy in 1939. He set up the Dinajpur Girls School in 1869. Maharani Shyam Mohini Devi was very keen to elevate the position of women in society. The movement which was launched against the oppression of women was later carried on by Hemprabha Devi, wife of Maharaja Girijanath Roy.[18]

Maharani Hemantkumari Devi of Rajshahi made sincere attempts to lay the foundation of Hemantakumari Sanskrit College in July 1904. Initially the classes began at Rajshahi College. Later, the structural development took place under the patronage of Maharani Hemantakumari. The Maharani Hemantakumari Hostel, Maharani Hemantakumari English High School at Zhawal and Maharani Hemantakumari School at Nandina of Mymensingh bear the testimony of her dedication towards education. Her most significant contribution was the foundation of Bhuban Mahan English High School in memory of her father in 1919.[19]

In 1851, the Deputy Magistrate of Natore established a school which was later merged with the Prasannanath Academy. The Deputy Magistrate applauded Raja Prasannanath Roy highly for this notable work and described this institution as a harbinger of better days for Rajshahi. He also founded the Rajshahi Girls' High School. Sharat Kumar Roy built a school namely Basanta Kumar M.E. School in memory of his elder brother. In 1910, Maharaja Jagadindranath Ray established the J.N. High School and constructed the present building of the school. He also offered huge grants for the Natore Girls' School and established a High School in Calcutta in memory of Rani Bhawani, Natore. The Dighapatia Raj family contributed to a great extent for the educational development of Rajshahi. The Rajshahi College, Promoth Nath Girls' High School, Sabitri Girls' High School, Basanta Kumar Agricultural College and a few other institutions received their patronage.[20]

THE DISTRICT OF JALPAIGURI

The upsurge of the Bengal Renaissance which engulfed Calcutta in the nineteenth and twentieth century also took long strides and reached Jalpaiguri town in no time. It is true that nineteenth-century Calcutta could boast of many luminaries and in this respect the Jalpaiguri town did not lag behind as a large number of social reformers, keen educationalists and education stalwarts accounted for a large section of population of the Jalpaiguri town. Being a tea industry centred town, Jalpaiguri attracted some great names of Bengali literature in various times. Such recurrent visits, by literary experts did not happen in the case of other towns of North Bengal. Nevertheless, inculcating educational interests and cultural consciousness among the inhabitants of this town were done by the honest efforts of some renowned personalities such as Tarini Prasad Roy, Jogesh Chandra Ghosh, Sasi Kumar Niyogi, Dr Charu Chandra Sanyal, Hriday Nath Bagchi, Satendra Prasad Roy, Birendra Chandra Ghosh, Jogodindra Raikot and so on. Most of them were renowned tea industrialists of contemporary Bengal. These stalwarts not only spread the name and fame of Jalpaiguri in Bengal but also at a national level. By the 1930s, Jalpaiguri had already achieved the status of a prospering town in literature. One landmark in regard to the Bengali tea planters of the Jalpaiguri town which will always remain vivid in the sociocultural history of the Jalpaiguri district was the establishment of various schools and colleges. They built a number of schools not only in every nook and corner of Jalpaiguri town but also in the neighbouring places which were adjacent to the gardens so that all the children could get some sort of education to bring a ray of hope for the younger generation.[21]

The Sadar Girls' High School was established in 1902 by Jalan Mian, a reputed educationist of the town. His wife Pyari Bibi, a Brahmo woman of Jalpaiguri town, established a primary school which was upgraded as an upper primary school in 1907. She was also the librarian of the library of the Brahmo Samaj in Jalpaiguri town. She got assistance from Sharat Pandit, a renowned educator of the then Jalpaiguri town. However, behind its growth and development, the role played by the Princess Suniti Debi of Cooch Behar deserves to be mentioned. She was said to have assisted the school by providing raw materials to lay the construction of building in 1912. The school was transformed to an English Medium school in 1921.[22]

Kamini Kanta Rahut, a renowned tea industrialist, established the Saudamani Girls' School in 1931. He also set up a primary school named Sishu Mahal to further the cause of primary education. Kamini Kanta Rahut, in memory of his father Ananda Chandra Rahut, established three important higher educational institutions in Jalpaiguri town such as Ananda Chandra College, Ananda Chandra Teachers Training College, Ananda Chandra College of Commerce. In the beginning of the twentieth century there was no provision for the youths of this district to get college education. Moreover, they had to face a lot of financial hardships in order to bear their expenses while pursuing college education in some other places. This resulted in the foundation of Ananda Chandra College in 1942 under the initiative of Kamini Kanti Rahut. He was said to have donated four acres of land and a grant of 25,000 rupees for the infrastructural development of the institution. In this great project he was helped by Tarani Mahan Chakrabarty, the ex-head master of Sonaulla High School and Debendra Kumar Chanda, the then assistant teacher of Jalpaiguri Sadar Girls' High School.[23] It is really commendable to say that a large number of notable educationists of Bengal started their careers from this heritage institution. Some of them were like Narayan Gangapadhyay, Kalyan Bhushan Chakrabarty, Dr Charu Chandra Sanyal and others.[24]

The Kadamtala Girls' High School was first started in the house of Madhusudan Karmakar in 1928. Bimala Roy, daughter of Madhusudan Karmakar and Anupama Debi, elder sister of Sri Pritinidhan Roy, were the first teachers of this school. It was upgraded as a higher secondary school in 1965. The contribution of tea planter Satyendra Prasad Roy towards its growth and development was really praiseworthy. The Jalpaiguri Central Girls' High School owed its origin to the initiative of Dr Charu Chandra Sanyal. In this mission, he was assisted by a group of leading personalities of the town like Tarani Mahan Chakrabarty, Dr. Dhiraj Mahan Sen, Shri Rukshini Kanta Bhowmick and others. It began its journey in the Sonaulla High School in the morning (6 to 10 a.m.) with four woman teachers and eighty-two girl students. Later the school was shifted to another area and the land was bought from its own fund. During his tenure as the Member of Parliament, Satyendra Prasad Roy provided adequate grants for the construction of the building. It was later inaugurated by Dhirendra Mahan Sen, the District Inspector of Schools. In 1959 it became secondary school and in 1965, it was upgraded to a higher secondary one. Satyendra Prasad Roy also started a fund named 'Tarini Prasad Roy Fund' in memory of his father, for the benefit of the needy students. The Sishu Mahal Primary School was established in 1944.[25]

The Fanindra Deb Institution (F.D.I.) was established by Prasanna Deb Raikat in memory of his father Fanindra Deb Raikot in 1917. During the 1930s Civil Disobedience Movement the whole of India was passionately involved in the independence movement; old and young—everyone being deeply moved with the *swadeshi* emotion and sentiment, called for quitting India. The students of the school could not remain aloof from this. As a consequence, the school authority received a financial setback from the government and all the grants stopped immediately. The monthly salary of a teacher was decreased from fifty to twenty. In this deplorable condition, Prasanna Deb Raikat extended his hand to Annada Charan Sen, the secretary of the school and thus the school survived the crisis.[26]

Prasanna Deb Raikat also started a primary school in memory of his mother Rani Amriteshwari on 2 January 1920. The first head master of the school was Tarani Mahan Chakrabarty. He dreamed to set up the school in the middle of the town. Munsi Muhammad Sonaullah came forward to fulfil his dream and hence he donated five thousand rupees, seven *bigha* of land along with six rooms of his palace. This school later came to be known as Sonaullah Institution. Next to it, P.D. Raikot established a school in the memory of his mother at Sannyasikata. At present it is popularly known as Sannyasikata High School. Khirodendra Deb Raikat, son of Jagadindra Deb Raikat was the first head master of this school.[27]

THE DISTRICT OF MALDA

The district of Malda was lagging far behind as compared to other districts of North Bengal in the field of Western education. One of the reasons for this was social and demographic diversity. As the district was overwhelmingly dominated by the Muslims and tribals, the progress of education could not be that much. At the initial stage the landowning and wealthy section of the society did not show much enthusiasm for the expansion of education but gradually they were seen to be enthusiastic.

A marked shift in the government's policy towards mass education can be noticed in Wood's Despatch in 1854. It, no doubt, initiated a broad change in the educational policy by encouraging the extension of educational facilities to the common people. As a result, the first Western educational institution called the Malda Zilla School was established in Malda in 1858. It was the first government school in North Bengal.[28]

By 1870 a number of English medium schools were established in the district. There was no college in the district until 1944. As a consequence, a number of students went to Rajshahi College and Berhampur Krishna Nath College for obtaining higher degrees. Thus, a new class of English educated gentry emerged in the last quarter of the nineteenth century who played an important role to develop the education and culture of the district. The first college in the district was the Malda College established in 1944.[29]

The rise of national consciousness was, no doubt, favoured by the spread of Western education. The nationalist leaders, being overwhelmingly influenced by the Swadeshi movement, took the initiative in laying the foundation of a number of national schools all over Bengal. The district of Malda did not lag behind in this field. Binoy Kumar Sarkar took the leading role in establishing the Malda Jatiya Shiksha Samiti in June 1907. In this mission, he was assisted by a group of leading personalities of the district like Radesh Chandra Seth, Bipin Bihari Ghosh and Maulavi Muhammad Nur Bux. Around eight schools with 748 students were set up by June 1908 at Malda, Qutubpur, Kaligram, Dharampur, Paranpur, Jadupur and Malatipur. Night schools were also set up at Qutubpur, Kaligram and Dharampur. For the development of female education, girls' schools came up at Kaligram and Dharampur.[30]

However, compared to the Hindu landlords, the Muslim ones were quite behind in this field. Muslim students were educated alongside the Hindus, but there were very few separate Muslim educational institutions in the district. Their views, however, began to change much later. The first attempt to improve their educational status in the district was the establishment of the Malda Muhamadden Association in 1890. Abdul Gani played a key role in laying the foundation of the institution. He also had to set up a Model Madrassa in the district in 1915. He was assisted to a great extent in this job by Kazi Azaharuddin who later founded the Jalalia Muqtab in 1916 for the development of women's education.[31]

The first girls' school established in the district was the Barlow Girls' School in 1871. It was the tireless effort of some renowned persons of the district like Panchanan Majumder. At first it got the recognition of a primary school from the government. The British government named the school as Barlow Girls' High School in 1871 in the memory of G.S. Barlow, the then Commissioner of Bhagalpur Division. However, the reputation, name and fame of the school was attained mostly during the period of Uma Sarkar, the head mistress of the institution from 1939 to 1986.[32]

CONCLUSION

Thus one may say that the contribution of the *maharaja*s and *zamindar*s for the cause of education was highly praiseworthy. The progress of education in Coochbehar was made possible under the supervision of Haughton and under the patronage of Maharaja Nripendra Narayan. Women's education took a new turn with the advent of Maharani Suniti Devi, the daughter of Keshub Chandra Sen. Suniti Academy established by Suniti Devi was recognized by the University of Calcutta as one of the leading centres of cultural awakening in nineteenth-century Bengal. Two more girls' schools came up in 1870s under the patronage of two leading personalities of the contemporary period namely Krishna Kumar Lahiri of Dinhata and Chhatrapati Singh of Mekhliganj.

Rani Sharat Sundari and Kumar Pradesh Narayan of Pootea, Rani Bhawani of Natore and the Raja of Dighapatia had distinguished themselves by their liberalism and generosity in promoting education in their respective places. They encouraged the culture of knowledge and offered adequate grants and scholarships for the development of education. The schools established by them have produced meritorious students who made significant contribution to the society.[33]

An urban centre gives rise to different functional activities on the basis of which urban social classification develops. This was true of the district towns of colonial Bengal. The Jalpaiguri town was a perfect example in this regard. The Bengali tea planters did not confine them in expanding their commercial interests. They also endeavoured to a great extent in setting up schools and colleges in the district. Such type of instances are very rare to find out in other districts of Bengal where sociocultural development took place mainly by the colonial rulers. The Jalpaiguri town stood out as an exception to this rule where sociocultural development took place mainly through the efforts of the Bengali tea-industrialists.

In all of this history of education, it is a misconception to credit Christian missionaries as being the pioneers ushering education in Darjeeling and the Duars. They were certainly the first to build schools, no doubt, but they had their own motives, which was to convert local people to Christianity. Contrary to this, the Bengali tea planters and *zamindars*, without any personal interest, contributed largely to the cause of education. Government education came in due course, therefore one cannot ignore their pioneering role in the field of education.

NOTES

1. *Coochbehar Select Records*, vol. II, Coochbehar State Press, 1884, p. 27.
2. Harendra Narayan Chauhdury, *Coochbehar State and Its Land Revenue Settlement*, Coochbehar State Press, Coochbehar, 1903, pp. 376-8.
3. Maharani Suniti Devi, *The Autibiography of an Indian Princess*, London, 1921, ed. Biswanath Das, Tarang Publication, Delhi, 1995, p. 12.
4. *Centenary Souvenir*, Acharya Brojendra Nath Seal, Calcutta, 1964, p. 55.
5. Amal Chattapadhyay, *Ananta Eshana Brajendranath Shil: Jiban O Chinta* (Life and Thought of Brajendranath Shil), Dip Publication, Kolkata, 1999, p. 22.
6. Upendra Nath Barma, *Thakur Panchanan Barmar Jiban Charit* (Biography of Thakur Panchanan Barma), Jalpaiguri, BS 1408, p. 3.
7. Ananda Gopal Ghosh, *Manishi Panchanan Barma O Tar Andalaner Uttaradhikar* (Panchanan Barma and the Legacy of His Movement), Sangbaden, Malda, 2015, pp. 64-5.
8. Sailen Debnath, *Essays on Cultural History of North Bengal*, National Library Publication, Siliguri, 2008, p. 104.
9. Anil Kumar Sarkar, 'Acahrya Brojendra Nath Shil and Victoria College', in Debabrata Chaki (ed.), *Uttar Prasanga,* Manju Printing Works, Coochbehar, West Bengal, 2014, p. 33.
10. Amal Chattapadhyay, op. cit., p. 26.

11. Ananda Gopal Ghosh, Bharater Swadhinata Andolane Deshiya Rajya Coochbehar: Prasanga Victoria College Chatra Samaj (1885-1947) (Role of the Princely State of Coochbehar in India's Freedom Struggle and the Students of Victoria College), in Gokul Sarkar (ed.), *Angikar*, autumn number, Dinhata, West Bengal, BS 1420, p. 46.
12. Harendra Narayan Chowdhury, *The Coochbehar State and Its Land-Revenue Settlement,* Coochbehar State Press, Coochbehar, 1903, pp. 325-6.
13. Annual Administrative Report, Coochbehar State Press, Coochbehar, 1903-4, p. 19.
14. Chhanda Chakrabarty, 'Coochbehar e Nari Shikshar Bibartan' (Evolution of Women Education in Coochbehar), in Ajitesh Bhattacharya (ed.), *Maduparni,* Coochbehar Jela Sankhya (Special Volume on the District of Coochbehar), Government of West Bengal, BS 1396, pp. 203-12.
15. Dick B. Dewan, *History of Education in Darjeeling Hill 1835-1985,* Indus Publishing Company, New Delhi, 1991, p. 172.
16. Maniruzzaman, *Zamindars of Bengal: Case Study of Selected Rangpur Zamindars 1793-1950,* Gatidhara, Dhaka, Bangladesh, 2011, pp. 171-2.
17. Maniruzzaman, *Rangpurer Itihas* (History of Rangpur), Gatidhara, Dhaka, Bangladesh, 2012, p. 306-7.
18. Kamalesh Goswami, *Raiganjer Itihas* (History of Raiganj), Dibaratrir Kabya Publication, Kolkata, 2008, p. 24.
19. S.M. Rabiul Karim, 'Rajshahi Zamindars: A Historical Profile in the Colonial Period (1765-1947)', unpublished PhD thesis, University of North Bengal, 2006, pp. 60-70.
20. Ibid., pp. 161-7.
21. Kamakhya Prasad Chakrabarty, *Sekaler Jalpaiguri Sahar O Samajik Jibaner Kichu Katha* (Few Words of Social Life of Contemporary Jalpaiguri Town), Sigma Information Technology Publication, Jalpaiguri, 2004, p. 66.
22. Suniti Bala Chanda, 'Jalpaiguri Jelar Eksho Bochore Stri Sikkhar Bikash' (One Hundred years of Development of Women's Education in the District of Jalpaiguri), in Charu Chandra Sanyal (ed.), *Jalpaiguri District Centenary Souvenir,* 1970, Jalpaiguri, p. 148.
23. Amiya Kumar Pakrashi, 'Jalpaiguri Jelay Siksha Bistarer Ruprekha' (An Outline of the Development of Education in the District of Jalpaiguri), in *Jalpaiguri District centenary Souvenir,* op. cit., p. 186.
24. Mahit Ghosh, 'Prayata Kamini Kanta Rahut Sambandhe Duti Katha' (Two Words about Late Kamini Kanta Rahut), in *Kamini Kanta Rahut Janma Shatabarshiki Bishesh Sankhya* (Birth Centenary Volume on

Kamini Kanta Rahut), Nikhil Bharat Banga Sahitya Sammalan, BS 1402, Jalpaiguri, p. 20.

25. Kamakhya Prasad Chakrabarty, 'S.P. Roy er Sankhipta Jibani', in *Satyendra Prasad Roy Janma Shatabarshiki Bishesh Sankhya,* Nikhil Bharat Banga Sahitya Sammalan, BS 1402, Jalpaiguri, p.14.
26. Amiya Kumar Pakrashi, op. cit., p. 175.
27. Umesh Sharma, *Jalpaigurir Raikot Bangsher Rajarshi* (Leading Personality of the Raikot Dynasty of Jalpaiguri), Jalpaiguri, 2003, p. 95.
28. Ashok Mitra, West Bengal District Census Handbook, Malda, 1951, Calcutta, p. 144.
29. G.E. Lambourn, *Bengal District Gazetteers,* Malda, Bengal Secretariat Press, Calcutta, 1918, p. 96.
30. Ashim Kumar Sarkar, *Nationalism, Communalism and Partition in Bengal: Maldah 1905-53,* Readers Service, Kolkata, 2013, p. 33.
31. Platinum Jubilee Souvenir, Jalalia Girls' School, Malda, 1994, p. 12.
32. Jatindra Chandra Sengupta, *West Bengal District Gazetteers, Malda,* Calcutta, 1969, p. 207.
33. Moksundar Rahman, *Natorer Maharani Bhawani* (Queen Bhawani of Natore), Rajshahi, 1988, p. 24.

CHAPTER 5

Growth and Development of Sabha-Samitis

INTRODUCTION

The nineteenth-century Bengal Renaissance was certainly a new phase in the intellectual history of Bengal. The middle-class consciousness was strengthened and its associational base was broadened from the Atmiya Sabha of 1815, through the Bengal British India Society of 1843 and the British Indian Association of 1851 to the Indian Association of 1876. It was flowing through other channels also like the Patriot's Association (1865), the Hindu Mela (1867) and the Students' Association (1875). The Brahmo Samaj movement became a potent and living force during this period, under the dynamic leadership of Keshub Chandra Sen.[1] Binay Sarkar has rightly remarked,

> These societies and associations were the harbingers of the new awakening in Bengal among the urban middle class, because Bengal or India had not known any such societies organized for collective thinking and discussion until the nineteenth century.[2]

Rajat Sanyal's *Voluntary Associations and The Urban Public Life in Bengal*, Nishith Ranjan Ray (ed.) *Public Associations in India From The Early Years of the Nineteenth Century to Independence*, Arun Kumar Chattarjee's *Unabinsha Shatabdir Sabha Samiti o Bangla Sahitya*, Manindra Nath Bandhapadhyay and Santosh Kumar Dey's *Unabinsha Shatabdir Sabha Samiti* need to be cited. The discussion of these books is related mainly to those associations which came up in Calcutta and its adjacent areas. Unfortunately, no serious study has yet has been made regarding the associations of North

Bengal. The area consisted of the districts of Dinajpur, Bogura, Pabna, Rajshahi, Rangpur, Malda, Darjeeling, Jalpaiguri and the Princely State of Coochbehar, parts of Purnea, Goalpara and part of the district of Kamrup. Professional historians appear to be reluctant to come forward to undertake this task in a concerted and coordinated manner. This is the vacuum that this chapter seeks to fill in.

SABHA-SAMITIS (ASSOCIATIONS) IN NORTH BENGAL

The first association of North Bengal, established in Coochbehar in 1859, was the Desha Hitaishani Sabha. A few British high officials such as Colonel J.C. Haughton and H. Beveridge contributed a lot towards its establishment. In 1864 it was renamed as Coochbehar Hitaishani Sabha. Its members were asked to repay their social debt by participating in welfare activities on behalf of the Coochbehar royal state.[3]

The Rajshahi Association was established on 21 July 1872. The fundamental objective was (a) to provide education, (b) to promote the cultivation of arts and science, (c) to assist in the development of healthy public opinion, (d) to promote sanitation, public health and some other objects of an altruistic nature. The president was Raja Prativa Nath Ray of Dighapatia and the secretary was Babu Saral Kumar Ghosh, M.A.[4]

In 1873, the Gyandayini Sabha was established in the village of Chatmahar, Pabna. The weekly *Gyanbikashini* was the mouthpiece of the association. For the purpose of publication, a printing press was set up by Raja Haranath Roychaudhury, the *zamindar* of Dubalahati, Rajshahi. On this occasion, it was written in *Grambarta Prakashika*, 'It was beyond our expectations that a printing press was set up in the village from where a weekly bought out named *Gyanbikashini*. Beside this two other weeklies named *Pallidarshan* and *Subadhini* were also published from the same printing house'. It was also stated:

> Attitude of few Bengali youths, after being received education from the Hindu College, have overwhelmingly been changed. Many of them were initiated

into Brahmonism. To stop this conversion and properly propagate the ideals of Hindu religion, a Dharma Sabha was established in Rajshahi. For this purpose, the authorities of the association had to publish a weekly named *Hindu Ranjika*. The office of the association was established by Anandanath Roy Bahadur, the Raja of Natore in 1272 BS.

Earlier there was no press in Rajshahi. All the numbers of this weekly were published from Dhaka which was very cost-effective. To remove this difficulty Raja Haranath Roychaudhury built a printing press at the expense of nearly one thousand rupees. This magazine used to publish articles particularly related to Hindu society and religion.[5]

The Varendra Anusandhan Samiti, established on 27 September 1910 in Rajshahi, with the object to explore and record the aspects of ancient history and culture of Bengal. In a conference of the Bangiya Sahitya Sammelan held on BS 1314 at Kasimbazar, the proposal for setting up an institution to study and explore the untold history of ancient Bengal was first raised by Ramasundar Trivedi. In the next two years, the proposal gained wide attention from the society. In the next two conferences of Bangiya Sahitya Sammelan held in Rajshahi and Bhagalpur respectively, the proposal was acclaimed highly by a group of intellectuals. As a consequence of the conferences, Varendra Anusandhan Samiti came into existence. The leading personalities behind its establishment were the historian Akshay Kumar Maitra, Maharaja Girija Nath Roy Bahadur, Ramaprasad Chanda the professor of Rajshahi Collegiate School and Sharat Kumar Roy.[6]

The building of the research society was constructed in 1911. Historian Akshay Kumar Maitra was the director, Sharat Kumar Roy the president and Ramaprasad Chanda was the secretary of this research society. Ramaprasad Chanda later became the head of the Archaeological Survey of India, Delhi. Most of the teachers of Rajshahi College like Dinesh Chandra Bhattacharya Professor of Sanskrit and Gulam Yazdani Professor of Persian and Arabian language were the members of the Samiti. He was later appointed as the Head of the Archaeological Society, Hyderabad. All of them were the disciples of Akshay Kumar Maitra. The first excavation in the historical sites of Paharpur was led by Akshay Kumar Maitra under the guidance of the Archaeological Survey of India. The entire excavation was assisted by the department of archaeology, University of Calcutta. R.C. Majumder has rightly commented, 'This regular excavation of an archaeological site through private efforts is the first of its kind in India, and may be regarded as the crowning glory of Akshay Kumar Maitra'.[7]

According to Nirmal Chandra Chaudhury, this excavation explored the ancient glory of Bengal during the Pala age. For the purpose of preceding the spirit of such excavations, Greater Indian Society was formed in Calcutta. Akshay Kumar Maitra was the key figure behind it. *Bharat Shilper Katha, Mir Qashim, Gauder Katha, Sagarika, Banger Puratattvasamgraha* and *A Short History of the Natore Raj* are some examples of his outstanding works. He was inspired by the works of Kangal Harinath Majumder. For the purpose of enriching people with the thought and works of Kangal Harinath, he started a number of cultural associations like Kumarkhali Sabha, Ekadashi Sabha, Adhyaksha Sabha, etc. For his Cast illuminating research works in history, the British government honoured him with the title 'Kaizar-i-Hind'.[8]

In 1899, he started the publication of a journal *Aitihasik Chitra* from Rajshahi which, though short-lived, did valuable work by publishing original work as well as translations of *Riyaz-us-Salatin* by Rampran Gupta and *Indika* by Bhabani Govinda Chaudhury. Akshay Kumar Maitra received great encouragement from Rabindranath Tagore who wrote a remarkable preface to its first volume, laying down lines of real independent research on local and regional history.[9] His collections of articles as well as mode of his writings ushered a new era of historical writings.[10] Akshay Kumar Maitra also built a museum in Rajshahi namely 'Shakuntala Natya Samiti'. It was renamed Victoria Theatre. He also wrote several plays in Bengali like *Basabdatta, Abahan* and *Asha.*[11] It is no exaggeration to say that Akshay Kumar Maitra was the leading Bengali historian of his day who opened up new possibilities of writing history, critical and well documented.

The Samiti published several rare books and manuscripts in Bengali. Side by side, publication in English and Sanskrit also continued. *Inscriptions of Bengal* (vol. III) by Nanigopal Majumder, *Gaudlekhamala* and *Gaudrajmala* (1322) by Rajanikanta Chakrabarty deserve to be mentioned here. Akshay Kumar Maitra later wrote an article in *Modern Review* where he explored the theme of the book *Gaurrajamala.*[12] A copy of the article was sent to Vincent Smith. Being overwhelmingly impressed with the article, he wrote, 'I have much pleasure in acknowledging the receipt of your guide and two pamphlets on the stones of Varendra which though small in bulk, contains much new and important historical information'.[13]

According to Samar Pal, the most significant contribution of Varendra Anusandhan Samiti was the establishment of Rajshahi Museum, one of the finest and smallest museums in Asia. It was the brain child of Sarat Kumar Bose. For this purpose, in 1912 he and Ramaprasad Chanda met the Divisional Commissioner of Rajshahi who made all the arrangements to meet the Governor-General of Bengal in Darjeeling. In August 1912, Lord Carmichael visited Rajshhai. The visit was marked by fireworks and illuminations. He was highly impressed to see the archaeological collections. As a consequence of this, he gave permission for the construction of the museum in Rajshhai. The foundation of this museum was laid by Lord Carmichael on 13 November 1916 and it was inaugurated by Lord Ronaldsay on 27 November 1919.[14] Sarat Kumar Bose sent Nani Gopal Majumder, the curator of the museum to Sir John Marshall the Director General of the Archaeological Survey of India to enrich him with information on the modern and advanced training on archaeological excavation. Sarat Bose allotted a fund for excavations in different parts of North Bengal. The building was constructed on the land provided by Raja Pramathnath Roy at the expense of 65,000 rupees. Several news and reports about this museum were published in contemporary Bengali periodicals like *Prabashi, Sahitya* and so on. The Varendra Research Society survived till 1963. But the museum is still there and now it is being administered by Rajshahi University.[15]

The Samaj Sanskarini Sabha, established in 1875, started a modernization movement in Darjeeling. The Nabya Ekta Sabha and the Himadri Harisabha founded for this purpose in Darjeeling in 1876 played a central role in the society.[16]

The Dinajpur Bhatpara Unnati Sadhani Sabha, established in 1878, contributed a lot to education and scholarships were offered to needy students. *Suhriday*, a yearly magazine in Bengali was the mouthpiece of the organization.[17] The same year, Maharaja Girijanath Ray laid the foundation of a literary Association called Pancha Ratna. The real inspiration behind it was Pandit Mahesh Cahndra Tarka Churamani. The Nitya Dharma Badhani Sabha came up in Dinajpur district in 1860 under the leadership of Babu Girish Chandra Chakrabarty and Pandit Amarnath Bhattacharya.[18] This was undertaken by a number of individuals like *zamindar* Radha Govinda Ray and Maharaja Girijanath Ray. The Bidhayani Sabha of Calcutta opened its branch in Dinajpur district in 1904 with the aim of promoting science and technical education. Maharaja Girijanath Ray was its first president. He also established the Dinajpur Natya Samiti in 1913. All the leading personalities of this cultural association were Brahmins like Nishikanta Ray Chaudhuri, Girija Mahan Niyogi and Kshitish Chandra Ray Chaudhuri. The Bengali poet Sharat Chandra Chattapadhyay and Tarashankar Bandapadhyay made regular visits there. Later it took the shape of the Raiganj Institute in 1934.[19]

The Debating Club of Darjeeling established in 1884 was a popular cultural association of Darjeeling. At the initial stage, its members were fifty in number. The royal families of Cooch-behar and Burdwan were its chief patrons. Through the munificence of tea industrialist Bipra Das Pal Chaudhury and the then Maharajadhiraja of Burdwan, it got its own building. It had primarily two fundamental objectives—(a) to improve the social, national and moral condition of the people; (b) to cultivate the power of speech and reason among its members. To promote a bond of cohesion among the local Bengalis, the association organized festivals like Durga Puja, Saraswati Puja, *Paela Baisakh* (Bengali Hindu New Year's Day) and dramatic as well as musical performances at its own auditorium.[20]

The Suniti Sancharini Sabha established on 8 January 1895 was a landmark in the history of women of Coochbehar State. This day was observed as the death anniversary of Keshub Chandra Sen by the Coochbehar Nababidhan Brahmo Samaj. However, all the members of the Suniti Sancharini Sabha were Brahmos and their main aim was to improve the living condition of women.[21]

The birth of Rangpur Sahitya Parishad in 1906 ushered in an era of golden age in the cultural history of North Bengal. Under its corroboration the *Uttarbanga Sahitya Sammelan* (North Bengal Literary Conference) was set up in Rangpur in 1908. Most of its members were *zamindar*s and lawyers by profession. Raja Jagadindra Deb Raikat, pleader Umagati Ray and Rai Saheb Panchanan Barma played a key role. It did not last long and continued for only twenty years.[22]

The foundation of Kamrup Anusandhan Samiti in 1912 was the immediate effect of the literary pursuits of Uttarbanga Sahitya Sammilini. Its main objective was to explore the unexcavated facts of the regional history of the North-East and North Bengal. The proposal of establishing Kamrup Anusandhan Samiti was first made in the fifth conference by *zamindar* Mrityunjoy Roychaudhury of Kundi and Amanatulla Ahmed of Coochbehar. They had the dream to enlighten people on the history and literature of a vast tract consisting of the districts of Dinajpur, Bogura, Pabna, Rajshahi, Rangpur, Malda, Darjeeling, Jalpaiguri the Princely State of Coochbehar, parts of Purnea, Goalpara and part of the district of Kamrup. This geographical region was known to them as 'Greater North Bengal'.[23]

Moreover, from the beginning of Uttarbanga Sahitya Sammilani, the participation of *zamindar*s and intellectuals of Assam in its several conferences was a very common feature. In the first conference, Priyanath Chakrabarty, Damodar Dutta Chaudhury, Satish Chandra Barua and others participated. Pravat Chandra Barua, the Raja of Gauripur sent a welcome address to the organizers. He was also the president of the reception committee of the third conference held at Gauripur on 22-3 January 1910. Dwijesh Chandra Chakrabarty, the Dewan of Gauripur (father of poet Amiya Chakrabarty) was the secretary. The president of the third conference was Padmanava Bhattacharya Vidyavinod, a renowned scholar and professor of Cotton College, Assam. Thus, it proved that there was a strong bond between the landholders and intellectuals of both Assam and Bengal and this finally laid the foundation of the Kamrup Anusandhan Samiti.[24]

Jitendranath Bhup Bahadur, the Maharaja of Coochbehar, was the main patron of Kamrup Anusandhan Samiti. Mahamahopadhyay Dhireswaracharyya Kaviratna, Padmanath Bhattacharya Vidyavinad, Taranath Kavyavinod, Pratap Chandra Goswami, Govinda Chandra Sharma, Uttam Chandra Barua, Rajani Kumar Das, Suresh Chandra Bandopadhyay, Umesh Chandra Dey, Gopal Krishna Dey, Mahamahopadhyay Hara Prasad Shastri, Nagendra Nath Basu and Akshay Kumar Maitrya were the founding members and contributed largely to its growth and development. Rangpur Sahitya Parishad was the first organization in colonial Bengal which first laid the foundation of an association designed exclusively to highlight the unexcavated history and archaeology of Assam. However, a branch of Kamrup Anusandhan Samiti was also established in Rangpur and Surendra Chandra Roychaudhury, the secretary of Rangpur Sahitya Parishad was the in-charge. But how long it continued is not known.[25]

The Rajbansi Kshatriya Samiti, founded in 1910, looked at government patronage for the upliftment of social status of their caste. It also sought to mobilize the masses. Only the Kshatriyas were eligible for membership of the association. In its fourth annual conference in 1913, it was decided that Mandali Samitis would be set up in every village to reach the common people. By 1918 a highly developed network of village organizations was operating under the Kshatriya Samiti. These Samitis were supposed to function as village governments and courts of arbitration, they would spread education and preach reforms of rituals and also function as cooperative societies for the economic improvement of the Rajbansi villagers.[26] The Rajbansi Kshatriya Samiti offered scholarships for the education of the poor Rajbansi students. With these students, a Kshatriya Chhatra Samiti was formed and its members were asked to repay their social debt by participating in welfare activities to help the poor members of the community.[27]

Sumit Sarkar shows that the Swadeshi movement was not only confined to boycott of foreign goods. It spread rapidly to the field of education also. National schools were springing up in different districts of Bengal.[28] According to Ashim Kumar Sarkar, Professor Binay Kumar Sarkar of Calcutta University played a leading role in establishing the National Education Council of Malda (Maldah Jatiya Shiksha Samiti) in June 1907. A group of leading personalities like Prankrishna Bhaduri, Bipin Behari Ghosh, Radesh

Chandra Seth, Md. Nur Baksh and Rajendra Narayan Chaudhuri were associated with the association. All were eminent lawyers and well known for their social work. The association had set up eight schools at Malda, Kutubpur, Kaligram, Dharmapur, Paranpur, Jadupur and Malatipur. Girls' schools were opened at Kaligram and Dharampur. It worked as a cultural and literary forum by organizing popular lectures, symposia, seminars and tried their best to foster the spirit of women's education. It also published periodicals for the new literates.[29]

The Bengali Association of Darjeeling was established in 1908 on land leased out by the Maharaja of Burdwan at Dowhill Road. The Bengali tea planters had an important role in setting up this cultural institution probably to pursue their cultural interests and social interactions. Through the munificence of S.B. Dey the Association got its building in 1930. Later it was named Raj Rajeswari Hall after the name of the wife of S.B. Dey.[30]

The Coochbehar Sahitya Sabha founded in 1915 (BS 1322) ushered an era of golden age in the history of Coochbehar. Maharaja Jitendra Narayan, Princess Indira Devi, Prince Victor Nityendra Narayan and Amanatullah Ahmed played an important role behind its foundation. It was the brainchild of Varendra Research Association, which had the fundamental goal to excavate the untold history, anthropology of the north-east region with special reference to Coochbehar. The mouthpiece of the association was *Paricharika* published by Nirupama Devi, wife of Victor Nityendra Narayan. The writings of Rabindranath Tagore, Akshay Kumar Maitra, Mrinalini Devi, Promoth Chaudhury and Suniti Devi were its main attraction.[31]

The Debating Club established by a group of leading tea planters like Tarini Prasad Roy, Jogesh Chandra Ghosh and Jogodindra Deb Raikot in 1917, marked the actual beginning of modernization in Jalpaiguri town.[32] Primarily, it was held at the residence of Jogodindra Raikot where literary discussions and cultural debates on heterogeneous subjects took place. The birth of the *Jalpaiguri Sahitya Samiti* in 1928 was the outcome of a group of people like Umapada Banarjee, Mohini Mohan Ghosh, Jitendra Nath Mukherjee, Priti Nidhan Ray and Promoth Nath Basu.[33]

The Hillmen's Association established in 1917 with the objective of educational and economical improvement of the hill people, creation of the spirit of cooperation and brotherhood and the protection of their civil rights. R.N. Sinha was the president and Rai Bahadur C. Tendupla, J.S. Lama were the vice-presidents. J.B. Thapa was the secretary. Swami Bisuddhananada had a close relationship with this association.[34] A group of members of the Samaj under the leadership of Bahadur Rai, founded the Hill people's Social Union in 1920 by the beginning of the twentieth century.[35] The Nepali Sahitya Sammelan, founded in 1924, marked the actual beginning of the growth and development of Nepali language and culture.[36]

In 1924, the All Bengal Student's Union established its first branch in Jalpaiguri. In contrast, the Muslim students of Jalpaiguri established a similar association named the 'Muhamadden Student's Association', with the aim of financially supporting the Muslim students. *Nawjawan* was the mouthpiece of this association.[37] Sahityika, a popular cultural association of the town, came up with the efforts of Jitendra Nath Mukherjee, a teacher by profession. A number of learned persons like Indubhushan Majumder, Principal of Ananda Chandra College, Upendra Nath Barman, Kumudini Chakrabarty, Ganesh Chandra Roy, Dr Charu Chandra Sanyal, Bhabaranjan Ganguly, Bhabani Ghosh, Debabrata Ghatak, Satyendra Mahan Moullick and others were associated with it. Articles, poems and short stories written by them were published several times in *Desh, Namer Antarale*, the short story written by Satyendra Mahan Moullick was published in the first issue of *Desh* in 1933. He was a lawyer by profession. The journey of Sahityika came to an end in 1945.[38]

The Jalpaiguri Cultural Institute was established on 7 September 1941. The next year, a literary conference was organized on 17 July by Pritinidhan Roy which was attended by several poets and writers.[39] Narayan Gangopadhyay of Ananda Chandra College, Jalpaiguri who later established himself as a renowned Bengali poet, read his article 'Jugo-Biplab O Sahitya' there.[40] The Muslim Sahitya Samiti, founded in 1931 by Tajmal Hossain maintained its distinction from the Bengali Hindu associations of Jalpaiguri town.[41] The Marwari Sangha was founded in Jalpaiguri town in 1931 to safeguard the interests of the Marwari people of the district both economically and educationally.[42] The Alipurduar Sahitya Parishad established in 1941 was the first cultural organization.[43] The Pallimangal Sammelan came up at Jalpaiguri town in the year 1943. Its chief founder and patron was Prasanna Deb Raikat. The fundamental aim of this association was to uplift the standard of living of the rural people.[44]

The Mahila Samiti of Jalpaiguri town established in 1928, was the first women's organization in North Bengal. Their goal was not limited only to women's emancipation; they also attempted to enrich the literary atmosphere as well. The setting up of Mahila Pathagar (female library) in 1945 was indeed a landmark in this direction.[45] At a later stage, the members of Jalpaiguri Mahila Samiti formed the Mahila Atmaraksha Samiti (Women Self-defence Association) which played an important role during the Tebhaga Movement in 1946. The Mahila Atmaraksha Samiti of Darjeeling district was established under the leadership of comrade Mira Chattarje.[46]

The Darjeeling branch of the All Bengal Women Conference was established in Darjeeling in 1930. It was popularly known as Saraj Nalini Dutta Memorial Association. The Sandhani Mahila Samiti of Kurseong was established in Kurseong for the benefit of local women of all communities. It had a prolonged relation with Brahmo Samaj of Kurseong.[47]

The Darjeeling branch of the All India Women Conference was established in Darjeeling town in 1947 for the welfare of women, children and destitutes. It distributed medicines and nourishing diet to the poor and needy patients, participated in community cooking, feeding the harijans and entertaining children on occasions of national importance. During the Chinese aggression, the organization donated woollen garments, magazines, food and first aid to the *jawans*. The Bangiya Mahila Samiti was established in Darjeeling on 23 June 1956. Its membership was restricted only to Bengali women. The Pulungdung Basti Mahila Samiti of Sukhiapokhri was established in 1965. It holds a literary class daily and imparts training in clay modelling, sewing and knitting besides organizing games for the members and staging cultural functions every year.[48]

CONCLUSION

The associations give one a complete picture regarding the socio-cultural history of North Bengal during the period of this study. Among scholars who made substantial contributions to highlight the history of North Bengal were Akshay Kumar Maitra, Ramaprasad Chanda, Sarat Kumar Roy of Dighapatia and others. It was Akshay Kumar Maitra who was the life and soul of not only the Varendra Anusandhan Samiti (Varendra Research Society) but also of the new movement for the reconstruction of Bengal history. This society rendered invaluable service to historical research by publishing original sourcebooks of Bengal history like *Ramcharitam* by Pandit Haraprasad Shastri (1910), *Gauda-lekhamala* by Ramaprasad Chanda (1912), and *Inscriptions of Bengal* by Nanigopal Sarkar (1929). *Aitihasik Chitra*, published by Akshay Kumar Maitra from Rajshahi, was India's first historical account written in any native language. The establishment of Coochbehar Sahitya Sabha, Bengali Association and Debating Club of Darjeeling the Rangpur Sahitya Parishad proves that the influence of the Renaissance was not confined in Calcutta; it took long strides in North Bengal, too. The *maharaja*s of Coochbehar, *zamindar*s of Rajshahi and Rangpur, Bengali tea industrialists of Jalpaiguri town played a key role in laying the foundation of these associations. They gave one new ideas of education, a new direction to life and brought great changes in society. But what needs to be focused here through the above discussion is that these associations remained confined to a small elite group (the so-called *bhadralok*) who were the economic and cultural beneficiaries of the colonial rule. Socially, they were wealthy Hindu and Muslims, and consolidated their position as landholders, pleaders and physicians. They had little contact with the toiling masses.

NOTES

1. Binoy Ghosh, 'The Press in Bengal', in Narendra Krishna Sinha (ed.) *The History of Bengal 1757-1905,* University of Calcutta, 1996, p. 228.
2. Binoy Ghosh, *Selections from English Periodicals of 19th Century Bengal 1878-80,* vol. VII, Papyrus, Calcutta, 1978, pp. X-XI.
3. Annual Proceedings of *Cooch Behar Hitaishani Sabha,* for the year of 1871-2, Coochbehar State Press, Coochbehar, 1873, p. 12.
4. List of Associations Recognized by Government of Bengal, Home Department (Pol), Bengal Government Press, Alipore, Bengal, 1946, p. 41.
5. Brajendranath Bandopadhyay, *Bangla Samayikpatra* (Bengali Periodicals), vol. I, Calcutta, B.S. 1379, pp. 208-9.
6. Muhammad Nasiruddin, 'Associations of Bengal: Their Activities and Role in Politics and Society 1851-85', unpublished PhD Thesis, Jadavpur University, p. 603.
7. Ananda Gopal Ghosh and Papiya Ghosh, *Uttarbanger Itihas O Samaj* (History and Society of North Bengal), vol. III, Sangbedan, Malda, 2017, pp. 53-4.
8. Nirmal Chandra Chaudhury, *Akshay Kumar Maitra: Jiban O Sadhana,* (The Life and Pursuit of Akshay Kumar Maitra), University of North Bengal, 1984, pp. 12-14.
9. Inaugural address by D.C. Sircar in the seminar Proceedings of Balurghat College, South Dinajpur, 4-5 February, 1982, p. 8.
10. Icchamuddin Sarkar, 'Akshay Kumar Moitra: His Ideas and Method of Interpretations as Reflected in his Historical Works', *Journal of the Asiatic Society of Bangladesh* (Hum.), vol. 67(1), 2022, p. 14.
11. Samar Pal, *Natorer Itihas* (History of Natore), vol. II, Rajshahi, 1984, p. 19.
12. Foreword, 'The Ancient Monuments of Varendra' by Akshay Kumar Maitra, Monograph-7, in K.C. Sarkar (ed.), *Varendra Research Museum,* June 1949, p. 26.
13. Fazlul Haque, 'Akshay Kumar O Varendra Gabeshana Jadughar [Akshay Kumar and the Varendra Research Museum]', in Tasiqul Islam (ed.) *Rajshahi Sahitya Patrika* (Literary Magazine of Rajshahi), October 1989, pp. 119-24.
14. Samar Pal, op. cit., p. 19.
15. Safiuddin Choudhury, 'Kumar Sharat Kumar Ray' (Prince Sharat Kumar Ray), in Safiuddin Choudhury (ed.) *Rajshahir Pratibha* (The Genius of Rajshahi), Rajshahi, 2000, p. 9.

16. Jahar Sen, *Himalaya Charcha O Darjeeling Prasanga* (Studying of Himalaya in the Context of Darjeeling), Cikitushi Prakashani, Kolkata, 2013, p. 52.
17. Muntasir Mamun, *Unish Shatake Bangladesher Samayik Patra* (Periodicals of Bangladesh during Nineteenth Century), Bangla Academy, Dhaka, 1985, p. 93.
18. Ananda Gopal Ghosh, 'Unish o Bish Shataker Uttarbanger Sabha-Samiti-Samaj' (Associations and Society of North Bengal during Nineteenth and Twentieth Century's), in Girindra Narayan Ray and Ankush Bhatta (eds.) *Maitrayani*, vol. 1, BS 1396, University of North Bengal, p. 41.
19. *Dinajpur Patrika*, winter issue, Paush Sankhya BS 1311, p. 168.
20. Muhammad Nasiruddin, op. cit., p. 611.
21. Swapan Kumar Roy, 'Prachin Cooch Behar-e Mudran Jantrer Abirbhab O Pragatir Unmesh (Growth and Development of Printing Press in Coochbehar)', *Kochbihar Jela Sankhya* (Special Volume on the District of Coochbehar), Government of West Bengal, BS 1413, p. 26.
22. *Rangpur Sahitya Parishad Patrika*, Rangpur, BS 1324, pp. 23-4.
23. Centenary Volume of Kamrup Anusandhan Samiti (Kamrup Research Society), Guwahati, 2010, p. 8.
24. Ananda Gopal Ghosh and Papiya Dutta, op. cit., pp. 73-7.
25. Proceedings of the Kamrup Anusandhan Samiti (Kamrup Research Society), Guwahati, 1993, p. 31.
26. Sekhar Bandyopadhyay, *Caste Politics and The Raj 1872-1937*, K.P. Bagchi Publication, Calcutta, 1990, p. 144.
27. Upendra Nath Barmen, *Thakur Panchanan Barmar Jiban Charit* (Biography of Panchanan Barma), Jalpaiguri, BS 1387, pp. 16, 29.
28. Sumit Sarkar, *Swadeshi Movement in Bengal 1905-8*, Peoples Publishing House, Delhi, 1978, p. 180.
29. Ashim Kumar Sarkar, *Nationalism, Communalism and Partition in Bengal Maldah 1905-53*, Readers Service, Kolkata, 2013, pp. 33-4.
30. K.C. Bhanja, *Darjeeling at a Glance*, Modern India Press, Darjeeling, 1941, p. 43
31. Swapan Kumar Ray, op. cit., p. 196.
32. Malay Shankar Bhattacharya, 'Nationalist Movement and Freedom Struggle in Some Selected Areas of Northern Bengal 1857-1947', unpublished PhD Thesis, North Bengal University, 1986, p. 12.
33. Bhubaneswar Mukhopadhyaya, *Jogesh Jiban* (Life of Jogesh), Jalpaiguri, BS 1371, p. 36.
34. Jahar Sen, op. cit., p. 63.
35. Amiya Kumar Banerjee, *West Bengal District Gazetteers: Darjeeling*, Calcutta, 1980, p. 583.

36. A.J. Dash, *West Bengal District Gazetteers: Darjeeling,* Calcutta, 1947, p. 279.
37. *Trisrota,* Jalpaiguri, 15 April 1928, p. 14.
38. Ananda Gopal Ghosh, *Jalpaigurir Sahityalekha O Ananya Prabandha* (Cultural History of Jalpaiguri and Other Essays), Sangbedan, Malda, BS 1417, p. 18.
39. Ananda Bazar Patrika, Calcutta, 8 Shrabon, 1349 BS.
40. *Trisrota,* Jalpaiguri, 7 June 1942, p. 27.
41. Kamakhya Prasad Chakrabarty, *Sekaler Jalpaiguri Sahar o Samajik Jibaner Kichu Katha,* Jalpaiguri (Few Words of Social Life of Contemporary Jalpaiguri Town), Sigma Information Technology Publication, 2004, p. 61.
42. Amiya Kumar Banerjee, op. cit., p. 586.
43. Narayan Chandra Saha, 'Jalpaiguri Jelar Marwari Samaj' (The Marwari Society of the District of Jalpaiguri), in Aravinda Kar (ed.) *Kiratbhumi* (Land of Kiartas), vol. 1, Jalpaiguri, 1994, p. 178.
44. Nirmal Chandra Chaudhury (ed.) *Raikat Bansha O Tahader Rajyer Sankhipta Bibaran* (A Concise History of the Raikat Dynasty and the State), by Jagadindradeb Raikat, Jalpaiguri, published by Uttarbanga Itihas Parishad (Historical Association of North Bengal), Jalpaiguri, 1389 BS, p. 45.
45. Bharati Ray, 'Freedom Movement and Women's Awakening in Bengal 1911-29', *Indian Historical Review,* July 1985-January 1986, p. 129.
46. Jibesh Sarkar, *Darjeeling Jelar Communist Andalan Prasange* (Regarding the Communist Movement in the District of Darjeeling), (vol. I), Ratanlal Brahman Memorial Trust, Siliguri, 2004, p. 104.
47. Ananda Gopal Ghosh, 'Darjeeling, Kurseong O Kalimpong Sahar Gathane Bangalider Abadan' (Contribution of Bengali People to the Formation of Darjeeling, Kurseong and Kalimpong Town), in Supam Biswas (ed.) *Himalay Banga: Prasanga Darjeeling Nama,* (History of Darjeeling in the Context of Himalaya), Readers Service, Kolkata, 2022, p. 76.
48. Amiya Kumar Banerjee, op. cit., pp. 587-8.

CHAPTER 6

Performing Art, Music and Culture

INTRODUCTION

The creative response of nineteenth-century Bengal to the stimulus of Western thought and culture has been felt a lot in literature and music. In nineteenth century, the only predominance in the field of drama was in the hand of the rich people of Calcutta or neighbouring areas. Basically, plays were performed for the recreation of Englishmen, Bengali landlords and servants. Bengali theatre (1795), Bidyotsahini Mancha of Kaliprasanna Singha (1858), theatre hall of Raja Pratap Chandra Singha at Belgachia (1858) and Jatindra Mahan Thakur were the main centres of performing plays and considered the greatest achievement of the period. Enthusiasm for the theatre which came over the Bengali society in the course of the seventh decade of the nineteenth century with the establishment of the Begachia Theatre, inspired the coming up of many more respectable amateur societies.[1]

There is a good number of works on the drama and music of colonial Bengal. Among the earlier works, Ajit Kumar Ghosh's *Bangla Nataker Itihas* (Calcutta, 1999), Ashutash Bhattacharya's *Bangla Natya Sahityer Itihas* (vol. I & II, Kolkata, 2004), Darshan Chaudhuri's *Bangla Theatre er Itiahs* (Kolkata, 1995), Kshetra Gupta's *Banglar Ranga Mancha* (Kolkata, 2008) discussed the history of theatre and drama in colonial Bengal. These books also provide a list of plays and dramatic personalities. But the focal point of their work is Calcutta and its adjacent areas. These books are completely silent about the plays that were staged in Jalpaiguri, Dinajpur, Malda, and the Princely State of Coochbehar. There was no mention of the artists from North Bengal who gave quality performance on the stages in Calcutta. Most importantly, there is hardly any discussion about the evening drama practice of the Bengali *babus* in their respective tea gardens. Hence an attempt has been made to make a study in this field.

THE PRINCELY STATE OF COOCHBEHAR

Coochbehar was a well-known name in the history of drama in Bengal. The setting up of the Khagrabari Dramatic Club in 1870 was truly a significant event in the history of drama in Bengal. The *maharajas* of Coochbehar not only patronized the institution with their munificence and enthusiasm but took an active part in the development of drama. It paved the way for popularizing drama and theatre in the royal state of Coochbehar. The staging of the plays was the result of the intense interest of a band of famous scholars which included a galaxy of names such as Purushotwam Vidyabagish, Siddhanath and Mohonath. They were renowned Brahmin scholars. Along with the practice of Sanskrit language and culture, they became interested in drama, writing, acting and stage setting as a part of a healthy social life.

The journey of this dramatic club started with the performance of the play 'Ratnabali'. At the initial stage, Sanskrit plays were performed but later Bengali plays too were staged. The famous play *Draupadi Parinay* by Pandit Siddhanath was staged here in 1884. This dramatic club had deep respect in the royal court. Maharaja Nripendra Narayan, was overwhelmingly impressed with the performance of the play *Harishchandra* and sanctioned adequate grants for renovating the building. As a consequence, the permanent stage of this club, popularly known as 'Karunamayi Hall', came into existence.[2]

This dramatic club, later came to be known as Young Men's Theatrical Club. With the founding of Lansdowne Hall in 1911, the club got the opportunity to perform on the stage there. The play 'Mughal Sandhya' written by Ashrukumar Dasgupta and Bimal Kumar Chakrabarty, staged at Lansdowne Hall in 1921, was highly appreciated. This led to the birth of Coochbehar Musical

Club in 1919. However, the Young Men's Theatrical Club, due to the dearth of money and enthusiasm, could not survive for long. The members of the royal family sometimes called upon to strengthen a troupe through the officials. But that effort was not fruitful. Around 1923, few playwrights of the Theatrical Club and Musical Club joined the Town Club, Coochbehar. In 1924, the journey of the Town Club in the field of drama and theatre started with the performance of the play 'Karnarjun'. This club attracted everyone's attention in everything from acting to stage decoration and scene planning.[3]

The Coochbehar Cultural Club, established in 1946, took the initiative to perform plays by female artistes of the town on the stage. They put up several famous plays like *Mirzafar, Dakghar, Down Train* and *Shahjahan.* This club, no doubt, played an outstanding role in conducting popular plays of modern times. Beyond the town, the tide of drama and theatre gained momentum in the subdivisions of Coochbehar. The Madanmahan Natya Samiti (1921) in Mekhliganj, Ashutosh Club in Mathabhanga, Vivekananda Club in Tufanganj, Jewells Club and Pioneer Club in Dinhata occupied a prominent position in the theatre world of Coochbehar. Under the management of Pragati Natya Sangha, there used to be a regular theatre competition with artistes from Bengal and Assam.[4]

The royal family of Coochbehar had a passion for sports and games. Maharaja Nripendra Narayan was a great lover of football and cricket. He founded the Bengal Gymkhana Club, Calcutta and also started the Coochbehar Cup Football Tournament in 1893. He was member of Mohun Bagan, the famous soccer club which received his patronage many times. The Maharaja also had a good cricket team. The first cricket tournament started in Coochbehar in 1907 under his patronage. Different Princely States of India represented the tournament with their cricket teams. The matches between them and the English cricketers were the biggest attraction of the tournament. He invited British officials from Calcutta and other parts of India to participate in shooting in the forests of Duars and Assam. Maharaja Jagaddipendra Narayan earned the reputation of a good and skilled cricketer. He led Bengal in Ranji

Trophy in 1943. He also led the Coochbehar XI in the IFA Shield Tournament held in Calcutta. Princess Gayatri Devi was an accomplished tennis and badminton players.[5]

THE DISTRICT OF DINAJPUR

One of the major mediums of urban culture in Dinajpur was drama along with singing. In 1904, drama reached its high watermark in Dinajpur with the establishment of Diamond Jubilee Theatre Hall. The prime role played in its founding was by Haricharan Sen. After a few years, with the same objective, a group of culturally motivated people of Balurghat took an initiative and thus the Balurghat Theatrical Association came up in 1909. After a few years, it came to be known as 'Balurghat Natya Mandir'. Radhacharan Bhattacharya, Umeshchandra Banerjee, Jadunath Roy, Chintaharan Mukherjee, Sashanka Sekhar Roy and others played a key role in laying the foundation of the theatre club. In 1920, the play *Bange Mussalman* written by Manmath Roy, the famous dramatist of Balurghat town, was staged there.[6]

In 1913, the Dinajpur Natya Samiti came into existence. They staged several famous plays like *Alamgir, Chandragupta, Priyambada, Billwamangal, Raja Pratapaditya, Prafulla, Manisha* and others. *Nishkriti* by Sharat Chandra Chattapadhyay and *Dui Purush* by Tarashankar Bondopadhyay were staged there under the direction of Sibprasad Kar. It is matter of pride that these two great novelists were both present in Dinajpur Natya Samiti during the performances of their plays. They were welcomed at Diamond Jubilee Hall with great joy and respect. Being highly honoured with the reception, Sharat Chandra has remarked that the artists of Dinajpur were not only skilled in acting but equally skilled in writing also. Tarashankar Bondopadhyay, watched the performances of Sibprasad Kar in the play *Dui Purush*, and told 'Dinajpur theatre has no comparison in the history of Bengal'. Such an incomparably beautiful staging of my play is possible only here and nowhere else. What I am not, what is not in my play, that undiscovered being of dramatic character, I found today by coming to Dinajpur to watch my play. Today I am blessed to see the true self through the eyes of the artist. The artists of Dinajpur are my namasya'. The style of production and performance of all these plays were close to that of the Girish era in the professional stage of Calcutta. These dramatic performances put new life to the cultural set up of Dinajpur.[7]

With the establishment of the Raiganj Institute in 1934, a permanent theatre came up in the town. Nirmal Ghosh, Sukumar Guha, Kamakhya Chatterjee and others played a pivotal role in laying the foundation of the theatre. Kamakhya Chatterjee acted in a female role opposite playwright Sishir Bhaduri at the Institute Hall of University of Calcutta.[8]

In 1942-3, Anti-Fascism Writers and Artists Association in Dinajpur organized programmes for patriotic songs and mass songs at various schools and colleges. Their main aim was to raise the spirit of nationalism among the youths. On 24 October 1944, this Association staged the play *Nabanna* written by Bijan Bhattacharya based on the Bengal Famine of 1770 in Dinajpur town. *Muktir Dak* (1923) and *Karagar* (1930), written by Manmath Roy accelerated the tempo of theatrical performances in Balurghat.[9] The Balurghat Town Club (1901), the Friends Union Club (1921) and Raiganj Town Club (1939) played the key role in popularizing theatre among the youths of the town.[10]

THE DISTRICT OF JALPAIGURI

Jalpaiguri, one of the most culturally traditional towns in North Bengal, had been practising music and songs for a long time. The cultural harvest was mainly literary. Earlier, playing music was not looked upon favourably in the middle-class society. Jagadindradev Raikot first realized the need for singing practice among the educated middle class of the town. As a consequence, the 'Sangit Samaj' came up in the town in 1917 at the household of the Raikot family. Every year great masters from different parts of India like Jaipur, Delhi and Agra used to come here and stay for a few months. The 'Students Association of Jalpaiguri Town' arranged several cultural competitions under the initiative of a group of young intellectuals like Sourindra Kumar Basu, Dhirendra

Nath Bagchi, Sushil Kumar Chakrabarty and Satyendra Prasad Roy. The main genres in such competitions were music, modern songs and recitations of poetry. The 'Prafulla Sangit Sangha' established in 1928 in the memory of Prafulla Sankar, a renowned classical singer of the town, opened up new directions in the rendering of music in the town. In December 1932, another music school was founded in the Brahmo Samaj Hall by a group of eminent persons of the town like Sorojendradev Raikot, Dinesh Chandra Roy and Selamat Hossain Khan. Through these schools, the standard of music in Jalpaiguri town gradually improved.[11]

Besides the Raikots, the Rahut family played a great role in spreading music and dance in society. With this objective, competitions were started on a large scale from 1942. Rabindracharcha gained wide attention among the people in the city under the patronage of the Rahuts. Sankar Mukhopadhyay, the great Rabindra Sangit singer of the period, played an outstanding role in this field. The establishment of the music school named Chandam in the premises of Arya Natya Samaj was a landmark in the cultural life of the town. Samarendradev Raikot brought in Indradev Sanyal, the famous dancer of that time, from Calcutta to teach the children of the town. With their tireless efforts, music and dance flourished to a great extent. After a few years, Indradev Sanyal returned to his own place and this gap was filled up by Taru Singh and his wife, the famous Manipuri dancer of that time. Among the five districts of North Bengal during the British Raj, Samarendradev Raikot of Jalpaiguri was the first artist who has the credit to record music. He was invited to different parts of Bengal to perform his music.[12]

Bengali theatre took a significant turn in Jalpaiguri town with the Swadeshi movement. A tendency to glorify the past and the essence of nationalism became the major theme of the plays. From 1905 to 1924 theatre was basically centred round the Arya Natya Samaj, established in 1902. Plays were staged every Saturday and Sunday and promoted by handbills in horse drawn carts. At that time dancing was inextricably linked with acting. A number of dramatic groups from different parts of Bengal and Assam took part in several programmes organized by the Arya Natya Samaj. It proved the contribution of this dramatic club in popularizing drama in the town to a great extent. Ganesh Roy and Tarapada Bandopadhyay had great respect for all the theatre workers of the town associated with drama. The historical play *Pratapaditya* had a great impact on the audience.[13]

Next to it was the Bandhab Natya Samaj, another famous theatre group in Jalpaiguri town. As far as it is known, a group of theatre lovers called the 'Friends Union Club' established in 1923, staged plays at the household of the Sanyals and others places. Next year, they formed a dramatic club called 'Friends Dramatic Club'. In Bengali, it was called Bandhab Natya Samaj. The founding members of this club were Nagendranath Mahalanwalis, Makhleshwar Rahman, Umapada Bandopadhayay, Ganesh Sanyal, Suren Dhar, Kalipada Maitra, Loken Bagchi, Nalini Chaudhury and others. Most of them were teachers and businessmen by profession. In 1924, the auditorium and green room of the theatre club were built on the land donated by Bibi Manjanneswa of the Nawab family. The much-needed electric lighting for theatres came to the town in the thirties with the help of this theatre club. Earlier, the performances took place in gas light.[14]

Gana Natya Sangha, another dramatic club of the town, started performing plays from the 1940s and continued till 1948. In the 1940s, this dramatic group used plays by local playwrights to perform them on various issues of society in different parts of the town. Drama was in great demand among the common people during the period.[15]

Beside the Jalpaiguri town, the area where plays were performed to a great extent was the Alipurduar town. Most of the people of this town came here from different parts of Bengal in search of better opportunity. A majority portion of them was associated with tea plantations and railways. Many of them were well educated. In addition to setting up schools and other literary institutions, they used to perform plays in gardens at leisure times. Though drama was their main object, they carried the torch of education to the remote corners also. The Edward Library,

Alipurduar High School and McWilliam Institute bear the testimony of these facts. Nilratan Mukherjee, Prafulla Majumder, Rasiklal Ganguly, Mani Mukherjee, Nagen Mukherjee and others played a key role in laying the foundation of these institutions. The McWilliam Institute, established under the guidance of Mc-William, the then Sub-Divisional Officer of the Alipurduar town, later came to be known as the Peace Memorial Institute in 1940s. It was the first theatre of the town. Many dramatic groups staged a number of plays, centred round the institution and provide a healthy cultural environment to the inhabitants.[16]

In the 1940s the tea gardens were scattered in the middle of the dense forest and were almost devoid of any means of transport. No reliable means of communication were available and people had to walk miles to reach their destination. Life was always at a risk as these forests were inhabited by wild animals. Even in the middle of this, the Bengali *babus* of the tea gardens continued their untiring efforts to create the right scene for entertainment. They were always striving to bring some exception in the dull and monotonous life in the tea gardens. Staging plays was one of their leisure activities. It also reflected their cultural life. It was not an easy task at that time to stage a play. Still, with the help of the untiring efforts of the tea garden staff, they succeeded in staging plays. In this enterprise they got full assistance from the owners of the gardens especially the Bengali industrialists. Whenever a play was to be staged in any garden, the entire locality buzzed with the news. Rehearsals continued for months together and the garden staff who were to participate, practised for hours in order to achieve perfection.[17]

From the mid-forties to the early forties, a number of theatre groups were formed in various tea estates and forest-dominated areas. The staff of the gardens, mainly the Bengalis who were popularly known as *babus* to the labourers, played an important role in establishing theatre groups in the duars. For example, the Kumargram theatre club, Chuapara Club, Jayanti Milan Sangha, Buxa Duars Staff Club. Sankash Dramatic Club, Friends Union Club deserved to be mentioned. These clubs hosted many historical and mythological plays for the recreation of people.[18]

By the end of the nineteenth century, the district town of Jalpaiguri, though young, occupied paramount position in North Bengal in terms of art, literature, culture and sports. In fact, sports culture developed there at the hands of the British. They were primarily club lovers. Apart from Jalpaiguri town, nowhere else in North Bengal could one see such a big European club. It was established in 1894. Along with it, Malbazar European Club, Western Duars European Club, Chulsa European Club, Dalgaon European Club and Chuapa European Club deserve to be mentioned. Among them, Chuapara and Chulsa Clubs were famous for golf and polo.[19] However, clubs and sports were introduced both by the British tea planters and railway officials mainly for their leisure activities. They were the first to start playing football and tennis in Jalpaiguri town. Peter McWilliam, the then Sub-Divisional Officer of Alipurduar, John Archibold Polwhele, Manager and Engineer-in-Chief of Bengal Duars Railway (BDR) at Domohani deserved special mention. They organized football matches many times. Beside the white tea planters and their managers, the railway officials, Bengali tea industrialists, lawyers and timber merchants were the ones who made the game of football interesting.[20]

THE DISTRICT OF DARJEELING

In Darjeeling hill, the most noteworthy recreation centre for the Bengali Hindus was the Nripendra Narayan Hindu Public Hall. Contributions from many Hindus including one of Rs. 1,000 from Maharaja Nripendra Narayan of Coochbehar and a grant of land by the Municipality in 1890 enabled the Bengali Hindus of Darjeeling to construct the building of this hall for religious and social purposes. It was used as a common meeting place for Hindus as well as for Puja celebrations. The Durga Puja, essentially a domestic festival, took an Anglo-Bengali character.[21]

A few Bengali drama enthusiasts staged plays in Siliguri with the establishment of Mitra Sammilani in 1909. It was from the second half of the twentieth century that the socio-economic conditions of Bengal and the essence of nationalism were reflected in the plays. The historical play *Harishchandra* had a huge impact on the audience in 1914. The performers were mainly the railway employees, official staff of the neighbouring tea gardens and a group of educated cultured people of the town. Dr Birendranath Chakrabarty, Atul Chandra Roy, Kartick Chandra Dey, Sharat Cahndra Duta and Jatindranath Gupta were some famous actors of that time. Plays staged at Mitra Sammilani like *Devala Devi, Sarala, Jaydev, Chandragupta, Chandidas, Bilwamangal* deserve a special mention.[22]

The plays staged there were mainly mythological and historical. But sometimes social plays were also performed. At that time, the scene on the stage was sometimes that of a village scene, and sometimes that of a street or a battlefield. A lamp or a row of candles on the stage served as full light. The performance usually started at 10 p.m., and it would be early morning by the time it ended, some actors who appeared on the stage could said to be at par with the acting talent of professional theatre artists of the then Calcutta. Sometime they also went to Jalpaiguri and Balurghat towns for stage performances. Sachindranath Nandi received a standing ovation from the audience by acting in the play *Pather Seshe.*[23]

The second theatre of Siliguri town, popularly known as Arya Samiti, came into existence in 1948. Most of its founding members were the railway employees. Tulsi Lahiri gained a lot of fame by acting in *Cheratar.* At the same time, the Saigal Institute, one of the most popular theatres of the town, came up. This institute was also popular for table tennis.[24]

In Darjeeling, the British tea planters and the government officials were fond of sports. G.W. Christison, one of the leading tea planters of the hill, was a good football player. Apart from tending the garden, he spent equal time for playing football. Every year he used to arrange annual matches at the playground of Tukvar tea estate.[25] In a report it was stated:

> the sports which began for his people gradually became one of the chief social functions of the district and for the last 13 years of their existence (1869 to 1892 with the exception of 3 years) a day was left in the Darjeeling Durga Puja programme for the Tukvar sports'.[26]

THE DISTRICT OF MALDA

The journey of theatre in the district of Malda began with the foundation of Malda Dramatic Club in 1896. It was founded by the initiative of a group of theatre loving people who came here from Rajshahi for their professional needs. The first play performed by them in the theatre named Rangmahal Laner Kache. At that time Chapai Nawabganj, Bholahat, Shibganj, Kanshat and Malda were the leading police stations in Rajshahi division where plays were staged to a large extent. A number of actors from these regions used to come to Malda for performing in these plays. The golden era in the theatre world of the district began with the foundation of B. Dey Hall, set up in 1901. It was named B. Dey Hall as the theatre was built by Brajen Dey, the then District Magistrate of Malda. He provided financial assistance to lay the foundation of the theatre. Beside his contribution, a number of theatre loving people like Haribhushan Das, Baidyanath Chaudhary, Pramathnath Dey, Abinash Bagchi and others incessantly endeavoured behind its foundation. A number of notable plays like *Mewarer Patan*, *Kulin Kula Sarbashya* were performed.[27]

It is true that the practice of drama in the district of Malda was centred on the B. Dey Hall but within a few years it spread beyond the town limits to the villages. In 1910, the Natya Mandir was built in Chapai Nawabganj. The first play staged there was *Debala Devi.* The artists of Harishchandrapur had a good reputation around the district. Their performance in the play *Alibaba* at B. Dey Hall was highly acclaimed. They surprised the audience to a great extent with their acting skills. Sometimes plays were staged in Harishchandrapur by making a bamboo stage. The use of light in the play *Bearing Post* organized by the Udayan Natyabithi Sangha in 1948 was literally the first use of light in the history of theatre in the district. During that time a number of theatre groups like Aloktirtha, Shilpi Parishad and Ruprangam came up in the drama atlas of the district. The play *Ferari Fauj* staged by Alaktirtha group directed by actor Rabindranath Bhattacharya in Minerva theatre, Kolkata in 1960 won the hearts of many theatre loving people. For example, Utpal Dutt, Shova Sen and Tapash Sen, the renowned figures of Indian theatre, were overwhelmingly impressed by seeing their performance. From this time comes the tide in the theatre of the district. Rabindranath Bhattacharya who migrated to the district from Naogaon after the Partition, formed single handedly a new theatre group called Natyabithi.[28]

Notable among the male performers who played female roles in the sixties were Dr Anil Kumar Dey, Pushpen Lahiri and Nitin Sen. Apart from drama, entertainment in Malda district during that period included mask dance and Gambhira songs. A new theatre group, popularly known as Makdumpur Dramatic Club, was formed in 1936 staged few plays at B. Dey hall. Rebati Maitra, a *peshkar* by profession, was the main inspiration behind its foundation. He himself used to write plays infused by the *swadeshi* spirit. In 1936, one of his plays *Mayer Puja* was staged at B. Dey Hall but the British government stopped the performance and confiscated the manuscript of the play as it contained revolutionary dialogues.[29]

The Apollo Club was formed in 1939. During the same period, a new theatre group named Malda Merchants Dramatic Club came into existence. The most prominent members of the club were merchants by profession like Suryakanta Dey, Haribhushan Das, Rasiklal Roy and Radheshyam Saha. Due to the conflict with the members of the Malda Dramatic Club, they came out from the club and formed their own dramatic club. The Muslim society of Malda did not lag behind in this field. Some prominent Muslim actors of that time were Farukh Ali, Jamal and others. In 1933 they established a theatre group named the Muslim Dramatic Club. From 1933 to 1939 they staged their performances at B. Dey hall.[30]

CONCLUSION

Thus one might say that the Renaissance influences which could be seen in Calcutta among the *bhadralok* community (progenitor of the *babu* culture), also reached out to the far flung areas of North Bengal where people reacted in their own way. The Bengali community of North Bengal, divided by caste and religion, though slow in their responses to the call of the Renaissance thoughts, were gradually embracing the fruits of Renaissance and started reshaping their cultural value system to suit the needs of the hours.

NOTES

1. Sashibhushan Dasgupta, *Bangla Sahityer Nabayug* (New Age in Bengali Literature), A. Mukherjee and Company, Kolkata, BS 1372, pp. 200-202.
2. Dipayan Bhattacharya, 'Raj Amale Coochbehar e Natya Charcha' (Practising Theatre and Drama in Coochbehar during the Royal Period)', *Bibriti,* Festive issue, Mathabhanga, Coochbehar, 2010, p. 62.
3. Sitangshu Sekhar Mustafi, 'Dinhatar Natyacarcha O Natyavinay Parikrama' (Theatre and Theatrical Performances in Dinhata), *Uttar Prasanga,* A Special Volume on Dinhata Subdivision, Coochbehar, 2016, p. 172.
4. Digvijay Dey Sarkar, 'Coochbehar Natyacharcha' (Practising Drama in Coochbehar), in Ajitesh Bhattacharya (ed.), *Madhuparni,* Coochbehar Zilla Sankhya (Special Volume on the District of Coochbehar), 1396 BS, pp. 297-308.
5. Gayatri Devi, *A Princess Remembers,* Rupa Publications, New Delhi, 1995, p. 61.
6. Kamalesh Goswami, *Raiganjer Itihas* (History of Raiganj), Dibaratrir Kabya Publication, Kolkata, 2008, pp. 289-91.
7. *Dinajpur Patrika,* B.S. 1340, Dinajpur, pp. 28-9.
8. Subrata Roy, 'Raiganjer Natyacharcha' (Theatre in Raiganj), in Ajitesh Bhattacharya (ed.) *Madhuparni,* Special Volume on the District of West Dinajpur, Balurghat, BS 1399, p. 426.
9. Dhananjay Roy, *Dinajpur Jelar Itihas* (History of the Dinajpur District), K.P. Bagchi, Kolkata, 2006, pp. 332-4.
10. Bhawani Prasad, 'Kheladhular Itibritta' (History of Sports), in *Dadhichi,* Autumn Issue, Balurghat, 1996, pp. 307-9.
11. *Janamat,* Autumn Number, Jalpaiguri, 4 October 1934.
12. Moushumi Chattapadhyay, 'Jalpaigurir Sangitcharchar Sekal Ekal' (History of Music Practice in Jalpaiguri), in Aravinda Kar (ed.), *Kiratbhumi* (Land of Kiratas), Festive Issue, vol. II, Jalpaiguri, 2008, pp. 338-9.
13. Souvenir, Arya Natya Samaj, for the year 1990-1, Jalpaiguri, 1992, pp. 22-3.
14. *Janamat,* Jalpaiguri, 23 April 1924.
15. Rabishwar Bhattacharya, 'Jalpaiguri Jelar Natya Charcha Sekal Ekal' (History of Practising Theatre in Jalpaiguri), in Arabinda Kar (ed.),

Kiratbhumi (Land of Kiratas), Winter Issue, vol. I, Jalpaiguri, 1994, pp. 321-5.

16. Sanchita Das, 'Alipurduarer Natyacharchar Utsa O Kramabikash' (Origin and Development of Theatre in Alipurduar), in Pabitra Bhushan Sarkar (ed.), *Matir Choya*, vol. 21, No. 15, Autumn Issue, Alipurduar, 1995, p. 139.
17. Piya Chatterjee, *A Time for Tea*, First published by Duke University Press in 2001, Published in South Asia by Zubaan, New Delhi, 2003, p. 138.
18. Supam Biswas, *Tea World of North Bengal*, Readers Service, Kolkata, 2016, pp. 74-6.
19. Kamakhya Prasad Chakrabarty, *Sekalar Jalpaiguri Shahar Ebong Samajik Jibaner Kichu Katha* (Few Words of Social Life of Contemporary Jalpaiguri Town), Jalpaiguri, 2004, p.107.
20. Reports on the State of Sports in Bengal, Calcutta, 1932, pp. 14-16.
21. A. Mitra, *West Bengal District Handbooks Darjeeling 1951*, West Bengal Government Press, Alipore, 1954, p. cxiii.
22. Nanu Mitra, 'Darjeeling Jelar Bangla Natak O Natyacharcha' (History of Bengali Dramas in the district of Darjeeling), in Ajitesh Bhattacharya (ed.), *Madhuparni*, Darjeeling Zilla Sankhya (Special Volume on the District of Darjeeling), 1996, p. 366.
23. Nripen Basu, 'Phele Asa Din Gulo' (Days Gone By), *Purabarta*, Published by Siliguri Municipality, Siliguri, 1992, p. 18.
24. *Annual Proceedings for the Year of 1973-74*, Arya Samiti, Autumn Number, 1974, Siliguri, pp. 12-16.
25. Paritosh Dutta, 'Darjeeling, Cha O Nanan Katha' (Tale of Darjeeling and its Tea), in Ajitesh Bhattacharya (ed.), *Madhuparni*, op. cit., p. 196.
26. Kumar Narayan Chaudhury, 'Kheladhulay Darjeeling Jela' (Sports in Darjeeling District), in Ajitesh Bhattacharya (ed.), *Madhuparni*, op. cit., p. 425.
27. Ranajit Devbhuti, 'Maldaher Natyacarchar Sankhipta Itibritta' (A Concise History of Practicing Theatre in Malda), *Uttarer Saradin*, A Bengali news weekly, Siliguri, 3 January 2013.
28. Ashim Goswami, *Malda Jelar Natya Andalaner Itihas* (History of Theatre Movement in the district of Malda), Malda, 2011, pp. 7-11.
29. *Maldaha Samachar*, Malda, 7 August 1936.
30. Irish Shabnam, 'Malda Jelar Natyacharcha' (History of Theatre in Malda), in Malay Sankar Bhattacharya (ed.), *Maldah Charcha*, Malda, 2011, pp. 276-7.

CHAPTER 7

Influence of the Renaissance on Muslim Community

INTRODUCTION

The Muslim community was divided primarily into two, namely *ashraf* (aristocrats) and *atraf* (lower class) and as such there was no middle class. The majority of the population was overwhelmingly agriculturists and they did not direct their attention towards the economic life of the urban areas. As a result of it, the Calcutta-centric Renaissance did not impact their life. Farazi and Wahhabi movements prevailed among the masses and this led them to ignore any such tradition and culture which did not have any relation to the Quran and Hadish. A huge number of culturally evolved Muslims found themselves in a state which was rather different from the mainstream lifestyle of that time. In order to spread Islam, the intellectuals started translating the religious scriptures into Bengali. So, in the garb of religion, different literary pieces were created by Bengali Muslims of North Bengal which in turn invented an independent style of writing. These writings throw a light on an independent intellectual expression of the Muslims. Immediately after this, the nationalist political ideas started influencing the community and a social resurgence movement was born as a result.[1]

CHANGED OUTLOOK IN THE NINETEENTH CENTURY

In the latter half of the nineteenth century, an urge to receive modern education could be perceived among the Muslim community under the patronage of Abdul Latif, the new leader of the Muslims of Bengal. In 1863, Abdul Latif established a cultural organization named Muhamadden Literary Society and this led to the thawing of the ice of age-old mentality of the Muslims. This society stood for Western education within the traditional Islamic education system, retaining full emphasis on Arabic and Persian learning. Sayyid Amir Ali and his Central National Muhamadden Association, on the other hand, advocated a total reorganization of Muslim education. Consequently, this paved the way for the origin of an educated Muslim middle class. In spite of many adversities, these Bengali Muslims strove hard to enlighten themselves through their deep emotional bonding with their mother tongue. Prose, poetry, play and criticism were all written by the Muslims in their mother language. These Muslims came forward and became aware about their cultural identity which prepared them for the demand of the times.[2]

The establishment of Madrasha Literary and Debating Society (1883), All Bengal Provincial Muslim Educational Society and Dinajpur Muslim Society (1904) bear testimony of the fact.[3] A good number of books and magazines in Bengali were published during the period. For newspapers and magazines, one may cite the names of *Balaranjika* (1873), *Sudhakar* (1889), *Mihir* (1892), *Hafez* (1892) by Seikh Abdur Rahim, *Hitakari* (1890) by Mir Musharaf Hossain, *Kohinoor* (1898) by Rahman Ali and *Nabanur* (1903) by Emdad Ali. As for books, the names of *Bishad Sindhu* (1875), *Jamidar Darpan* (1873), *Gojibon* (1889) by Mir Mosharaf Hossain, *Ray Nandini* and *Anal Prabaha* (1915) by Ismail Hossain Siraj Kusumanjali and *Premer Har* (1898) by Mojammel Hauque—all these reveal the picture of an intellectual awakening among the members of the Muslim community. Some of these poets and writers are honoured names in the literature of Bengal. Dr Anisuzzaman in his book *Muslim Manash and Bangla Sahitya* has expressed that the origin of Muslim renaissance can be traced back to 1870.[4]

If there is any peak to be accessed then the history of 10 years had surely reached that destination. Sirajul Hauque in his book *Muslim Sahitya Samaj: Samaj Chinta O Sahitya Karma* has opined that these 10 years clearly indicate the intellectual excellence and activities among the Muslims. Taking cue from the magazine *Sikha*, Kaji Abdul, Abul Hossain, Motahar Hossain and others started a similar movement like the Young Bengal Movement and named its Young Muslim Movement. During this period especially in 1930s, through different magazines, gatherings and intellectual discussions, they had tried to hit the age-old blind faiths of the community. They put forward the ideas of humanism, intellectualism and shed the dark social and cultural faiths vehemently declaring that that time was the time of reason and intelligence, Bengali was the mother tongue and without literary practice no race, no community could develop themselves.[5]

INFLUENCE OF THE RENAISSANCE ON MUSLIM COMMUNITY IN NORTH BENGAL

This Muslim renaissance had deep impact and spread like wild fire in northern part of Bengal during the latter half of the nineteenth century and beginning of the twentieth century. Releasing themselves from the age-old customs and religious bindings, a good number of young Bengali Muslim youths came forward to set an example to others that the time called for social progress through intelligence and reason. The Muslim community in the northern part of Bengal was somewhat less impacted by the nineteenth-century Renaissance. One of the foremost reasons was that this community had no profound relationship with Western civilization and culture. They could not accept the British rule easily and for a long time refused to take the advantage of modern English education. The impact of Renaissance remained confined mainly to the higher strata of the Hindu society and it failed miserably to influence either the Muslims or the lower-caste Hindus including the Adivasis.[6]

Salauddin Ahmed has rightly said that Sayyed Amir Ali was the pioneer of the Islamic renaissance in the second half of the nineteenth century like Rammahun Roy of the Hindu Bengali Renaissance of the first half of the nineteenth century. Historically it is an acknowledged fact that the Muslims of India or Bengal had accepted neither the Company's rule nor the Western education policy. Both the Bengali Muslims or the Ashraf Muslims had never sent their wards to the English educational institutions. No Muslim students took admission in Rangpur Zilla School or Rajshahi School. The *Bamabodhini Patrika* gave the information that the Eden Girls School of Dacca established in 1878 had 153 girl students in 1880 but the number of Muslim girls was only one. The foundation stone of the Presidency College was laid in 1817 but it was opened up for the Muslim student's from 1873. No Muslim girl was allowed to pursue her education in Bethun School between 1849-97.[7]

EMERGENCE OF MUSLIM INTELLIGENTSIAS

Traditionally, Rangpur was a cradle of Muslim nationalists. The personalities who left their mark on the history of Rangpur were intellectuals such as Nurul Amin, Abu Hossain Sarkar, Ahmed Hossain and so on. The notable freedom fighter Surendra Mahan Ghosh of Rangpur held them in high esteem and mentioned two names specifically that of Nurul Amin and Abu Hussain whom he regarded highly due to their untiring efforts towards work related to social welfare. Surendra Mahan Ghosh was the deputy of Fazlul Hauque and the leader of Krishak Praja Party. He was later elected as the member of Bengal Legislative Council.[8]

The book named *Bartaman Sankat O Mussalmander Kartabya* written by Muhammad Amanul Hauque Afendi was an outstanding literary work. It was banned by the British on 31 August 1939. The literary progress of the time was also enriched by poet Fajlul Karim whose books titled *Layla Majnun* and *Afganistaner Itihas* are worth mentioning here. He started publishing a magazine named *Basana* from Rangpur in 1908 and the main theme of the magazine was Hindu-Muslim culture, social welfare and progress of both. But its publication was cancelled by the British in 1910 who alleged the magazine of promoting anti British ideas. Sheikh Riyajuddin wrote two books titled *Sachitra Arab Jatir Itihas* and *Jib Hatya and Gokorbani.* He also wrote an elaborate biography of Sir Sayed, a towering personality of Muslim community. He was also the secretary of 'Bangiya Lathiyal Samiti'. Sheikh Fajlur put immense effort for the development of the backward sections of Bengali Muslim society, as well as spreading the light of education among the illiterate masses.[9]

Nafarudin was an inhabitant of Shyampur village. His first historical novel was published in 1929. It was titled *Bhagyalipi.* As a writer, he also contributed regularly to a number of magazines published at that time. Those were *Moslem Darpan, Moslem Hitaishi, Dinajpur Patrika* and *Desher Bani.*[10] Maulana Abdulla Baki was a knowledge seeker. He was also a dedicated political person. He was a symbol of self-consciousness among the people of his district. Based on Islamic ideas, he wrote a large number of books. Impressed with his expertise about Muslim scriptures, a cultural society of Poland conferred on him the membership of their society. Maulana Abdul Rahman, Aftab Uddin Chaudhury, Fazlur Rahman, and other intellectual *satyagrahi*s contributed their intellectural and informative writings to different magazines such as *Nawroj.* Saukat Ali was a distinguished novelist, story writer, essayist and critic. *Pingol Akash* was his remarkable masterpiece. He was a professor of Bengali language and literature at Jagannath college, Dhaka. Yusuf Ali Bhagbi editor of the Bengali periodical *Kased,* Hemayet Ali editor of the Bengali periodical *Nawraj,* Abdullah Kafi editor of the Bengali periodical *Satyagrahi,* Samsuddin Ahmed author of the book *Muslim Rule in India,* Wazed Hossain Khan and others were some contemporary Muslim intellectuals of undivided Dinajpur.[11]

Jawhar Ali was a distinguished educationist of the Muslim community. The book *Jawheral Momenin* written by him was highly recognized.[12] Abdul Baki was a professor in the Arabic language department of the Islamia College in Calcutta. In 1934, he published a monthly magazine named *Jagaran.* Eknuddin Ahmad was another renowned person of Dinajpur district who dedicated himself to literary works. He was such an accomplished writer that his presence could be seen in every field of literature. He earned fame by contributing regularly to a social magazine named *Shantiniketan.* In 1904, due to his efforts, the Muslim Sabha was set up in Dinajpur. In 1924, he presided over the first meeting of the Bangiya Muslim literary Society in Calcutta.[13]

Many Muslim intellectuals worked as contributors towards the history of the district. Golam Hussain arrived at Maldah to work under George Woodny at his business firm. He wrote a historical account titled *Riyas-Us-Salatin* in Persian language, when he was requested by Woodny. This is the only historical account about the rights of Muslims written in Persian language. His achievement was that he tried to recreate the literature of Muslim reign carved on the ruins of Gaur Pandua, and fix the sequence of historical events in an orderly manner, on the basis of date and year. Maulvi Abdus Salam translated *Riyas-Us-Salatin* into English. In 1907, historian Rampran Gupta translated this masterpiece into Bengali and earned acclamations from fellow historians. Akimuddin and Munhsi Nasiruddin of Malda district were both prolific writers of *puthi* literature.[14]

Abdul Gaffar Siddiqi, a highly knowledgeable person, wrote *Mussalman O Banga Sahitya.* Elahi Baksh, started collecting regional historical folklores from different sources and compiled them into a large, valuable book in Persian, and it was titled *Khursid-i-Jahannuma.* Such was the quality of the book that, the colonial rulers copied all the 498 pages of the book dedicated to Bengal. Later on, he translated this into English. Abdul Karim worked under Gulam Rashid. He was a connoisseur of Persian language and had great interest in history. He inherited the large collection of books of Gulam Rashid. Rashid's library had more than 1,000 rare books in Persian and Urdu. Historian Elahi Baksh dedicated his book *Khursid* to his intimate friend, Karim.[15]

Another towering historian from Malda was Abid Ali. The book which he wrote after extensive research about the ruins of Gaur Pandua was titled *Memories of Gaur Pandua.* He was inspired to write the book by Lord Curzon himself. In 1930, an abridged and edited version of the book was published after revaluation/ inclusion of the role of H.E Stepleton.[16]

Sheikh Suleman was a lyricist who wrote regularly in the magazine *Krishna Charan.* In the first half of the twentieth century, Maulavi Abdul wrote a play *Najibullah.* He was the editor of the weekly *Alfa Akhbar.* It started circulation in 1914 in Malda. Safiur Rahman, a distinguished Gambhira artist, published a collection of folk songs and named it *Gambhira.* In 1918, at the Pabna literary meet, Rabindranath handed him the gold medal himself. He was a pioneer of modern Gambhira song. Muhammad Sufi and Suleman Master were very popular among the Gambhira singers as expert lyricists. Muhammad Abdul Karim was a resident of Shyampur Bajitpur in Malda district. He published a Bengali play titled *Jagatmahini* in 1875. This was the second play written by a Muslim in Bengali. He also wrote another book titled *Ashabrikkha*, published in BS 1299. The literary society of Bengal conferred upon him the title of 'Sahitya Bisharad'.[17]

In the literary field of Malda, Nur Muhammad was a distinguished personality showing his skill as a poet, novelist, story writer, essayist and critic. His literary creations include the famous novel *Utsab, Muslim Bina* and *Asche Bochor* in Bengali. He also started a literary and cultural society named *Gourbanga.* He was the editor as well as attached with the management of a number of magazines like *Ajan, Akbar* and *Adina.* The collection of poems *Swarnakkhar* was written by a Muslim poetess, Begum Aziza. Mosharaf Hussain, a resident of Malda district, was a distinguished social worker, journalist and teacher. Maulavi Abdul Aziz had mastered Arabic as well as Persian. He was a benevolent and sensitive person. He was a lawyer but was also greatly interested in historical research.[18]

FOUNDATION OF MUHAMADDEN ASSOCIATIONS AND THEIR SOCIOCULTURAL DEVELOPMENT

The Central Muhamadden Association, a noteworthy institution of its time, established its branch in Malda in 1884. The founder president was Ershad Ali Khan Chaudhury, *zamindar* of Nator. Maulavi Haidar Ali and Maulavi Muhammad Yaqub helped him immensely to lay its foundation. This association was fully loyal to the British and its main aim was to fulfil the interests of their community.[19] To improve the condition of womens education, a girls school came up, known as Rajshahi Girls' High School and the main figures behind its creation was Mirza Yusuf Ali, the President of the Central Muhammaden Association, Rajshahi and

Sirajuddin Ahmed, a physician by profession who donated land for the construction of its building. Hajilal Muhammad, a *zamindar*, played a key role in establishing the Rajshahi Muhammadan Association, in which leading Bengali Hindus cum historians like Akshay Kumar Maitra, Sasadhar Roy, Rakhaldas Bandopadhyay and Ramaprasad Chanda were patrons. Also he helped Sarat Kumar Roy, *zamindar* of Dayarampur Estate, Dighapatiyar to lay the foundation of Rajshahi Varendra Musuem.[20]

The Muhamadden Association of Rajshahi was established in 1884 under the patronage of Ershad Ali Khan Chaudhuri, a *zamindar*. The Association had several aims and objectives—(a) promoting education and cooperation among the Muhamadden of the district, (b) to bring the wants and grievances of the Muhamadden community to the notice of the British government and the overall advancement of the community. Any adult Muhamadden gentleman was eligible to become a member of the Association. Most of its members were *zamindars*, *talukdars*, pleaders, *mukhtars*, *jotedars*, *pirs* (religious heads), merchants and traders. The president was Maulavi Muhammad Haidar Ali, M.A. and the secretary was Maulavi Muhammad Yakut. The building of the Association was first constructed in 1891 by Mirza Yusuf Ali which later became the Rajshahi Girls' School. The Anjuman Hemayat Islam of Rajshahi (1891) by Maulavi Hasan Ali and Nur-Ul-Iman of Rajshahi were established with the object to promote education among the Muhamadden community.[21]

The Bogra National Muhamadden Association was established in 1884 with the aim to safeguard the interests and spread of education among the Muhamadden population of the district. The founder president of the Association was Sayyed Shobhan Chaudhury and the secretary was Md. Abdul Karim.[22]

The Muhamadden Association of Rangpur was established in 1887 under the aegis of Central National Muhamadden Association, Calcutta. It advocated special measures to spread education and expressed loyalty to the British Raj. The founder president of the Association was Abdul Majid Chaudhuri, the *zamindar* of Mahipur. He also laid the foundation of Islam Mission in the district. The Association assisted the Rangpur Madrashah financially to establish the students' hostel. Hajilal Muhammad also contributed generously to set up the Anjuman Mafidul Islam Samiti in 1906. The Nur-Al-Iman was established in 1893 and the key figures behind it were Muhammad Yusuf Ali, Abdul Aziz, Saberuddin Ahmad, Munshi Muhammad Ali and others. This association was fully devoted to serve the poor students for their educational enrichment.[23]

The Muhamadden Association of Malda was founded by a group of elite Muslims of M'alda town in 1890. It was the branch of Central National Muhamadden Association, Calcutta. The fundamental objective was to improve the social, political and educational condition of the Muhamadden community. Membership was open to all educated Muhamaddens. Most of the members were leading pleaders, landowners, tradesmen and physicians. Business was transacted by an elected committee of 30, mostly residents of English Bazar. Maulavi Muhammad Ismail Chaudhuri was the president and Abdul Aziz Khan was the secretary of the Association. Both were staunch propagators of pan-Islamic ideology. In the year 1895, Mr Price the then District Magistrate and *zamindar* Chaudhury Mohayedur Rahaman became its honourable president and working president respectively. Their appeal to the British government was to appoint only Muslim members in the District Education Department to a large extent. This Association raised the demands for introducing Islamized Bengali language rather than Musalmani Bengali language. The major response to their demand was the formation of 'All Bengal Muslim Literary Association' at Malda town in 1899.[24]

The Muhamadden Association of Dinajpur was founded in 1904 with the aim to improve the sociocultural and political condition of the Muslim community. Its founder president was Eknuddin Ahmed, a *zamindar* by profession. He was the founder of 'Nawraj Sahitya Sabha' and president of All India Muslim Literary Conference held in Calcutta in 1917. He was also a prolific writer. His two monographs namely *Shantiniketan* and *Islam Dharmaniti* published in Dinajpur magazine in 1891 attained wide acclamation of the contemporary intellectual society.[25] Most of the members of the Muhamadden Association of Dinajpur were pleaders and landholders. During the visit of the British Official Ramfiled Fuller in December 1905, the Association, under the guidance of Eknuddin Ahmed and Maharaja Girijanath Roy, welcomed him with great joy. At the initial stage, they supported the Congress and actively participated in the Swadeshi movement. A few leaders of this association like Munshi Soleman, Munshi Fakirullah and Eknuddin Ahmed organized the Boycott and Swadeshi movement in the district. In the 1940s the Association was inclined towards the Muslim League and raised their voices for a separate Muslim country.[26]

The Anjuman-i-Islamia of Darjeeling was established on 5 December 1860 and was made up of 225 Muslim residents who had come from the plains. It was the first branch of Anjuman-i-Islamia in North Bengal. Advancement of education, socio-religious regenerations among the Muhamadden of the district and instilling loyal sentiments in the youths of the community were some of its radical aims. It imparted education, religious or otherwise, to Muslim boys and girls and helped them by awarding stipends for the pursuit of higher studies. Its first president was S. Sujauddin and vice-presidents were H. Karim Baksh and M. Alam. The first secretary was Aziz Ahmed.[27]

The Muhamaden Association of Jalpaiguri came up in 1894 under the leadership of Jotedar Eknuddin Ahmad and tea industrialist Khan Bahadur Rahim Baksh. It strove to develop the notion of pan-Islamic ideology and spirit of education among the Muslim community of the town. This association had a strong link with the National Muhamadden Association founded by Sayyed Amir Ali in Aligarh. They had a strong relationship with the local Rajbanshi Muslims which grew under the initiative of Sonaulla Saheb.[28]

The Anjuman-i-Islamia of Rajshahi was founded in the year 1891. Its fundamental aim was the promotion of loyalty towards the British government and the promotion and protection of the social, political, educational and other rights and interests of the Muhamadden community. The association was made up of selected members of the Muhamadden community residing in the town and the interior of the district, with an executive committee consisting of president, a secretary, a joint secretary, an assistant secretary, a treasurer and members.[29]

The Anjuman-i-Islamia of Jalpaiguri was founded in the year 1892. Respectability was the qualification required for a membership of the Anjuman; the majority of members belonged to the landholding class. Maulavi Mehrajuddin Ahmad was its founder. Tea industrialist Khan Bahadur Musharruf Hussain was the first president and Maulavi Kazi Abdul Khaleque was the secretary. The Ahmadiya Association came up at Jalpaiguri town in 1927. Its main aim was to sow the seed of Islamism among the Hindus.[30]

The Anjuman-i-Islamia of Dinajpur was established in the year 1894 and was formed with 103 Muslim residents of the district. Its main objective was to promote the well-being of the Muhamadden of the Dinajpur district and to ameliorate their educational, social and religious status. Its first president was Maulavi Muhammad Kader Baksh, vice-presidents were Muhammad Isa, Khorasad Ali Chaudhuri and Maulavi Ainuddin Ahmed. The first secretary was Maulavi Hasan Ali Ahmed.[31]

The Anjuman-i-Islamia of Malda was founded in 1909 by Abdul Aziz Khan. He was the chairman of English Bazar Municipality (1900-1912). Its chief ends were to promote the well-being of the Muhamadden of the district. The Anjuman Makhaerul Islam of Malda town was set up in 1900. Hasimuddin Mian, the native *zamindar* of Bargharia village was its chief founder. Its main aim was to propagate the morality of Islam and disdain Hinduism.[32]

Abdul Hamid, a renowned Khilafat leader, was arrested when he visited Darjeeling in connection with the Khilafat movement. He was sentenced to one year of rigorous imprisonment. He was a good orator. He was the main person behind the setting up of Anjuman-i-Islamia in Darjeeling hill. Mirza Samsuddin of Darjeeling took great interest in studying the social life and implementing his understanding in real life. His deep knowledge was highly appreciated by the learned people of the society. Abdul Bor was a familiar name to the Muslim youths engaged in freedom struggle. This spirited person took the initiative in setting up Janakalyan Samiti during the food and other crises in 1944, and started vigorous movement.[33]

Rahim Box of Jalpaiguri had the unique identity of being the first Indian tea planter. He was knowledgeable, virtuous and a refined gentleman. Owing to his educational zeal, the British government conferred upon him the title of Khan Bahadur. Muhammad Sahebjan Hauque Chaudhury was another person who left no stone unturned for the social reformation movement for Muslims. A glaring instance of this is his setting up of a primary school in 1885. Abdul Karim, Abu Bakkar, Abdul Gani, Wahliyar Rahman and Munshi Aftabuddin were also very much involved in intellectual enlightenment of the masses.[34]

Muhammad Sonaulla comes first and foremost in the social progress movement. It is acknowledged widely that he inspired and nurtured many new talents. In 1923, he contributed so handsomely to Deshbandhu's Swaraj fund that even Deshbandhu himself was amazed. His patriotism, logical thinking and historical insight enamoured Deshbandhu and as such was consequently conferred the title 'Ashir-Ul-Mulk' by him. Sonaulla School, Dinbazar Mosque, Karimunnesha Primary School, Dinbazar market—all these owed their origin to his efforts. Sofikul Islam, Sofiuddin Muhammad, Abdur Rahman, Abdur Rahman, Musharaff Hussain tried relentlessly to bring to light many unheard, unquoted historical episodes of the Muslims of the district.[35]

Sir Ahmed Fazlur Rahman was a distinguished person of the district. In 1912, he returned to his native country after completing BA Honours in history from Oxford University. He worked as a professor in Aligarh and Dhaka University. He also chaired as the joint secretary of University of Calcutta commission and was also the first provost of Sanimulla Muslim hall (1921-7). Later on, he became the chancellor of Dhaka University and further an elected member of federal public service commission. He achieved the unique honour of being conferred Knighthood by the British.[36]

In the 1930s, Khan Chaudhury Amanatulla Ahmed had the unique identity of being the first writer of the history of Coochbehar. He wrote the first and foremost book on Coochbehar titled *Coochbeharer Itihas* (History of Coochbehar) in Bengali. It was translated into English by Sharat Chandra Ghoshal, a distinguished person of the district. In the literary field, Abbasuddin was a distinguished person showing his skill as a folk singer. He was widely popular for the Bhawaiya folk song. He later recorded Khirol and Chatka which were famous in Goalpara district, Coochbehar and Rangpur. He found patrons in a number of erudite poets and scholars of the time like Bidrohi Kabi (Rebel Poet) Kazi Nazrul Islam, Palli Kabi (Pastoral Poet) Jasimuddin, Acharya Dinesh Chandra Sen, Guru Saday Dutta and many more. The poet Jasimuddin dedicated his book *Rangila Nayer Majhi* (1935) to Abbasuddin. He was honoured with the 'Kabya Ratnakar' award by Arya Sahitya Samaj for his profound contribution in Sanskrit literature. The Shilpakala Academy award in 1979 added another feather to his cap. Another renowned Bhawaiya singer of the district was Nayeb Ali, commonly known as Tepu. He was very popular for the song *Diner Sobha Suruj Re.* The agricultural economy of North Bengal has been captured vividly in such folk songs. The happiness and joy, pains and anxieties have been nicely depicted in the lyrics of Bhawaiya songs. Maulavi Jafar Ali Ahmed, Maqbul Hossain, Jafir Uddin Bakshi, Jahiruddin Sayyed and Altaf Hossain were some eminent contemporary Muslim intellectuals of the district. Abdul Karim was a distinguished person of the district who wrote a number of plays like *Madhumala, Rupadhanakanya, Haldi Sanai, Maruchmati Kanya* and *Mahua Sundari.*[37]

CONCLUSION

In view of the above discussion, it is obvious that the social profile of the Muslim community of North Bengal, particularly the upper class known as Ashraf, was seemingly more progressive. They earned a lot as business owners and were landed aristocrats as well. They showed their acts of magnanimity by benevolent dispensations. Simultaneously, the growth of a professional middle class group in Jalpaiguri was indeed remarkable. Musharraf Hussain, a philanthropist of this town, was given the title of Nawab which was an exceptional honour in the whole of North Bengal. A.F. Rahman was the first Indian Vice-Chancellor of Dhaka University (1934-6) and the British government conferred him with the title of 'Night'. The number of Muslims honoured with the title of 'Khanbahadur' and 'Raybahadur' by the British government was much higher in Jalpaiguri in comparison to that in other districts. It is worth noting that the Muslims of Jalpaiguri succeeded both in commercial and industrial (mostly in tea plantations) enterprises. No other district could claim such exemplary instances of success. Had there been no Partition, it is thought that they would have flourished much more. After the Partition, they moved to East Pakistan where they developed a similar socio-economic set up as successful businessmen, industrialists, doctors, lawyers and similar professional groups. Now, the question remains as to why the Muslims of other districts, could not in comparison fare well in comparison.

However, if one tries to get to the bottom of the problem, one sees that their beneficial approach were often preconditioned by some factors which overshadowed the image of their progressive character.

This newly-emerged privileged group following, the onset of colonial economy could be seen in almost equal terms among their Hindu counterparts elsewhere in Bengal, who acted as a comprador class to collaborate with the British interests, and were the offshoots of the so-called Bengal Renaissance. Unlike the newly-emerged European trading community as a response to the Renaissance, they were neither free and independent of the control of the ruling class in terms of running their business, nor did they have any agenda to be at one with the toiling masses for a greater cause like what was evinced in the prerogatives of the European Renaissance-led economic groups.

Moreover, their faithfulness to the British, degenerated our indigenous economy. So the narrative of the nineteenth-century Renaissance and its ramifications for an imagined transformation of Bengal society as a whole, was an over simplification of the much acclaimed Renaissance effect. Yet, whatever progressive changes they brought about, were often hijacked by the religious overtones of both the Hindu and Muslim communities undermining the spirit of mutual love and respect. In fact, this was backed by the age-old agenda of the cultural communalism which received further indulgence from the British policy of divide and rule.

One example of such a sinister move on the part of the landed Muslim aristocracy was seen to mobilize the Muslim peasantry not to join the Tebhaga movement launched for the sake of peasants' better lot in Boda, Patgaon and Pachagarh regions of North Bengal. This was done by dividing them on the question of religious identity and also being influenced by the political aims of the Muslim League. Similar attitudes among the Congress leaders, backed by landed gentry, tried to disassociate the common peasants from such movements. Such moves were also seen when the Hindu landed class turned back at the growing discontent among the peasants and tried to diffuse the same. Their class interest at times was strengthened by petty religious fervour. Already there was an underlying current of antagonism among the Congress and the League leaders on communal lines for attaining separate states after the Independence of India.

But there is no denying the fact that the role of the social reforms together with the spirit of cultural awakening emanating from English education and Western progressive ideas, brought about a qualitative change in the mindset of the so-called 'native' and 'savage' people to enable them to take part in the freedom struggle and form a sense of pride in their Indian identity.

Finally, it can be said that both the Hindu and Muslim members played active role in some of these *sabha*s and *samitie*s. The tide of social reforms engineered by these associations had engulfed a large section of the society across North Bengal. The reforms had influenced more Hindus than the Muslim people. It is striking that being in majority in some of the areas, they were on the back foot. Perhaps this could be the reason why numerically their associations were less than those of the Hindus. Yet, they participated in movements on issues like social change, education and politics. Newly-educated youths came forward to lead the institutions with new vigour. These societies acted in bridging gaps between the different groups of people with multiple identities. The Anjumans, despite their religious leanings, tried to ensure overall development in the Muslim society. They insisted on the spread of education, though indirectly, they were opposed to Western education. The *sabha*s and *samiti*s, bent on educational activities, left an enormous influence on the local students' community striving for disciplined life, extension of women's education and social services. It was noticed in the Muslim society that there was a gradual transformation from a moribund, immovable society to a responsive and dynamic set up. Thus the Renaissance and the reform movement became stronger among the Muslim community as a whole.

NOTES

1. W.W. Hunter, *A Statistical Account of Bengal*, vol. VII, D.K. Publishing House, Delhi, 1974, p. 47.
2. Sekhar Bandopadhyay, *From Plassey to Partition,* Orient Longman, New Delhi, 2004, p. 268.
3. J. Maitra, *Muslim Politics in Bengal, 1855-1906: Collaboration and Confrontation,* K.P. Bagchi & Co., Calcutta, 1984, p. 24.
4. Anisuzzaman, *Muslim Manas and Bangla Sahitya* (Muslim World and the Bengali Literature), Charulipi Prakashani, Dhaka, Reprint 2014, p. 29.
5. Sirajul Hauque, *Muslim Sahitya Samaj: Samaj Chinta O Sahitya Karma* (The Muslim Literature and Society: Social thought and Literary Works), Kathaprakash Publication, Dhaka, Bangladesh, third edition, 2019, pp. 10-12.
6. Amalendu De, 'The Social Thoughts and Consciousness of the Bengali Muslims in the Colonial Period', in *Social Scientist*, vol. 23, No. 4/6 (April-June, 1995), p. 16.
7. Ananda Gopal Ghosh, 'The Syndrome of Nineteenth Century: Bengal Renaissance in North Bengal with Special Reference to the Minorities and the Non-caste People', in Shyamal Guharoy et al., (ed.), *History and Thought of India: Essays in Memory of Professor P.K. Bhattacharyya*, Abhijeet Publications, New Delhi, 2022, p. 205.
8. Muhammad Maniruzzaman, *Rangpurer Itihas* (History of Rangpur), Gatidhara Prakashani, Dhaka, 2012, p. 282.
9. Dhananjay Roy, *Uttarbanga Unish O Bish Shatak* (North Bengal during Nineteenth and Twentieth Centuries), Dip Prakashan, Kolkata, 2002, p. 202.
10. *Dinajpur Patrika*, 1322 BS, Dinajpur, p. 87.
11. Muhammad Maniruzzaman, *Dinajpurer Itihas* (History of Dinajpur), Gatidhara, Dhaka, 2010, pp. 40-4.

12. *Dinajpur Patrika*, Magh 1322 BS, p. 102.
13. Waqil Ahmed, *Unish Shatake Bangali Musalmaner Chinta Chetanar Dhara* (The Trend of Thought of Bengali Muslims during Nineteenth Century), vol. 1, Bangla Academy, Dhaka, first edition, 1983, p. 404.
14. *Aitihasik Chitra*, 1315 BS, Rajshahi, pp. 90-2.
15. Sk. Abdul Khayer, *Mussalmani Puthi Sahitya* (Manuscripts of Muslim Literature), Book Space, Kolkata, 2016, p. 103.
16. Maulana Abid Ali, *Memories of Gaur Pandua*, H.E. Stepleton, Bengal Secretariat Bok Depot, Calcutta, 1931, p. 37.
17. *Maldaha Samachar*, A News Daily, Malda, 24 June 1925.
18. Palash Goswami et al. (eds.), *Utsarita Alo*, Malda, 2010, p. 65.
19. Mazharul Islam, *Nawabganjer Itihas O Aitihya* (History and Heritage of Nawabganj), Anandadhara Publication, Dhaka, 2009, p. 30.
20. Md. Maziruddin Mian, 'Varendra Anchaler Sahitya Ahdunik Yug' (Modern Age in the Literature of Varendra Region), in *Rajshahir Itihas*, vol. 1, Bagura, 1965, p. 995.
21. S.M. Abdul Latif, 'Shatabdir Aitihyabahi Sanghathan: Rajshahi Association' (A Traditional Organisation throughout the Century), in Tafiqul Islam (ed.), *Rajshahi Association Sahitya Patrika* (Literary Magazine of Rajshahi Association), First Issue, 1987, pp. 16-17.
22. *List of Associations Recognised by Government of Bengal*, Home Department (Pol.), Bengal Secretariat Press, Alipore, Bengal, 1946, p. 40.
23. Mamun Muntasir, *Unish Shatake Purba Banger Sabha Samiti* (Associations of East Bengal during Nineteenth Century), Dacca University, 1983, p. 96.
24. *Sudhakar* 12 Magh BS 1296, Calcutta, p. 14.
25. Ali Mehrab, *Dinajpurer Rajnaitik Andalaner Itihas* (History of Political Movement in Dinajpur), Naoroja Sahitya Majalisa, Dinajpur, 1965, p. 57.
26. *List of Associations Recognised by Government of Bengal*, op. cit., p. 46.
27. Amiya Kumar Banerjee et al., *West Bengal District Gazetteers, Darjeeling*, Calcutta, 1980, p. 583.
28. Ananda Gopal Ghosh, 'Jalpaiguri Jelar Musalman Samaj' (Muslim Society of Jalpaiguri District), in *Madhuparni*, Jalpaiguri Zilla Sankhya, BS 1394, Jalpaiguri, p. 129.
29. *Sudhakar*, 2nd Chaitrya 1296 BS, Calcutta, p. 8.
30. Ananda Gopal Ghosh, 'Unish o Bish Shataker Uttarbanger Sabha-Samiti-Samaj' (Associations and Society of North Bengal during Nineteenth and Twentieth Century's), in Girindra Narayan Roy and Ankush Bhatta (ed.), *Maitayani*, University of North Bengal, 1999, p. 39.

31. Ahmed Rafiuddin, 'The Role of Associations and Anjumans in the Political Mobilization of the Bengal Muslims in the later Nineteenth Century', *Bangladesh Historical Studies*, vol. IV, 1979, p. 41.
32. *List of Associations Recognised by Government of Bengal*, op. cit., p. 41.
33. Dhananjay Roy, op. cit., p. 205.
34. Supam Biswas, *Tea World of North Bengal, Readers Service*, Kolkata, 2020, p. 39.
35. Umesh Sharma, *Jalpaigurir Ray Bahadur Khan Bahaur* (Ray Bahadur and Khan Bahadur of Jalpaiguri), Grantha Tirtha, Kolkata, 1997, p. 156.
36. Ananda Gopal Ghosh and Nilangshu Sekhar Das, *Uttarbanger Itihas O Samaj* (History and Society of North Bengal), vol. I, Dipali Publishers, Malda, 2009, p. 38.
37. *Dainik Basumati*, A News Daily, Siliguri, 2 November 1997.

Conclusion

In the trend of writing regional history of Bengal in the last phase of the nineteenth century and the beginning of the twentieth century, a group of historians and researchers have chosen North Bengal. Whatever may be the reason behind it, it is true that for many centuries the history of Bengal was centred on North Bengal as a whole. The history of Bengal means the history of Pundravardhana and Varendra region. The *Divyavadana* has mentioned Pundravardhana as a large territory in the east. Pundra as a territory was first mentioned in the Mahasthangarh inscription. Mahasthangarh was the capital of the Pundra region or Northern Bengal. Pundravardhana in the ancient times corresponded to the northern geographical division of Bengal and encompassed the areas which included the districts of Malda, North Dinajpur, South Dinajpur, a part of Murshidabad, Bagura, Rajshahi, Pabna and Rangpur.

One of the major reasons for this was definitely the geographical aspect of North Bengal and its superiority as the oldest cultural region of Bengal. The name and fame of the ancient history of North Bengal spread beyond Bengal to the whole of India. The history of Bengal resolves around two ancient cities, Mahasthangarh in Bogura and Bangarh in Dinajpur district. Their image did not fade in any way until the advent of the Sultanate period. Over the ages foreign travellers and researchers have paid attention to the history and culture of the region. Their memoirs and travelogues have mentioned these places. Following the footsteps of Akshay Kumar Maitra, Ramaprasad Chanda, Munshi Jayanath Ghosh and Bhagawati Charan Bandopadhyay, the study of North Bengal gained another dimension later under the tutelage of Rajendralal Acahrya, Khan Amanatullah Ahmed, Kalipada Lahiri, Nihar Ranjan Roy and others. It is interesting to note that till date no major research works have been published on these great sons of North Bengal.

The trend of writing regional history like Jaynathmunshi's *Rajopakhyan* (1833), Shyamdhan Mukhopadhyay's *Murshidabader Itihas* (1864) and Babu Ananda Chandra Ghosh's *Kuchbiharer Itihas* (1865) which started in various parts of North Bengal throughout the nineteenth century, influenced and encouraged many enthusiastic people to study the history of the region. Along with many historians from all over India and Bengal, some of them were Jagaddipendradev Raikot (*Raikot Bamsha O Tahader Rajyer Sankhipta Biabran*, 1883, Jalpaiguri), Bhagawati Charan Bandopadhyay (*Kuchbiharer Itihas*, BS 1291), Kalinath Chaudhury (*Rajshahir Sankhipta Itihas,* 1901) and Jadav Chandra Chakrabarty (*Kuchbihar Rajyer Sankhipta Biabran*, 1883). During this time, some other famous people were able to highlight the regional history of Bengal as a whole with special importance. For example, Swarup Chandar Roy (*Subarna Gramer Itihas,* 1891), Kantichandra Rarhi (*Nabadwiptattwa*, BS 1300), Kedarnath Majumder (*Dhakar Bibaran,* 1909), Jatindra Mahan Roy (*Jessore-Khulnar Itihas,* vol. 2s, 1914) and Sudhir Kumar Mitra (*Hooghly Jelar Itihas O Banga Samaj,* 1948) deserve to be mentioned. In short, a special wave of writting regional history through the Bengali language stirred the whole of Bengal and some people of Varendra region responded to it in time. As a consequence of this, the publication of the above-mentioned works and books have survived the passage of time.

The intellectual society in North Bengal during the nineteenth century had developed in two ways—one centred on the royal court of Coochbehar and the other as a result of the British rule. However, there was a special difference between the character and structure of the intellectual society centred on this royal court and the intellectual society that developed under the British rule. It is true that there was not much barrier in the practice of learning in the royal state of Coochbehar. The intellectual society was ruled and controlled by the Brahmins and Kshatriyas. The Brahmin community of Coochbehar belonged to Mithila and Sylhet. This second Brahmin group was popularly known as the Kamrupi Brahmin.

The second characteristic of the intellectual society that grew in Coochbehar was that a large section of them were outsiders, mainly hailing from different parts of Bengal on the basis of professions in the royal court. Most of them were Brahmos and therefore, the impact of Brahmo religion played a praiseworthy role in developing the educational and cultural environment in Coochbehar. Moreover, the consequence of the marriage between Maharaja Nripendra Narayan and Suniti Devi heralded the beginning of the modernization of the state. A number of educational institutions and cultural associations came up. The Victoria College, established in 1888, under the encouragement of Maharaja Nripendra Narayan Bhup Bahadur, had the pride of place in higher education not just all over Bengal but in north-eastern India. A large number of students outside Bengal, mainly from Assam, used to come there for higher studies. A hostel named Brahmo Boarding was set up for them. Many of them later earned name and fame in their professional life. A number of teachers who had nationwide fame, served the college for a period of time. During the reign of Maharaja Nripendra Narayan, there were around 329 primary schools in Coochbehar. For the spread of women's education, a school named Suniti Academy was established.

The Sahitya Sabha, established in 1915, became a prized possession of the people as far as Bengali language, literature and culture were concerned. Victor Nityendra Narayan made the Sahitya Sabha a medium for the publication of various literary works ranging from the epic to the novel and even to music. Publication of periodicals like *Sukatha*, *Paricharika* played a key role in spreading Brahmo ideas and thought in the state. His wife, Nirupama Debi took the initiative to publish an illustrated version of the monthly magazine *Paricharika* from 1323 BS Nirupama Debi's poetry acquired its own unique place in Bengali literature. She was probably the first accomplished modern writer of Coochbehar. In short, they were torch bearers of the renaissance movement in Coochbehar. Their efforts raised Bengali language and literature in Coochbehar to great heights.

The intellectual society of the district of Malda developed in a very small way. The reason for this is twofold. First, Malda district is a traditional historical region. In *Akbarnama*, there is a reference to Malda as an important centre for trade and commerce. Tavernier referred to Malda in his travel accounts. Alexander Hamilton described Malda as a large town, well inhabited and frequented by merchants of different countries. The town of Malda stood as a juncture between the productive centres of North Bengal and North-Eastern Bengal. Trade and commerce in Malda was fully controlled by the merchants from Agra, Benares and Gujarat. Every year they purchased and shipped cotton and silk fabrics. Goods made in Malda were also exported to Dhaka, Murshidabad and Rajmahal. At Berhampore, Rampur Boalia and English Bazar, there were many silk merchants who had their business houses and conducted their business transaction to different parts of India and abroad.

Second, Malda was the first district in North Bengal which came under the British rule. Moreover prior to the advent of British rule in India, an intellectual society centred on Gaur developed there during the Sultani rule. After coming in contact with English silk traders and merchants, a Western style society developed there. It was the first district in North Bengal to start an English medium school. The first girls' school was also set up there, callled Barlow Girls School. It was the only district where two municipalities were formed in the nineteenth century, the English Bazar municipality and Old Malda municipality. Above all, as one of the leading trade communication centres, Malda was visited by several people and merchants of the country. As a result, a modern yet basically Indian intellectual society developed there in late nineteenth century.

The local intellectual society of the district had a pivotal role in developing the cultural environment. For example, Radesh Chandra Seth, Bipin Bihari Ghosh, Baladevananda Giri and Haridas Palit deserve mention. All of them were lawyers by profession. It was they who inspired the contemporary intellectual society to the national thought. A massive national and homeward flow of new awakeing was created in the urban society of Malda.

Malda had another advantage. That is many landlord families who were highly fond of education and culture, played an exemplary role in setting up a printing press, libraries and *sabha-samitis* as well as undertaking publication of books and monographs. Beside all these factors, the intellectual society of Malda was benefited to a great extent as the district was situated next to the district of Rajshahi. Naturally the cultural atmosphere of Rajshahi left an overwhelming impact on the social and cultural life of the district.

Rajshahi, overwhelmingly dominated by the Varendra Brahmins and Kayastha landlords, was the heart of the learned society of colonial Bengal. The first college of North Bengal was started in Rajshahi, even the first intellectual society named 'Rajshahi Association' was established there. A learned society grew up there centred around the Association. In Rajshahi, Rabindranath Tagore visited the household of his friend Loken Palit who was a judge, several times. During the days of his stay there, a number of high-level academic discussions took place. Sarat Kumar Roy, the *zamindar* of Dighapatia, Maharaja Jagadindranath Roy of Natore, Akshay Kumar Maitra, Rajani Kanta Sen and Dinendra Kumar Roy used to come to those discussions. They were, no doubt, the pillar of the intellectual society of Rajshahi. The *zamindars* of Rajshahi contributed to a great extent to enrich the education and culture of their estates by establishing a number of schools, colleges along with other cultural institutions. It helped the people to come to terms with the cultural awakening of nineteenth-century Bengal. With the passage of time, they became aware of the cultural enlightenment and their cultural awakening later reflected with the setting up of two literary organizations namely the Rajshahi Association (1872) and Varendra Research Museum (1912). As a researcher, it is believed, that culture and civilization of the Varendra region needs to be highlighted to a great extent because Rajshahi and Pabna, were both the torch bearers of Varendra culture. Ashok Mitra, I.C.S., discussed this phase of history in his autobiography *Tin Kuri Dash.*

Next to Rajshahi, Rangpur was the heartland of North Bengal. In earlier days, Rangpur was geographically a vast district. The climate and environment of Rangpur were conducive to living except for malaria and Kalazar. The administrators of the British government from Murshidabad or Calcutta used to come to work there with great reluctance. John Gegas, the first Supervisor of

Rangpur (1769-71), breathed his last in Rangpur due to malaria. Despite all these adversities, Rangpur became a city of migrants in the last phase of the nineteenth century. Many of them played a pivotal role in developing a cultural environment there. For example, Umesh Chandra Gupta, father of Barrister Atul Chandra Gupta, Dr Krishnadhan Ghosh, father of the great revolutionary and saint Aravinda Ghosh, Gopal Chandra Sen, the Honourable Vice-Chancellor of Jadavpur University, Satyendranath Sen, the Honourable Vice-Chancellor of University of Calcutta and many more, deserve to be mentioned. In the middle of the nineteenth century, the *zamindars* of Rangpur, apart from their subject oriented welfare, began to promote cultural and literary enterprises. Their efforts were fruitful and as a consequence, Rangpur Sahitya Parishad, Rangpur Public Library, Uttarbanga Sahitya Sammilini came into being.

It is true that the episode of the Coochbehar marriage (6 March 1878) split the Brahmos and did much to weaken their organization as a whole but it ushered a new era in the Princely State of Coochbehar. The central figure behind the setting up of Sadharan Brahmo Samaj in Coochbehar was Ray Kalikadas Dutta Bahadur, the Dewan of the Princely State of Coochbehar. During his tenure, Brojendra Nath Shil, the principal of Victoria College, became the president of Sadharan Brahmo Samaj for a few days. With the efforts of Brojendra Nath Shil, almost every branch of literature reached its height in Coochbehar. The first worshipping temple of Sadharan Brahmo Samaj (New Dispensation Church) led by Keshub Chandra Sen was set up in Coochbehar in 1880. In no time the Brahmo religion became the state religion in Coochbehar. The Brahmo movement in Coochbehar had a very great influence on the education and cultural development of the place. Keshub Chandra Sen provided the movement with a better organizational structure and ideological consistency. The most outstanding outcome of Brahmo movement in Coochbehar was the Renaissance.

Through its emphasis on freedom of individual thought and intensely rationalistic approach, Brahmonism infused a new spirit into the nineteenth-century cultural life of North Bengal and hastened the march towards social and cultural regeneration. The role of the Brahmo society in the development of the intellectual society of North Bengal was significant. In the second half of the nineteenth century, the branches of the Samaj came into existence almost in every districts of North Bengal. Although the number of Brahmos was very few, their exordium in the formation of intellectual practice and cultural environment was really unique. Among the eight districts of North Bengal during the British period, the impetus of the movement was greatly felt in the royal state of Coochbehar. The influence of Brahmo movement in Coochbehar had a very notable bearing on the education and cultural development of the place. The Brahmo movement gained a new lease of life in North Bengal with the marriage between Nripendra Narayan, the Maharaja of Coochbehar and Suniti Devi, the eldest daughter of Keshub Chandra Sen. The Renaissance movement of Coochbehar had active participation from people belonging to different professions like landholders, Dewans, Deputy Magistrates, pleaders, physicians and teachers. Their cultural outlook was mostly a blend of the East and the West. This golden era saw a flourishing of talent in every field.

The study to trace the cultural history of North Bengal was first started by the Varenra Anusandhan Society. They had published many books, monographs and articles and thus, had given birth a new study, popularly known as North Bengal studies. But their attempt received a major setback with the Partition of India in 1947. However, the curse of Partition did not stop the study the history and culture of North Bengal for a long time. This situation has been gradually disappearing. A new epic centre of North Bengal study has been developing at a rapid pace in Jalpaiguri, the divisional headquarter of the Jalpaiguri Division and the 'Capital of the Green Colony'. In fact, after the Partition, the intellectual helm of affairs of North Bengal has shifted from Rajshahi-Rangpur to Jalpaiguri. The leading personalities of Jalpaiguri at that time were fully capable of providing leadership in all spheres of life of North Bengal from writing to sports. Dr Charu Chandra Sanyal, Dr Rebati Mahan Lahiri, Nirmal Chandra Chaudhury, Upendra Nath Barman and Dr Arun Bhushan Majumder were the torch bearers of North Bengal studies. A group of intellectuals in different parts of North Bengal evolved who came forward and played a leading role in the study of North Bengal. So an atmosphere of reviving and restoring the study of North Bengal was developed all over North Bengal.

This received a further boost with the establishment of the North Bengal University in 1962 under the tutelage of Dr Bidhan Chandra Roy, the then Chief Minister of West Bengal. The foundation of the University was indubitably the turning point in the intellectual history of North Bengal. It gave rise to new hopes and expectations amongst the regional intellectuals. North Bengal was earlier the centre of higher education of the Pundravardhana-Varendra region. It included major portions of the districts of Bagura, Rajshahi, Rangpur and Dinajpur in present Bangladesh. The name and fame of Jaggadal Mahavihara (College) and Sompura Vihara were proverbial. The Chinese pilgrims noticed the existence of both the Hinayana and Mahayana systems in the Varendra region. The Chinese traveller Fa-hien, Hiuen Tsang and Itsing gave a vivid description of Buddhism in Pundravardhana. Hiuen Tsang said that there were more than 300 *bhikshus*, both Hinayana and Mahayana sects who practised Buddhism and near about three thousand schools of both the sects in Pundravardhana. Many places in Rajshhai are still associated with the name 'Vihara'. A place named Bhikshupara (quarter of the *bhikshus*) exists about ten miles west of Rajshahi. The Somapura Mahavihara situated at Paharpur was the most famous Buddhist learning centre of Pundravardhana. It was built by the second Pala King Dharmapala. According to Dharmakayavidhi and Madhyamaka Ratnapradipa, Taranath's account that Devapala, the successor of Dharmapala built it after his conquests of Varendra. After one thousand years, North Bengal again became the centre for higher education of the concerned region and the surrounding regions of the Himalayan foothills, Nepal Terai and western Assam.

Dinajpur town was the heartland of the intellectual society of the entire district. Balurghat was another centre of intellectual discourse of the district, where an intellectual society developed in the first decade of the twentieth century. It was a well-known name in the history of dramatic literature in Bengal.

In Jalpaiguri district, intellectual society was almost absent in the nineteenth century. The Jotedars had no role in laying the foundation of an intellectual society there. Most of the educated people of the town were outsiders who migrated into the district mainly for professional reasons. A major section of them worked in neighbouring tea gardens and railways. They were very busy with their work related activities and spent most of their time in striving for financial prosperity. As a consequence, one could not see any major steps taken by them to build educational and cultural institutions in their place of living. Thus one may say that the history of Jalpaiguri vis-à-vis the district in the nineteenth century was a complete history of financial enhancement. However, the scenario began to change from the first decade of the twentieth century. The advent of Bengali youths from different parts of Eastern Bengal in search of better profession and livelihood, changed the whole situation. A notable feature of their life was that they, along with their entreprenural and business activities, devoted their life for the growth and development of education and culture. The societies that were formed, particularly those following their contact with enlightened Europeans, became essentially beneficial and educative for all the inhabitants of the district.

The situation in the Darjeeling district was completely different from other districts of North Bengal. It was a thoroughly colonial town comprising of outsiders. Darjeeling was born out of the British love for mountains as much as for being the gateway of business outside India. The weather was suitable for the Europeans more like the one back home. While Chittagong was the garden of Bengal, Darjeeling was the sanatorium of the province. The British government declared the Darjeeling hill as the 'Summer Capital of Bengal' in the year 1879. The hill town also served as major producing grounds of very specific corps like tea and cinchona. A large number of English medium schools were built around the whole of Darjeeling hill. By the end of the nineteenth century there were ninety-five schools run by the missionaries in the Eastern Himalayan region—Darjeeling, Kurseong, Kalimpong, the Duars and Sikkim. Kurseong was considered as the hub of

English medium schools as compared to other hill stations such as Shillong, Garhwal, Dehradun and Guwahati. Consequently, Darjeeling evolved as the centre stage of politico-cultural events and strategic-economic dynamics. These factors ostensibly accelerated the process of advent of a large number of wealthy educated Indians in Darjeeling. Among them the Bengali elites (*bhadraloks*) of Calcutta ranked first. The presence of the upper and middle class Bengali people sought to inhabit the same social space that the Europeans themselves occupied. The *sabha* and *samitis* first grew there with the encouragement of the educated professional Bengali people. The royal families of Coochbehar, Burdwan, Mayurbhanj and the Natore Estate, have all contributed to a great extent in developing an intellectual society in Darjeeling. The Nepali intellectual society emerged much later in the third decade of the twentieth century and had a different character and structure.

Bibliography

A. PRIMARY SOURCES

I. Government Reports and Proceedings

Administrative Reports of Coochbehar for the year of 1916-1917, Coochbehar State Press, Coochbehar, 1917.

Adam, *Reports on the State of Education in Bengal,* Calcutta, 1836.

Annual Administration Report of the Coochbehar State, 1889-90.

Annual Proceedings of Cooch Behar Hitaishani Sabha, for the year 1871-1872, Coochbehar State Press, Coochbehar, 1873.

Annual Proceedings for the year of 1973-4, Arya Samiti, Autumn Number, 1974, Siliguri.

Annual General Administration Report, Rajshahi Division, 1886-87.

Annual Administrative Report of Coochbehar for the year 1904-5, Coochbehar State Press, Coochbehar, 1905.

Annual Administration Report of the Department of General Administration and Criminal Justice of the Coochbehar State for the year 1921-22, Coochbehar State Press, Coochbehar, 1922.

Coochbehar Select Records, vol. II, Coochbehar State Press, 1884.

Greene, Rev., *Report of Dinajpur Mission*, 1953.

List of Associations Recognised by Government of Bengal, Home Department (Pol), Bengal Government Press, Alipore, Bengal, 1946.

Proceedings of the Coochbehar State Council 1892-94, Coochbehar State Press, 1907.

Proceedings of the Government of Bengal, General (Political) Department, February 1864, No. 53 and 58.

Proceedings of the Kamrup Anusandhan Samiti (Assam Research Society), Guwahati, 1993.

Proceedings of the Rangpur Sahitya Parishad Patrika, Rangpur, BS 1315.

Proceedings of the First Conference of Uttarbanga Sahitya Sammelan, Rangpur, 27 June 1908.

Proceedings of the Uttarbanga Sahitya Sammilani, for the year 1910-11, Rangpur, 1911.

II. Government Reports, Gazetteers and Statistical Accounts (Published)

Acharya Brojendra Nath Seal Centenary Souvenir, Calcutta, 1964.

Banerjee, Amiya Kumar, *West Bengal District Gazetteers: Darjeeling*, Calcutta, 1980.

Bell, F.O., *Final Report on the Survey and Settlement Operations in the District of Dinajpur 1934-40*, Bengal Secretariat Press, Alipore, 1941.

Bengal District Gazetteers, Bogra, Bengal Secretariat Press, Calcutta, 1913.

Bengal District Gazetteers, Rajshahi, Bengal Secretariat Press, Calcutta, 1923,

Centenary Souvenir, Khagrabari Dramatic Club, Coochbehar, 1971.

Centenary Volume of Kamrup Anusandhan Samiti, Guwahati, 2010.

Dash, A.J., *Bengal District Gazetteers, Darjeeling*, Bengal Secretariat Press, Calcutta, 1947.

Grunning, John F., *Eastern Bengal and Assam District Gazetteers: Jalpaiguri*, The Pioneer Press, Allahbad, 1911.

Hamilton, Buchanan, F.W., *The History, Antiquities, Topography and Statistics of Eastern India*, vol. II and III, Calcutta, 1801.

Hartley, A.C., *Final Report on the Survey and Settlement Operations in the District of Rangpur 1931-38*, Bengal Secretariat Press, Alipore, 1940.

Hunter, W.W.W., *A Statistical Account of Bengal*, vol. VII, D.K. Publishing House, Delhi, 1974.

Hunter, W.W.W., *A Statistical Account of Bengal*, vol. X, London, 1876.

Lambourn, G.E., *Bengal District Gazetteers, Malda*, Bengal Secretariat Press, Calcutta, 1918.

Majumder, Durgadas, *West Bengal District Gazetteers, Coochbehar*, Government of West Bengal, Calcutta, 1977.

Mitra, A., *West Bengal District Handbooks Darjeeling 1951*, West Bengal Government Press, Alipore, 1954.

O'Malley, L.S.S., *Bengal District Gazetteers, Darjeeling*, Logos Press, New Delhi, 1907.

Platinum Jubilee Souvenir, Jalalia Girls' School, Malda, 1994.

Sengupta, Jatindra Chandra, *West Bengal District Gazetteers, Malda*, Calcutta, 1969.

Strong, F.W., *Eastern Bengal District Gazetteers, Dinajpur*, Allahabad, 1912.

Vas, J.A., *Bengal District Gazetteers Rangpur*, Allahabad, 1911.

III. Newspapers and Periodicals

Aitihasik Chitra, Rajshahi.

Dainik Basumati, Siliguri.

Bharatabarsha, Kolkata.
Janamat, Jalpaiguri.
Coochbehar Sahitya Sabha Patrika.
Paridarshak, Pabna.
Coochbehar Samachar.
Rajshahi Association Sahitya Patrika.
Dharmatattwa, Kolkata.
Sudhakar, Kolkata.
Dinajpur Patrika, Dinajpur.
The Mussalman, Kolkata.
Gyanbikashaini, Pabna *Trisrota*, Jalpaiguri.
Uttar Malda Sambad, Malda.

B. SECONDARY SOURCES

PRINTED BOOKS IN BENGALI

Ahmed, Ali, *Bangla Muslim Granthapanji* (Index of Muslim Books in Bengali Language), Bangla Academy, Dhaka, 1992.

Ahmed, Wakil, *Unish Shatake Bangali Musalmaner Chinta-Chetanar Dhara* (The Trend of Thought of Bengali Muslims during Nineteenth Century), vol. I, Bangla Academy, Dhaka, Bangladesh, First Edition, 1983.

Anisuzzaman, *Muslim Manas and Bangla Sahitya* (Muslim World and the Bengali Literature), Charulipi Prakashani, Dhaka, Reprint 2014.

Bandopadhyay, Bhagawati Charan, *Kuchbiharer Itihas* (History of Coochbehar), Coochbehar State Press, Coochbehar, 1882.

Bandopadhyay, Brajendranath, *Bangla Samayik Patra* (Bengali Periodicals), vol. I, Kolkata, BS 1379.

Bandopadhyay, Brajendranath, *Bangla Samayikpatra* (Contemporary Periodicals of Bengal), (vol. I), Calcutta, 1379 BS.

Barma, Upendra Nath, *Thakur Panchanan Barmar Jiban Charit* (Biography of Thakur Panchanan Barma), Jalpaiguri, BS 1408.

Basak, Amarendra (ed.), *Centenary Volume, Tufanganj Subdivision*, Coochbehar, 1992.

Chakrabarty, Dipesh, *Itihaser Janajiban O Ananya Prabandha* (History, Public Life and Other Essays), Ananda Publication, Kolkata, 2011.

Chakrabarty, Kamakhya Prasad, *Sekaler Jalpaiguri Sahar o Samajik Jibaner Kichu Katha* (Few Words of Social Life of Contemporary Jalpaiguri Town), Sigma Information Technology Publication, Jalpaiguri, 2004.

Chakrabarty, Rajanikanta, *Gaurer Itihas* (History of Gauda), Rangpur Sahitya Parishad, Rangpur, Kolkata, BS 1317.

Chattapadhyay, Amal, *Ananta Eshana Brajendranath Shil: Jiban O Chinta* (Life and Thought of Brajendranath Shil), Dip Publication, Kolkata, 1999.

Chaudhury, Kalinath, *Rajshahir Sankhipta Itihas* (A Short History of Rajshahi), Calcutta, BS 1308.

Chaudhury, Nirmal Chandra, *Akshay Kumar Maitra: Jiban O Sadhana* (The Life and Pursuit of Akshay Kumar Maitra), University of North Bengal, 1984.

——, *Raikat Bansha O Tahader Rajyer Sankhipta Bibaran,* (A Concise History of the Raikat Dynasty and the State), by Jagadindradeb Raikat, Jalpaiguri, published by Uttarbanga Itihas Parishad (Historical Association of North Bengal), Jalpaiguri, 1389 BS.

Chaudhury, Saifuddin, *Kumar Sharat Kumar Roy* (Prince Sharat Kumar Roy), Bangla Academy, Dacca, 2002.

Dasgupta, Sashibhushan, *Bangla Sahityer Nabayug* (New Age in Bengali Literature), A. Mukherjee and Company, Kolkata, BS 1372.

Devi, Sabitri, *Swargiya Kumar Gajendranarayan* (Late Prince Gajendranarayan), Kolkata, 1928.

Dutta, Prankrishna , *Kalikatar Itibritta* (History of Calcutta), Pushtak Bipani, Kolkata, 1981.

Ghosh, Ajit Kumar, *Rammohan Rachanabali* (Essays on Rammohan), Haraf Publication, Kolkata, 1973.

Ghosh, Ananda Gopal and Soumendra Prasad Saha, *Uttarbanga Itihas O Samaj* (History and Society of North Bengal), vol. II, Sangbedan, Malda, 2015.

Ghosh, Ananda Gopal and Sumana Das Barman, *Uttarbannger Itihas O Sanskriti* (History and Culture of North Bengal), vol. VIII, Sagnik Books, Kolkata, 2022.

Ghosh, Ananda Gopal, *Jalpaigurir Sahityalekha O Anyanya Prabandha,* (Cultural History of Jalpaiguri and Other Essays), Sangbedan, Malda, 1396 BS.

——, *Manishi Panchanan Barma O Tar Andalaner Uttaradhikar* (Panchanan Barma and the Legacy of His Movement), Sangbaden, Malda, 2015.

Ghosh, Shaktibrata, *William Carey er Sahitya Sadhana* (Literary Pursuits of William Carey), Burdwan, 1980.

Ghosh, Ananda Gopal and Papiya Ghosh, *Uttarbanger Itihas O Samaj* (History and Society of North Bengal), (vol. III), Sangbedan, Malda, 2017.

Goswami, Kamalesh , *Raiganjer Itihas* (History of Raiganj), Dibaratrir Kabya Publication, Kolkata, 2008.

Hauque, Fazlul, *Maharaja Jagadindranath Roy* (King Jagadindranath Roy) Bangla Academy, Dhaka, 1992.

Hauque, Sirajul, *Muslim Sahitya Samaj: Samaj Chinta O Sahitya Karma* (The Muslim Literature and Society: Social thought and Literary Works), Kathaprakash Publication, Dacca, Bangladesh, third Edition, 2019.

Islam, Mazharul, *Nawabganjer Itihas O Aitihya* (History and Heritage of Nawabganj), Anandadhara, Dhaka, 2009.

Khastagir, Asish, *Unish Shataker Bnagla Chapakhana* (Printing Press of Bengal during Nineteenth Century), Sopan, Kolkata, 2014.

Khayer, Sk. Abdul, *Mussalmani Puthi Sahitya* (Manuscripts of Muslim Literature), Book Space, Kolkata, 2016.

Maitra, Akshay Kumar, *Bharat Shilper Katha* (A Tale About Indian Art), Calcutta, 1982.

Mamun, Muntasir, *Unish Shatake Purbabanger Mudran O Prakashana* (Press and Publications of Eastern Bengal during Nineteenth Century), Bangla Academy, Dhaka, 2006.

——, *Unish Shatake Bangladesher Samayik Patra* (Periodicals of Bangladesh during Nineteenth Century), Bangla Academy, Dhaka, 1985.

——, *Unish Shatake Purba Banger Sabha Samiti* (Associations of East Bengal during Nineteenth Century), Dhaka University, 1983.

Maniruzzaman, Muhammad, *Rangpurer Itihas* (History of Rangpur), Gatidhara, Dhaka, Bangladesh, 2012.

Mehrab, Ali, *Dinajpurer Rajnaitik Andalaner Itihas* (History of Political Movement in Dinajpur), Naoroja Sahitya Majalisa, Dinajpur, 1965.

Mukhopadhyaya, Bhubaneswar, *Jogesh Jiban* (Life of Jogesh), Jalpaiguri, BS 1371.

Pal, Samar, *Natorer Itihas* (History of Natore), (vol. II), Natore, Rajshahi, 1984.

Palit, Haridas, *Maldaher Radeshchandra* (Radeshchandra of Malda), Calcutta, BS 1318.

Patra, Samir and Sekhar Bhowmik (ed.) *Akshay Kumar Maitra Smarak Grantha* (Book in Memory of Akshay Kumar Maitra), Ashadip, Kolkata, 2012.

Rahman, Moksudur, *Natorer Maharani Bhawani* (Queen Bhawani of Natore), Rajshahi, 1988.

Rahman, Moksundar, *Natorer Maharani Bhawani* (Queen Bhawani of Natore), Rajshahi, 1988.

Ray, Bimal Prasad, et al., *Natorer Katha O Kahini* (Words and Stories of Natore), Calcutta, 1981.

Roy, Dhananjay, *Dinajpur Jelar Itihas* (A History of Dinajpur District), K.P. Bagchi, Kolkata, 2006.

——, *Uttrabanga Unish O Bish Shatak* (North Bengal during Nineteenth and Twentieth Century's), Dip Prakashan, Kolkata, 2002.

Sarkar, Jibesh, *Darjeeling Jelar Communist Andalan Prasange* (Regarding the Communist Movement in the District of Darjeeling), (vol. I), Ratanlal Brahman Trust, Siliguri, 2004.

Sen, Jahar, *Himalaya Charcha O Darjeeling Prasanga* (Studying Himalaya in the Context of Darjeeling), Cikitushi Prakashani, Kolkata, 2013.

Sen, Jaladhar, *Atmajibani O Smrititarpan*, (Autobiography and Memoir), ed. Baridbaran Ghosh, Jiggyasa Agency Limited, Kolkata, BS 1367.

Sharma, Umesh, *Jalpaigurir Ray Bahadur Khan Bahaur* (Ray Bahadur and Khan Bahadur of Jalpaiguri), Grantha Tirtha, Kolkata, 1997.

——, *Jalpaigurir Raikot Bangsher Rajarshi* (Leading Personality of the Raikot Dynasty of Jalpaiguri), Jalpaiguri, 2003.

Shastri, Shibnath, *Ramtanu Lahiri O Tatkalin Brahmo Samaj* (Ramtanu Lahiri and the Contemporary Brahmo Samaj), New Age Publishers, Third Edition 2009, Kolkata.

PRINTED ARTICLES IN BENGALI

Acharya, Chittaranjan, 'Carey Dinajpure Chay Bachar' (Six Years of William Carey in Dinajpur), in Dhananjay Roy (ed.), *Anchalik Itihas Charchay Dinajpur Jela* (Study the Regional History of the District of Dinajpur), Sanskrit Pushtak Bhandar Publication, Kolkata, 2009.

Basu, Nripen, 'Phele Asa Din Gulo' (Days Gone By), *Purabarta*, Published by Siliguri Municipality, Siliguri, 1992.

Bhattacharya, Dipayan, 'Raj Amale Coochbehar e Natya Charcha' (Practising Theatre and Drama in Coochbehar during the Royal Period), *Bibriti,* Festive issue, Mathabhanga, Coochbehar, 2010.

Chakrabarty, Chhanda, 'Coochbehar e Nari Shikshar Bibartan' (Evolution of Women Education in Coochbehar), in Ajitesh Bhattacharya (ed.), *Maduparni,* Coochbehar Jela Sankhya (Special Volume on the District of Coochbehar), Government of West Bengal, BS 1396.

Chanda, Suniti Bala, 'Jalpaiguri Jelar Eksho Bochore Stri Sikkhar Bikash' (One Hundred years of Development of Women's Education in the District of Jalpaiguri), in Dr. Charu Chandra Sanyal (ed.), *Jalpaiguri District Centenary Souvenir,* 1970, Jalpaiguri.

Chattapadhyay, Moushumi, 'Jalpaigurir Sangitcharchar Sekal Ekal' (History of Music Practice in Jalpaiguri), in Aravinda Kar (ed.), *Kiratbhumi* (Land of Kiratas), Festive Issue, vol. II, Jalpaiguri, 2008.

Chaudhury, Dilip, 'Darjeeling Jelar Sadharan Granthagar O Granthagar Andalan' (General Library and Library Movement in the District of Darjeling), in Ajitesh Bhattacharya (ed.), *Madhuparni,* Darjeeling Jela Sankhya, November 1996.

Chaudhury, Kumar Narayan, 'Kheladhulay Darjeeling Jela' (Sports in Darjeeling District), in Ajitesh Bhattacharya (ed.), *Madhuparni,* Darjeeling Zilla Sankhya (Special Volume on the District of Darjeeling), 1996.

Choudhury, Safiuddin, 'Kumar Sharat Kumar Ray' (Prince Sharat Kumar Ray), in Safiuddin Choudhury (ed.), *Rajshahir Pratibha* (The Genius of Rajshahi), Rajshahi, 2000.

Das, Bhupendranath, 'Canchal Rajbari' (The Royal Palace of Canchal), *Uttar Malda Sambad,* Autumn Number, BS 1411, Malda.

Das, Sanchita, 'Alipurduarer Natyacharchar Utsa O Kramabikash' (Origin and Development of Theatre in Alipurduar), in Pabitra Bhushan Sarkar (ed.), *Matir Choya,* vol. 21, No. 15, Alipurduar, 1995.

Das, Subodh Chandra and Biman Chakrabarty, 'Kuchbehar Rajye Brahmo Andalan' (Brahmo Movement in the princely state of Coochbehar), in Ajitesh Bhattacharya (ed.), *Madhuparni,* Kuchbehar Jela Sankhya, BS 1396.

Dey Sarkar, Digvijay, 'Coochbehar Natyacharcha' (Practising Drama in Coochbehar), in Ajitesh Bhattacharya (ed.), *Madhuparni,* Coochbehar Zilla Sankhya (Special Volume on the District of Coochbehar), 1396 BS.

Dutta, Paritosh, 'Darjeeling, Cha O Nanan Katha' (Tale of Darjeeling and its Tea), in Ajitesh Bhattacharya (ed.), *Madhuparni,* Darjeeling Zilla Sankhya (Special Volume on the District of Darjeeling), 1996.

Gangopadhyay, Bhabaranjan, 'Jalpaiguri Jelar Sambadpatrer Sankhipta Itihas' (A Concise History of the News Dailies in the District of Jalpaiguri), in Charu Chandra Sanyal (ed.), *Jalpaiguri District Centenary Volume,* Jalpaiguri, 1970.

Ghosh, Ananda Gopal, 'Bharater Swadhinata Andolane Deshiya Rajya Coochbehar: Prasanga Victoria College Chatra Samaj (1885-1947)' (Role of the Princely State of Coochbehar in India's Freedom Struggle and the Students of Victoria College), in Gokul Sarkar (ed.), *Angikar,* autumn number, Dinhata, W.B., BS 1420.

Ghosh, Ananda Gopal, 'Uttarbange Brahmo Dharma O Samaj Andalan' (Brahmo Religion and Socio-religious Movement in North Bengal), in Mayukh Das (ed.), *Itihascharcha* (Studies in History), vol. I, Kolkata, 2016.

——, 'Unish o Bish Shataker Uttarbanger Sabha-Samiti-Samaj' (Associations and Society of North Bengal during Nineteenth and Twentieth Century's), in Girindra Narayan Ray and Ankush Bhatta (eds) *Maitrayani,* vol. 1, BS 1396.

——, 'Darjeeling, Kurseong O Kalimpong Sahar Gathane Bangalider Abadan' (Contribution of Bengali People to the Formation of Darjeeling, Kurseong and Kalimpong Town), in Supam Biswas (ed.), *Himalay Banga: Prasanga*

Darjeeling Nama, (History of Darjeeling in the Context of Himalaya), Readers Service, Kolkata, 2022.

Ghosh, Mahit, 'Prayata Kamini Kanta Rahut Sambandhe Duti Katha' (Two Words about Late Kamini Kanta Rahut), in *Kamini Kanta Rahut Janma Shatabarshiki Bishesh Sankhya* (Birth Centenary Volume on Kamini Kanta Rahut), Nikhil Bharat Banga Sahitya Sammalan, Jalpaiguri, BS 1402.

Hauque, Fazlul, 'Akshay Kumar O Varendra Gabeshana Jadughar' (Akshay Kumar and the Varendra Research Museum), in Tasiqul Islam (ed.), *Rajshahi Sahitya Patrika,* October 1989.

Latif, S.M. Abdul, 'Shatabdir Aitihyabahi Sanghathan: Rajshahi Association' (Rajshahi Association: A Traditional Organisation throughout the Century), in Tafiqul Islam (ed.), *Rajshahi Association Sahitya Patrika* (Literary Magazine of Rajshahi Association), First Issue, 1987,

Mamun, Muntasir, 'Banglay Brahmo Samajer Itibritto' (History of Brahmo Samaj in Bengal), in Atanu Sashan Mukhopadhyay (ed.), *Dashdishi Patrika,* Kolkata, 2014.

——, 'Varendra Theke Prakashita Sambad Samoyikpatra' (Newspapers and Periodicals published from Varendra), in Icchamuddin Sarkar (ed.), *Aitihye O Itihase Uttarbanga* (North Bengal—Its History and Heritage), N.L. Publishers, Assam, 2002.

Mian, Md. Maziruddin, 'Varendra Anchaler Sahitya Ahdunik Yug' (Modern Age in the Literature of Varendra Region), in *Rajshahir Itihas,* vol. 1, Bagura, 1965.

Mitra, Nanu, 'Darjeeling Jelar Bangla Natak O Natyacharcha' (History of Bengali Dramas in the district of Darjeeling), in Ajitesh Bhattacharya (ed.), *Madhuparni,* Darjeeling Zilla Sankhya (Special Volume on the District of Darjeeling), 1996.

Mitra, Ranajit Kumar, 'Jelar Samayik Patra Patrika' (Contemporary Newspapers and Periodicals of the District), in Ajitesh Bhattacharya (ed.), *Madhuparni,* Jalpaiguri Jela Sankhya, BS 1394.

Mustafi, Sitangshu Sekhar, 'Dinhatar Natyacarcha O Natyavinay Parikrama' (Theatre and Theatrical Performances in Dinhata), *Uttar Prasanga,* A Special Volume on Dinhata Subdivision, Coochbehar, 2016.

Pakrashi, Amiya Kumar, 'Jalpaiguri Jelay Siksha Bistarer Ruprekha' (An Outline of the Development of Education in the District of Jalpaiguri), in Charu Chandra Sanyal (ed.), *Jalpaiguri District Centenary Souvenir,* 1970, Jalpaiguri.

Prasad, Bhawani, 'Kheladhular Itibritta' (History of Sports), in *Dadhichi,* Autumn Issue, Balurghat, 1996.

Roy, Ratna, 'Unish Shataker Nabajagaran O Uttarbanga' (Nineteenth Century Bengal Renaissance and North Bengal), in Kali Krishna Sutradhar and Samit Saha (ed.), *Uttarbange Nabajagaran O Samajik-Sanskritik Andalan* (Renaissance and Sociocultural Movement in North Bengal), Abhijeet Publication, New Delhi, 2024.

Roy, Subrata, 'Raiganjer Natyacharcha' (Theatre in Raiganj), in Ajitesh Bhattacharya (ed.) *Madhuparni,* Special Volume on the District of West Dinajpur, Balurghat, BS 1399.

Roy, Swapan Kumar, 'Prachin Kochbihare Mudran Jantrer Abirbhav O Pragatir Unmesh' (Growth and Development of Printing Press in Coochbehar), *Kochbihar Jela Sankhya* (Special Volume on the District of Coochbehar), Government of West Bengal, BS 1413.

Saha, Narayan Chandra, 'Jalpaiguri Jelar Marwari Samaj' (The Marwari Society of Jalpaiguri District), in Aravinda Kar (ed.) *Kiratbhumi* (Land of Kiartas), vol. 1, Jalpaiguri, 1994.

Saha, Sanjay, 'Jharer Pakhi-Nirupama Devi' (The Storm Bird-Nirupama Devi), in Debashish Das (ed.), *Coochbehar Rajnagarer Andarmahal,* Bibrita Sahitya Prakashani, Malda, 2015.

Sarkar, Anil Kumar, 'Acahrya Brojendra Nath Shil and Victoria College', in Debabrata Chaki (ed.), *Uttar Prasanga,* Manju Printing Works, Coochbehar, W.B., 2014.

Shabnam, Irish, 'Malda Jelar Natyacharcha' (Practising Drama in Malda), in Malay Sankar Bhattacharya (ed.), *Maldah Charcha,* Malda, 2011.

Sharma, Umesh, 'Jalpaigurir Shatabarshiya Brahmo Samaj: Munshi Jalaluddin' (Hundred Years of Brahmo Samaj in Jalpaiguri: Munshi Jalaluddin, in Arabinda Kar (ed.) *Kiratbhumi,* vol. XXIX, Jalpaiguri, 2015.

Subir Roy, 'Jalpaigurite Brahmo Samaj' (Brahmo Samaj in Jalpaiguri), in Ajitesh Bhattacharya (ed.), *Madhuparni,* Jalpaiguri Jela Sankhya, BS 1394.

Printed Books in English

Abid Ali, Maulana, *Memories of Gaur Pandua,* H.E Stepleton, Bengal Secretariat Book Depot, Calcutta, 1931.

Ahmed, Chaudhury Amanatulla Khan, *A History of Coochbehar,* Coochbehar State Press, 1936.

Azad, Abul Kalam, *Khwaja Najimuddin Muslim Hall and Public Library,* Granthatirtha, Dinajpur, 1970.

Bandyopadhyay, Sekhar, *From Plassey to Partition,* Orient Longman, New Delhi, 2004.

——, *Caste Politics and The Raj 1872-1937,* KP Bagchi Publication, Calcutta, 1990.

Bhanja, K.C., *Darjeeling at a Glance,* Modern India Press, Darjeeling, 1941.

Biswas, Supam , *Tea World of North Bengal,* Readers Service, Kolkata, 2016.

——, *The Empire Wrote Future: The British in North Bengal,* Abhijeet Publications, New Delhi, 2024.

Bose, Sugata and Ayesha Jalal, *Modern South Asia History , Culture, Political Economy,* Oxford University Press, New Delhi, Second Edition, 2004.

Chatterjee, Piya, *A Time for Tea,* First published by Duke University Press in 2001, Published in South Asia by Zubaan, New Delhi, 2003.

Chaudhury, Harendra Narayan, *Coochbehar State and its Land Revenue Settlement,* Coochbehar State Press, Coochbehar, 1903.

Collet, S.D., *The Life and Letters of Raja Rammohan Roy,* ed. D.K. Biswas and P.C. Ganguly, Calcutta, 1962.

Das, Biswanath (ed.), *Autobiography of an Indian Princess* (Memory of Maharani Suniti Devi), Vikas Publishing House, New Delhi, 1995.

Dasgupta, Ranajit, *Economy, Society and Politics in Bengal: Jalpaiguri 1869-1947,* Oxford University Press, Calcutta, 1992.

Debnath, Sailen, *Essays on Cultural History of North Bengal,* National Library Publication, Siliguri, 2008.

Devi, Gayatri, *A Princess Remembers,* Rupa Publications, New Delhi, 1995.

Dewan, Dick B., *History of Education in Darjeeling Hill 1835-1985,* Indus Publishing Company, New Delhi, 1991.

Dozey, E.C., *A Concise History of Darjeeling since 1835,* N.L. Publishers, 2011, Siliguri.

Ghosh, Ananda Gopal et al., (ed.), *Sesquicentennial Commemoration Volume of Jalpaiguri District (1869-2019),* Kunal Books, New Delhi, 2020.

Ghosh, Binoy, *Selections from English Periodicals of 19th century Bengal 1878-80,* vol. VII, Payrus, Calcutta, 1978.

Hamilton, Buchanan, *The History, Antiquities, Topography and Statistics of Eastern India,* vol. II and vol. III, 1801, Calcutta.

Khan, Abid Ali, *Memories of Gaur and Pandua,* Bengal Secretariat Press, Calcutta, 1924.

Kopf, David, *The Brahmo Samaj and the Shaping of Modern Indian Mind,* Princeton University Press, 1997.

Maitra, J., *Muslim Politics in Bengal, 1855-1906: Collaboration and Confrontation,* K.P. Bagchi & Co., Calcutta, 1984.

Pal, Bipin Chandra, *Memories of my Life and Times,* Modern Book Agency, Calcutta, 1973.

Sanyal, Charu Chandra, *The Meches and the Totos* (Two Sub-Himalayan Tribes of North Bengal), Calcutta, 1973.

Sarkar, Ashim Kumar, *Nationalism, Communalism and Partition in Bengal: Maldah 1905-1953,* Readers Service, Kolkata, 2013.

Sarkar, Sumit , *Swadeshi Movement in Bengal 1905-08*, Delhi, Peoples Publishing House, 1978.

Sen, A.P., *Hindu Revivalism in Bengal 1872-1905,* Oxford University Press, Delhi, 1993.

PRINTED ARTICLES IN ENGLISH

Bharati Ray, 'Freedom Movement and Women's Awakening in Bengal 1911-29', *Indian Historical Review,* July 1985-January 1986.

Biswas, Dilip Kumar, 'Brahmo Samaj', in Narendra Krishna Sinha (ed.) *History of Bengal 1757-1905,* University of Calcutta, Second edition June 1996, Calcutta.

De, Amalendu, 'The Social Thoughts and Consciousness of the Bengali Muslims in the Colonial Period', in *Social Scientist,* vol. 23, No. 4/6 (April-June, 1995).

Ghosh, Ananda Gopal and Ratna Roy Sanyal, 'Growth of Public Opinion in North Bengal: A Case Study of Newspapers and Periodicals (1870-1947)', *North Bengal University Review,* 1993.

Ghosh, Benoy, 'Press in Bengal', in Narendra Krishna Singha (ed.), *The History of Bengal 1757-1905,* University of Calcutta, 1996.

Mallick, S.P. , 'The Boundaries of Jalpaiguri', in Charu Chandra Sanyal (ed.), *Jalpaiguir District Centenary Souvenir,* Jalpaiguir, 1970.

Mitra, Ramesh Chandra, 'Education', in Narendra Krishna Sinha (ed.), *The History of Bengal (1757-1905),* University of Calcutta, 1996.

Rafiuddin, Ahmed, 'The Role of Associations and Anjumans in the Political Mobilization of the Bengal Muslims in the later Nineteenth Century', *Bangladesh Historical Studies,* vol. IV, 1979.

Sarkar, Icchamuddin, 'Akshay Kumar Moitra: His Ideas and Method of Interpretations and Reflected in his Historical Works', *Journal of the Asiatic Society of Bangladesh* (Humanities), vol. 67(1), 2022.

UNPUBLISHED PHD THESES

Bhattacharya, Malay Shankar, 'Nationalist Movement and Freedom Struggle in Some Selected Areas of Northern Bengal 1857-1947', PhD Thesis, University of North Bengal, 1986.

Das, Kamalesh Chandra, 'The Modernisation of a Princely State of Coochbehar under Maharaja Nripendra Narayan (1863-1911)', PhD Thesis, University of North Bengal, 1989.

Jana, Bhakti Pada, 'Evolution of Public Libraries in Colonial Bengal: 1800-1947', unpublished PhD thesis, Vidyasagar University, 2020.

Karim, S.M. Rabiul, 'Rajshahi Zamindars: A Historical Profile in the Colonial Period (1765-1947)', PhD thesis, University of North Bengal, 2006.

Mukherjee, Sibsankar, 'Emergence of Bengali Entrepreneurship in Tea Plantation in Jalpaiguri Duars 1879-1933', unpublished PhD thesis, University of North Bengal, 1978.

Nasiruddin, Muhammad, 'Associations of Bengal: Their Activities and Role in Politics and Society 1851-85', PhD Thesis, Jadavpur University.

Index

Abbasuddin 40, 98, 152
Ahmadiya Association, Jalpaiguri 151
Ahmed, Amanatullah 38, 55, 81,152
Ahmed, Eknuddin 145, 149
Ahwan 60
Aitihasik Chitra 18
Ali, Abid 146
Ali, Nayeb 40, 153
Alipurduar Sahitya Parishad 122
Ananda Chandra College 35, 104
Anisuzzaman (Dr.) 142
Anjuman-i-Islamia 150-51
Aravinda Pathagar, Jalpaiguri 67
Arya Library, Dinajpur 65
Arya Natya Samaj, Jalpaiguri 67, 132
Arya Samiti, Siliguri 136
Assam Desh Hitasadhani Sabha 22
Assam Sahitya Sabha 21
Assamese Literary Society 21
Atmaraksha Samiti 122
Atmiya Sabha 30, 112
Azad Hind Pathagar, Jalpaiguri 68

Bahadur, Ray Kalikadas Dutta 36
Balurghat Natya Mandir 130
Banaras Hindu University 79
Bandhab Natya Samaj, Jalpaiguri 133
Bandopadhyay, Charu Chandra 31
Baneswar Shiva temple 43
Bangiya Sahitya Parishad 90
Bangiya Sahitya Sammelan 22
Barlow Girls' School, Malda 107
Barooah, Jagannath 21
Barooah, Manik Chandra 21
Barooah, Pramathesh 41
Barua, Pravat Chandra 41, 80, 118
Basu, Rajnarayan 42
Bell, F.O. 64
Bengal Land Holder's Association 88-90
Bengal-Duars Railway 22,135
Bengali Association, Kurseong 68, 120
Bengali Babu of tea gardens 68, 134-5
Bengali tea entrepreneurs 35, 103
Bhagabati Devi Pathagar 62
Bhanjadeo, Maharaja Ramchandra 42
Bhatpara Unnati Sadhani Sabha 51
Bhattacharya, Annada Charan 96
Bhattacharya, Padmanabha 80
Bhupal Chandra Vidyapith 84, 102
Bidyotsahini Sabha 17
Bina Printing Press 58
Bogra National Muhammaden Association 148
Bose, Bhagwan Chandra 34-5
Brahmamandal 36
Brahmo Samaj 15, 18, 27, 30; Coochbehar 36-8; Darjeeling 31-3; Dinajpur 31; Jalpaiguri 33-6; Malda 31 Siliguri 33
British East India Company 15
Buchanan 76
Buchanan, Francis 64
Buddhism 13, 166

Calcutta Public Library 61
Carey, William 16, 63
Carmichael College 20-1
Carmichael, Lord 19, 101, 116
Chakrabarty, Dipesh 80, 91
Chakrabarty, Harimahan 35
Chakrabarty, Ishan Chandra 51
Chakrabarty, Jadav Chandra 38, 53
Chakrabarty, Nilmani 34

Chakrabarty, Rajanikanta 80, 115
Chakrabarty, Troilokyonath 32, 43
Chanda, Harimahan 30
Chanda, Ramaprasad 114
Chandragupta Maurya 13
Chaudhuri, Abdul Majid 148
Chaudhury, Abul Hassan 18
Chaudhury, Ashutosh 81-2, 89
Chaudhury, Ershad Ali Khan 147-8
Chaudhury, Nirmal Chandra 18, 115
Chinese Pilgrims 166
Churaman Dramatic Society 83
Colonel Haughton 65,113
Coochbehar Club Football Tournament 129
Coochbehar Cultural Club 129
Coochbehar Darpan 28
Coochbehar Gazette 53
Coochbehar Musical Club 42
Coochbehar Sahitya Sabha 38-9, 65, 120
Coochbehar State Library 65
Coochbehar State Press 53-4
Cotton College, Assam 21
Curzon, Lord 41, 97, 146

Darjeeling 19
Das, Chittranjan 69, 82
Das, Debendra Prasad 32
Das, Pulin Bihari 98
Dasgupta, Ashrubala (Dr.) 60
Dasgupta, Khagendranath 60
Debating Club, Darjeeling, 117
Debating Club, Jalpaiguri 13
Deshbandhu District Library 69
Devi, Brindeshwari 50, 100
Devi, Hemprava 84
Devi, Indira 44, 66
Devi, Maharani Sharatsundari 86
Devi, Maharani Shyam Mohini 102
Devi, Maharani Siddheshwari 85
Devi, Maharani Sucharu 33
Devi, Mohini 38
Devi, Nirupama 37-38
Devi, Pransundari 83
Devi, Sucharu 38
Devi, Suniti 18, 43, 104
Dhaka 14, 34
Dhaka Anushilan Samity 98
Digdarshan Press 50
Dighapatia Raj Family 12
Dinajpur Bhatpara Unnati Sadhani Sabha 116
Dinajpur Girls' School 84
Dinajpur Muslim Society 142
Dinajpur Natya Samiti 117, 130
Dinajpur Patrika 52, 55
Diwani 15
Dutta, Babu Prankrishna 37
Dutta, Sashibhushan 32

Edward Memorial Hall 62
Edward Memorial Library, Alipurduar 67
English Bazar 16
European Clubs 135

Fanindra Dev Institution 107
Fuller, Ramfiled 150

Gambhira 57
Ganesh, Raja 85
Gangopadhyay, Narayan 121
Gani, Abdul 107
Gaudalekhamala 17
Gaur 13
Ghosh, Ananda Gopal 12, 23
Ghosh, Harachandra 23
Ghosh, Jogesh Chandra 58
Ghosh, Purna Chandra 58
Ghosh, Surendra Mahan 144
Ghoshal, Sharat Chandra 38
Goalpara 20
Gourbarta 56
Government Bhutia Boarding School 32
Grambarta 16-17, 113
Grihastha 57

Guha, Amalendu 21
Guha, Girish Chandra 33
Guptas 15
Guwahati 34
Gyanankur 51
Gyandayini Sabha, Pabna 113

Haldar, Motilal 32-3
Haldibari PVN Library 66
Hamid, Abdul 151
Hillmen's Association 121
Himadri Harisabha 116
Hindu College 22-3
Hindu Ranjika 51
Hitasadhani Press 21
Hossain, Tajmal 121
Hunter, W.W. 36
Hussain, Gulam 146
Hussain, Musharruf 151

Islam, Kazi Nazrul 55, 99

Jalaluddin, Munshi 34
Jalark 60
Jalpaiguri Central Girls' School 105
Jalpaiguri Cultural Institute 121
Jalpaiguri Press 58
Jalpaiguri Sahitya Samiti 120
Janamat 58-59
Jones, Keneth 27

Kamrup Anusandhani Samiti 21, 81
Kaviranjan, Bijayratna Sen 54
Khagrabari Dramatic Club 42, 14
Khalek, Abdul 61
Khan, Abdul Aziz 151
Khastagir, Ananda Charan (Dr.)31
Kolkata 11, 14
Kopf, David 11, 27
Krishnakali Press 56
Kuchbihar Darpan 55
Kuchbihar Patrika 53
Kuchbihar Sahitya Sabha 55
Kuchbiharer Itihas 53

Kumari, Maharani Hemanta 86, 102
Kumarkhali Sabha 16
Kurseong 33

Lansdowne Hall 40, 65
Lytton, Lord 88

Madan Mahan temple 41
Maharaja of Burdwan 19
Maharani Girls High School 19
Maharani Girls' High School 19, 31-3, 100
Mahila Atmaraksha Samiti 68
Maitra, Akshay Kumar 15, 18, 50, 52, 80, 114
Majumder, Harinath 16-18, 115
Majumder, Lila 32
Majumder, Pandit Dinanath 54
Majumder, Ramesh Chandra 87, 115
Malda Jatiya Shiksha Samiti 109, 121
Malda Muhammadan Association 109
Malda Zilla School 106
Maldaha Samachar 56
Mamun, Muntasir 49
Marnai School 82-3, 102
Mathuranath Press, Rangpur 16
Mehtab, Bijay Chand 41
Mitra Sammilani, Siliguri 135
Mitra, Krishna Kumar 33
Mitra, Premendra 61
Modern Art Printers 59
Moshahari, Prabhu Dayal 35
Muhammad, Nur 147
Muhammaden Associations 147-50
Mukherjee, Ashutosh 19, 39, 82
Mukhopadhyay, Balai Chand 55
Mukhopadhyay, Tribhanga 100
Muslim Sahitya Samiti, Jalpaiguri 121

Nabadwip 13
Nabya Ekta Sabha, Darjeeling 116
Narayan, Harendra 19
Narayan, Kumar Gajendra 37, 41, 43

Narayan, Maharaja Harendra 55, 94
Narayan, Maharaja Jagadipendra 65
Narayan, Maharaja Narendra 95
Narayan, Maharaja Nripendra 18, 33, 40, 42, 99-100
National Council of Education 97
Natore Raj family 86
Nawraj Sahitya Sabha 149
Nishan 58, 61
Nitya Dharma Badhani Sabha 117
Nityendranarayan, Victor 37
Niyogi, Sashi Kumar 59
North Bengal Landholders Association 79
North Bengal State Railway 22
Nripendra Narayan Hindu Public Hall 19, 135

Pabna Darpan 51
Pabna Edward College 20
Pal, Bipin Chandra 33, 35
Palit, Haridas 58
Pallidarshan 51
Pallimangal Sammelan 122
Pancha Ratna 117
Paricharika 38
Pataliputra 13
Pathagar, Subhashini 68
Planters' Press Limited 58
Polwhele, John Archibold 135
Pradayini Sabha 22
Pragjyotishapur 13
Prasannanath Academy, Natore 88, 102
Pundravardhana 13, 17, 159

Rahman, Fazlur 152
Rahut, Kamini Kanta 104
Raikat, Jagadindradeb 80
Raikat, Prasanna Deb 39, 122, 105
Raj Rajeshwari Hall 120
Rajbanshi Kshatriya Samiti 119
Rajendra Smriti Pathagar 68
Rajshahi Association 13, 88, 113
Rajshahi College 89
Rajshahi Muhammaden Association 146
Rajshahi Sambad 50
Rampur Boaliya Dharmasabha 51
Rangpur Bartabaha 49, 78
Rangpur Digprakash 50, 53
Rangpur Sahitya Parishad 11, 63, 76-7, 118
Rani Amriteshwari 104
Rani Bhawani of Natore 76, 87, 103
Rani Brindamayee Girls School 79
Rani Janaki Ballav Sen of Dimla 79
Raychaudhuri, Tapan 11
Renaissance in Assam 21
Rogers Library, Coochbehar 65
Ronaldsay, Lord 116
Roy Ananda Charan (Dr.) 33
Roy, Bidhan Chandra (Dr.) 166
Roy, Girijanath 84
Roy, Gurucharan 50
Roy, Maharaja Girijanath 81, 102, 117, 150
Roy, Maharaja Jagadindranath 87-8
Roy, Parbati Charan 32
Roy, Pritinidhan 59
Roy, Raja Jagadindranath 61
Roy, Raja Pramathnath 116
Roy, Rammohun 15, 28
Roy, Sarat Kumar 63, 90, 102
Roy, Satyendra Prasad 105
Roy, Tarini Prasad 58
Roychaudhury, Kali Chandra 78-9, 101
Roychaudhury, Mahima Ranjan 62, 78, 101; Malda 15, 23; Malda College 107; Malda Dramatic Society 137
Roychaudhury, Raja Haranath 113
Roychaudhury, Ramanimohan 62
Roychaudhury, Sambhu Chandra 50, 61
Roychaudhury, Surendra Chandra 77, 78, 101

Sadar Girls' High School 104
Sadharan Brahmo Samaj, Coochbehar 36-7
'Samaj Para', Jalapiguri 35
Samaj Sanskarini Sabha, Darjeeling 116
Samprakash 17
Sancharini Sabha, Coochbehar 117
Sangit Samaj, Jalpaiguri 131
Sanyal, Charu Chandra (Dr.) 1635
Sanyal, Dewan Nilkamal 52
Sanyal, Jyotish Chandra 58, 59
Saptashashtri, Madan Mahan 41
Saraswati Samiti, Dinajpur 85
Sarkar, Binoy Kumar 57, 81, 107
Sarkar, Ganga Govinda (Dr.) 33
Sarkar, Hemlata 31
Sarkar, Jadunath 81
Sarkar, Nilratan (Dr.) 33
Sarkar, Sumit 119
Sarkar, Sushovan 23
Sashanka 11
Satyagrahi 56
Saudamani Girls' School 104
Sen, Chandi Charan 35
Sen, Dinesh Chandra 87
Sen, Janaki Ballava 62
Sen, Keshub Chandra 18, 32, 34, 36, 42
Sen, Kunjabihari 43
Sen, Madhusudan 31
Sen, Rajanikanta 50
Seth, Radesh Chandra 52, 56, 80
Sharma, Tarabandhu 51
Shastri, Hara Prasad 81
Shastri, Sibnath 29, 30, 33, 35
Siddheshwari Institution 20
Sikdar, Nagendra Nath 58
Sil, Brojendra Nath 37, 95-7
Singh, Brojeshwar 55
Singha, Brajendra Chandra 52
Sircar, Panchanan 96
Smith, Vincent 116
Somapura Mahavihara 164
Strong, F.W. 83, 84
Sukatha 54
Sulabha Samachar 17
Summer Capital of Bengal 167
Suniti Academy 100

Tagore, Debendranath 30
Tagore, Rabindranath 82, 90
Tarai Library 71
Tarkachuramani, Sashadhar 44
Thomas, John 64
Tindharia 33
Tripathi, Amalesh 12
Trisrota 58-9
Trivedi, Ramasundar 114

Udyog Bidhayani Sabha 51
University of Calcutta 96, 101
Uttarbanga Rahstriya Granthagar 66
Uttarbanga Sahitya Sammilani 13, 21, 78, 79-83

Varendra Research Institute 13, 21, 63, 114, 116
Victoria College 41, 44, 95-8
Victoria Public Library 63
Viharas 13

Woodburn Library, Bogura 63

Young Bengal Movement 22-3
Young Men's Theatrical Club 40, 128

Zamindars of Bhupalpur 20
Zamindars of Canchal 20